THE BIRTH OF
LOUD

LEO FENDER, LES PAUL, AND
THE GUITAR-PIONEERING RIVALRY
THAT SHAPED ROCK 'N' ROLL

IAN S. PORT

SCRIBNER

NEW YORK   LONDON   TORONTO   SYDNEY   NEW DELHI

SCRIBNER
An Imprint of Simon & Schuster, Inc.
1230 Avenue of the Americas
New York, NY 10020

First Scribner hardcover edition January 2019

SCRIBNER and design are registered trademarks of The Gale Group, Inc., used under license by Simon & Schuster, Inc., the publisher of this work.

For information about special discounts for bulk purchases, please contact Simon & Schuster Special Sales at 1-866-506-1949 or business@simonandschuster.com.

The Simon & Schuster Speakers Bureau can bring authors to your live event. For more information or to book an event, contact the Simon & Schuster Speakers Bureau at 1-866-248-3049 or visit our website at www.simonspeakers.com.

Interior design by Michelle Marchese

Manufactured in the United States of America

10 9 8 7 6 5 4 3 2 1

Library of Congress Cataloging-in-Publication Data

Names: Port, Ian S. author.
Title: The birth of loud : Leo Fender, Les Paul, and the guitar-pioneering rivalry that shaped rock 'n' roll / Ian S. Port.
Description: New York : Scribner, [2019] | Includes bibliographical references.
Identifiers: LCCN 2018024537 (print) | LCCN 2018026518 (ebook) | ISBN 9781501141768 (eBook) | ISBN 9781501141652 (hardcover) | ISBN 9781501141737 (pbk.)
Subjects: LCSH: Electric guitar—History. | Electric guitar makers—United States. | Fender, Leo, 1909–1991. | Paul, Les.
Classification: LCC ML1015.G9 (ebook) | LCC ML1015.G9 P66 2019 (print) | DDC 787.87/190922—dc23
LC record available at https://lccn.loc.gov/2018024537

ISBN 978-1-5011-4165-2
ISBN 978-1-5011-4176-8 (ebook)

To my parents,
who gave the gifts of love, writing, and music.

CONTENTS

An if ya listen, you'll hear a movin', an' a sneakin', an' a rustlin', an'—an' a res'lessness. They's stuff goin' on that the folks doin' it don't know nothin' about—yet. They's gonna come somepin outa all these folks goin' wes'—outa all their farms lef' lonely. They's comin' a thing that's gonna change the whole country.

JOHN STEINBECK, *THE GRAPES OF WRATH*, 1939

PROLOGUE

The screams came in waves, hysterical and elated, punctuated by applause. Then the camera found them: five men in matching striped shirts, teetering with nerves, grinning like children. The Beach Boys. A clap on the snare drum sent the song rumbling to life, and the players at the stage's front tapped their feet to stay in time. Punches from the drum kit underpinned a sheen of male voices in harmony. But fighting for prominence was another noise—a throaty, splattering sonic current.

Curious instruments hung over the striped shoulders of the men in front. Two of the instruments were painted white, with thin bodies and voluptuous curves that suggested spaceships, or amoebae, or the human torso. Behind their players sat cream-colored cabinets the size of refrigerators, massive speakers barely visible inside, components in a new system of noisemaking. These sleek guitars transformed single notes and chords into flows of electrons, while the amplifiers converted those electrons into wild new tones—tones that came out piercingly human despite their electric hue.

There was no piano, no saxophone or trumpet, no bandleader, no orchestra. Besides their drums and voices, the Beach Boys wielded just these bloblike guitars, each dependent on electricity, each able to produce ear-piercing quantities of sound, and nearly all bearing the name *Fender*. Their amplified blare seemed to encourage the shrieks of fans buffeting the stage, their bodies swaying to the thrumming joys of "Surfin' USA."

When this scene played in American movie theaters just after Christmas 1964, it was a vision of the future. It was part of a filmed rock 'n' roll concert—the very first—that also showed the Rolling Stones seething and strutting, and James Brown pulling off terpsichorean heroics unlike anything most of the American public had yet seen. *The Teenage Awards Music International Show* looked like one more entry in a procession of frivolous teen movies, but it arrived with the shock of the new. It was a multiracial assemblage of the day's most famous pop stars, captured on film alongside bikini-clad go-go dancers and howling youths. Movie critics mostly sniffed. "Adults, unaware of the differences between these numerous young groups, view the combined efforts as fairly monotonous," went a typical assessment. But a new order was establishing itself.

One of its precepts was racial equality, or at least the sincere pursuit of such. It was a celebration that both targeted and was beholden to the American teenager. And it prized music played on electric instruments that gave individual musicians a vast new sonic palette—and volume level—with which to express themselves.

Only fifteen years earlier, this scene would have been unrecognizable. Popular music had been the domain of dedicated artisans, trained pros in tuxedos who read notes on paper and sat on bandstands in disciplined regiments, led by a big name in a bow tie. Crooners like Bing Crosby acted out songs written for them by others, and sang for adults, not young people. Nearly everyone who joined them on the pop charts had white skin.

But in the boom years after World War II, teenagers had wrested control of the market for pop music, and many lacked their parents' racial prejudice. Singers like Chuck Berry and Bo Diddley, and later Marvin Gaye and the Supremes, rose onto charts once ruled by whites. These cultural changes were accelerated by a complementary revolution in the technology of music-making. By the night *The T.A.M.I. Show* was filmed in 1964, anyone with the right equipment could achieve volumes that would reach hundreds or thousands of onlookers. The new rulers of music could manipulate electric guitars and amps to produce a universe of evocative or alien new sounds.

One company had done more than any other to usher in the technology that was changing listeners' aural experiences. One company had made electric guitars into ubiquitous leisure accessories, by supplying cheap, sturdy instruments to amateurs and professionals alike. This firm was the first in its industry to align itself with the tastes of young people, among the first to paint guitars bright red and later metal-flake blue and purple, first to give its models sexy monikers like the Stratocaster and the Jaguar.

Competitors had long mocked the creations of the Fender Electric Instrument Company, but this Southern California upstart had an asset unlike any other—a self-taught tinkerer whose modesty was utterly at odds with the brash characters who used his tools. Clad in perpetually drab workmen's clothes, preferring to spend most of his waking hours designing and building in his lab, Clarence Leo Fender toiled endlessly to perfect the tools that ushered in pop music's electric revolution, yet he couldn't play a single instrument himself. Instead, he trusted musicians, whom he loved, to tell him what they wanted. In the waning days of World War II, Leo Fender had started building guitars and amplifiers in the back of his radio repair shop. By that night in 1964, the company he'd built dominated the burgeoning market for electric instruments.

At least, for the moment.

Showing off their striped, short-sleeve shirts, the Beach Boys appeared clean-cut and respectable, apparently (if not actually) innocent young men. To close out *The T.A.M.I. Show*, a quintet of Brits arrived wearing modish dark suits and expressions of bemused insouciance, even outright hostility. The lead singer's dark hair fell in curls down to his collar as he prowled the stage, thick lips pressed up against the microphone, hunting and taunting his young quarry. To his left, a craggy-faced guitarist beat on an unfamiliar instrument. That small, solid-bodied guitar responded with snarls and growls, a thick, surging sound that couldn't have been more different from the thin rays of light that had emanated from the Beach Boys' Fenders.

The earlier act embodied rock 'n' roll life as a teen idyll, a carefree jaunt in which sex was mentioned only euphemistically, and hardly ever as a source of conflict. Minutes later, the Rolling Stones made rock into a carnal fantasy, a dim mélange of ego and lust, betrayal and satisfaction. Already labeled rock 'n' roll's bad boys, the five young Brits embraced the role in performance and offstage, viewing the Beach Boys—another band of white men using electric guitars to play music first created by black men—as entrants in a completely different competition.

The Rolling Stones *did* sound new and distinct. And part of what then fueled the difference was an instrument discovered in a secondhand music shop in London, a secret weapon for producing the nasty tones this outfit preferred. It was a guitar, made by the venerable Gibson company, that bore the name Les Paul. Thanks to Keith Richards and certain other British rockers, this Les Paul guitar would soon rise again to become Fender instruments' prime companion and rival—just as the man it was named after had been many years earlier.

For Les Paul himself was as emphatic and as colorful as human beings come, as loud and public as Leo Fender was quiet and private: a brilliant player and a gifted technician, a charmer and a comedian, a raconteur and a tireless worker who hungered for the top of the pop charts. Out of his roots in country and jazz, Les Paul had invented a flashy style of playing that was immediately recognizable as his own, a style that would help define the instrument for generations of ambitious guitarists. But almost since the moment he began playing, Les Paul had found existing guitars inadequate. He knew what he wanted and what he thought would make him a star: a loud, sustaining, purely electric guitar sound. Nothing would give it to him.

His search for this pure tone—and through it, fame—led him to California, to a wary friendship with the self-taught tinkerer Leo Fender, who was interested in the same problem. The two men began experimenting together, pioneering the future of music. But when Les finally managed to drag the guitar out from its supporting role and deposit it at the center of American culture—and when a radical new electric guitar design finally became reality—their friendship fractured into rivalry. The greatest competitor to Leo Fender's instruments was soon a Gibson model with Les Paul's signature emblazoned in gold. From then on, it was Fender vs. Gibson, Leo Fender vs. Les Paul, their namesake electric guitars battling for the affections of a vast generation of players inspired by the new sound of rock 'n' roll.

For a brief period this competition seemed to abate. But soon after Keith Richards appeared in *The T.A.M.I. Show* using his Gibson Les Paul, his peers in the British rock scene would find that this instrument could produce tones then out of reach of any other guitar—including a Fender. The Gibson Les Paul could become molten, searing, heavy: sounds for which it was never intended, but which were now wildly desirable. This guitar's look and sound would go on to virtually define a new style of blues-based hard rock.

So almost from the moment the Beach Boys and the Rolling Stones shared a stage in *The T.A.M.I. Show*, the old Fender-Gibson rivalry, that competition between the unassuming Leo Fender and the attention-seeking Les Paul, reignited. Once begun, this showdown—between bright and dark, thin and thick, light and heavy, West and East, new and old—would consume countless future musicians, as it still does to this day.

But both men's instruments would also further a larger struggle. Whether in the hands of Chuck Berry or Buddy Holly, Jimi Hendrix or the Velvet Underground, Sly and the Family Stone or Led Zeppelin, Prince or the Runaways, Bad Brains or Sleater-Kinney, electric guitars would be used to make music with a tolerance—stated, if imperfectly applied—for people of different racial and ethnic identities. The music fueled by these instruments sought a single audience, or at least one ever-expanding group of listeners, who thought of themselves, however improbably, as young. And perhaps this bias toward diversity and youth explains some of the hostile words so casually published in 1964.

For there were proper adults in the audience of the Santa Monica Civic Auditorium on the night *The T.A.M.I. Show* was filmed. There were grown-ups sitting in the many movie theaters where it played. Were they really so bored by James Brown and the Rolling Stones, Marvin Gaye and the Beach Boys? Or did they perhaps sense that young people, armed with Leo Fender's and Les Paul's powerful new tools, might finally finish the cultural revolution they'd long been threatening?

1.

"THE ELECTRIC GUITAR SPELLED MONEY"

NEW YORK CITY, 1940–1941

On Sunday afternoons, Les Paul would bolt awake at his apartment in Queens and rush across the East River into Manhattan. There was something he needed to build, something he could only build there.

It was never in the mornings, because Les Paul was allergic to mornings. It had to be in the afternoons, after Les had had time to sleep off the previous nights: those rabid jazz jam sessions up in Harlem or on Fifty-Second Street, and the big-band swing concerts he sometimes played before them. Sundays were often the only day of the week when Les didn't have a rehearsal, or a radio concert, or a live gig. He could have spent them with his family, with the wife he'd brought to New York from Chicago, the woman who was about to have his first child. But Les Paul had a sound in his head that needed to get out.

After arising well into the middle of the day, he'd throw on some rumpled clothes, dash alone out of his tiny apartment, and barrel back across the Fifty-Ninth Street Bridge toward the same crowded, smoky island from which he'd just returned a few hours earlier. He'd nose his sedan down through the clogged avenues of Manhattan to Fourteenth Street, where a proud Renaissance Revival building stood near the corner of Seventh Avenue, its upper floors occupied by the Epiphone stringed instrument factory.

The factory was ostensibly closed on Sundays, but Les had made an arrangement with the owner. When the lanky twenty-six-year-old approached those stately front doors and flashed his goofy smile, a watchman let him in and showed him upstairs. The guard turned on the lights and the lathes and the sanders in the empty workshop, and demonstrated how they worked. Then he left Les Paul alone inside that cavernous room, left him to build a tool that could create the sound Les heard in his head.

Les had been hearing the sound for almost half his life—ever since he was a kid playing hillbilly tunes and telling cornball jokes to anyone in Waukesha, Wisconsin, who'd listen. Born Lester Polsfuss on June 9, 1915, to a mother who'd adored and spoiled him from the start, Les had picked up the harmonica at age eight, discovering by accident that he could make it sound better by soaking it in boiling water. As a child, he'd torn apart and reassembled his mother Evelyn's player piano, her telephone, her phonograph—even her electric light switches. He adored radio—loved listening to the *Grand Ole Opry* with Evelyn, a devoted country fan; loved building a simple earpiece radio; loved tinkering with a fancier receiver he shared with a friend.

But for all Les's passion for electric gadgets and their mysteries, nothing captivated him like the guitar. After he'd first encountered the instrument, backstage at a hillbilly concert in Waukesha, he'd thrown himself at it, racing to master it as if there were some countdown clock only he was aware of. By his early teens, as the leader of a nascent band, Les was climbing out of his upstairs bedroom at night and talking his way into taverns to scope out older players, memorizing their chords and licks. Soon, he had an epiphany about the guitar and the radio, his two favorite things. The first device had a crippling weakness, he'd learned, and the second seemed to offer a way to fix it.

At fourteen, he often performed solo at a barbecue stand outside of

Waukesha, in a dirt parking lot where the customers, chewing drippy beef sandwiches in their cars, made a captive audience. In the warm summer just before the Great Depression, Lester Polsfuss—or "Red Hot Red," as he then called himself—earned generous tips. He'd set up at the edge of the parking lot and warble out old hillbilly tunes like "I'm a Stern Old Bachelor" ("I change my socks three times a year / With no one to complain"), blow harmonica, and crack jokes while the highway travelers half listened in their Model Ts. To make himself more audible across the noisy lot, Les had cleverly wired a microphone into the circuit of his mother's portable radio, transforming it into a primitive public address system.

One afternoon at the barbecue stand, a carhop brought a note up to young Red Hot Red. It was not a request, nor a compliment; rather, it complained that while listeners could hear Les's voice and his harmonica, they could not make out his guitar. That little acoustic instrument, a Troubadour model Les had bought with $3.95 in paper-route earnings out of the Sears, Roebuck catalog, couldn't carry on its own over the hungry voices and rattling motors in the parking lot.

Les got an idea. One afternoon, he rode his bicycle over to his father's service station and borrowed the guts of George Polsfuss's radio and phonograph set. Back at the barbecue stand, Les ran his microphone through his mother's radio, as usual. But this time, he took his father's phonograph needle and jammed it into the top panel of his guitar—the wood panel vibrated by its strings. Then he ran the phono needle wire into his father's radio, thinking that the connection might transfer the sound of the acoustic guitar into the radio's electric circuit and speaker, thus amplifying it.

Guitar plus radio: it proved a magical combination. Les's voice and harmonica blared out of one electronic speaker, and his guitar—raw and muddy, but *louder*—plunked from another. The barbecue crowd could now hear the whole range of Red Hot Red's act: voice, harmonica, and scratchy guitar. They were agog. His tips that afternoon tripled (or so Les, in his often fanciful memory, recalled). Young Lester Polsfuss had learned, as he later put it, that "the electric guitar spelled money."

But not only money. Les saw that overcoming the guitar's pathetic volume could propel his career—that the sonic prominence of his instrument could, and would, determine his prominence as a performer.

Eleven years later, on those restless Sunday afternoons in New York, Les Paul was still trying to amplify the guitar with an electric speaker. He was now a rising star, having persuaded a well-known bandleader into making a place for the Les Paul Trio inside his forty-five-piece jazz orchestra. Fred Waring's Pennsylvanians did two live shows every evening from the Vanderbilt Theatre on Forty-Eighth Street, their sets broadcast on radio stations coast-to-coast during prime evening hours. *DownBeat* magazine had championed the wily guitar runs Les added to Waring's broadcasts, declaring his rambunctious, jokey group a highlight among the tuxedoed, self-serious swing regiment. From the parking lot of a Wisconsin farm town, Les had talked himself—with the help of his incandescent talent—into one of the most prestigious and well-paid staff jobs in American music.

Yet he wasn't satisfied. Not with the rigid schedule of the job, not with the staid music he had to play for it, and not at all with the sound of his instrument.

The guitar had come a long way in the eleven years since Les repurposed his father's phonograph set. Electric guitars had appeared on the market in 1932, as players wrestled against the oldest limitation of their instrument: volume. A guitar was inherently a marvelous thing—Beethoven himself had called it a "miniature orchestra," since it covered four octaves and could be used to play lush chords as well as sprightly melodies. But while versatile and portable, the guitar's low volume sharply limited its usefulness. Those six strings worked far better in a parlor, or around a campfire, than in a big hall, competing with other instruments.

Having improved so much of daily life in the early twentieth century, electricity seemed fit to improve the guitar, too. By 1940, many firms sold guitars that employed electric power to increase their volume. In New York, Les relied on a Gibson model, considered state-of-the-art, that had hit the market only three years earlier. Yet for all the promise electricity seemed to hold for boosting the guitar's volume and sound, Les found the result deeply disappointing.

What passed for an electric guitar in 1940 was actually an acoustic instrument in every respect but one. Les's Gibson ES-150 had a thick, hollow body with F-shaped holes in the top to project sound, just like any acoustic model. Its key difference was a black metal bar under the strings, called a pickup, that turned the strings' vibrations into an electromagnetic signal and sent that through a cable to an amplifier. Les's instrument wasn't a completely electric guitar, then, but a hybrid. It had been designed mainly to produce a warm, airy acoustic tone. The pickup allowed the player a small boost in volume via connection to an amplifier. But this electric sound was optional, and limited. If Les turned up the amplifier too loud, the sound from the amp would reverberate inside the guitar's body, get captured by the pickup, and emit howls of feedback, ruining a performance.

What Les really wanted, what he'd dreamed about almost since that parking lot afternoon in Waukesha, was a purely electric tone from a purely electric guitar. No woody warmth. No acoustic cavity. Just the crisp electric signal from the vibrating steel strings, made loud—as loud as he wanted—by an amplifier. No instrument available in New York in 1940 could do that. So on those Sunday afternoons, alone, often exhausted, driven by his insatiable curiosity, Les set out to make one.

He began with a rough plank of pine, four inches by four inches, about two feet long. Just solid, dense wood—what could have been a section of fencepost. This was to be the entire body of the guitar.

To one end of it, Les glued a spare Epiphone guitar neck (he had talked the Epiphone factory owner into contributing to this experiment). In the center, he attached a homemade electric pickup—essentially a magnet wrapped thousands of times with copper wire—that would transform the strings' vibrations into an electric signal. When he'd bolted on hardware and strings, Les Paul regarded his strange contraption. It looked like a lumberyard mutant, a stick bound with steel cables, a wood shop project—which is what it was. He called it the Log.

On the Sunday evening he finished the project, Les took the Log to a little place called Gladys' Bar in Sunnyside, Queens. He pulled his mutant guitar up on the small stage, fired up his Gibson amplifier, and strummed a chord. The purely electric sound he'd so long dreamed of came splattering out of the little speaker. It was thin and sharp, prickly and alien. It possessed none of the mellow warmth, the woody grace, of a hollow-body electric—but it did have some of the qualities Les had dreamed of.

Because there was no acoustic cavity, Les could turn up this Log guitar unusually loud without creating any feedback. And because its dense, solid-wood body didn't absorb vibrations easily, the strings themselves vibrated longer than on an acoustic instrument, giving each note a lyrical sustain. Les thought this strange guitar sounded pretty good. Frustratingly, though, no one in the room even noticed. Here was a four-by-four stick of wood, strung up and plugged into an amplifier—and a young man daring to use it as a guitar. Not one person in the audience would have seen a wooden board made into a guitar before, yet none seemed to care one bit.

Thinking it over, Les wondered if the Log's plain appearance might be the problem. Over subsequent Sundays, he went back to the Epiphone factory, sawed an old acoustic guitar body in half, and attached its sides to the Log like wings. Now the instrument looked like a standard guitar, but with a curious block of solid wood running through its middle.

The evening he finished the addition, Les took the Log back to the bar. This time, when he went onstage to jam, there was a huge reaction. Everyone seemed captivated by the thin, bright sound of the Log, and they bombarded him with questions about the guitar and the amplifier. Les had learned, as he would later put it, that audiences "listen with their eyes." Because his instrument now looked like something strange and substantial, the crowd noticed its powerful volume and sustaining tone. They seemed so captivated that Les—ever prone to dissatisfaction with a thing he'd just achieved—began to wonder if he could make a solid-body guitar that would sound even better than the Log.

Les continued playing and jamming around New York until one steamy afternoon in May 1941. He was goofing around that day with some fellow musician friends in the basement of his Queens apartment building. Pouring sweat, he touched his electric guitar and a metal microphone stand at the same time, completing a circuit and sending a jolt of electricity through his body. He screamed for help, but it took the others a few crucial seconds to figure out that he was being electrocuted.

When they kicked away the mic stand, all feeling was gone from Les Paul's hands. The jolt had torn his muscles; he was facing weeks in the hospital, and his future as a performer seemed suddenly unclear. Electricity, the very force Les believed would give him the prominence he so desired, had thrown everything into jeopardy. He was now a guitar player who couldn't play the guitar.

In the wake of the accident, Les quit Fred Waring's Pennsylvanians and moved back to Chicago, where he'd lived before venturing to New York. While his body healed, and with his playing sidelined, Les continued to work on the Log, increasingly convinced of the advantages of an electric guitar with a solid body. That year or the following one, Les recalled, he got a meeting with leaders at the Gibson guitar company. Founded in 1902 in Kalamazoo, Michigan, Gibson made the guitars that Les publicly endorsed and played. The company had been in the vanguard of fretted instrument design for decades but its executives, some of whom had been running things since its founding, were on the verge of selling to younger owners.

Still only twenty-six years old, Les Paul arrived at his appointment full of hope, and with the Log in tow. With characteristic audacity, Les held out his huge, unvarnished hunk of a guitar and told the managers that Gibson should consider building something like it: an electric guitar with a solid body that would allow unlimited volume and increased sustain. He insisted that the Log's pure electric tone, produced entirely by an amplifier, revealed new vistas of opportunity for the instrument by eliminating the ceiling on its volume.

The Gibson crew managed to suppress their laughter, but only barely. They declined Les's idea out of hand, quickly showing the bright-eyed young man and his craft project out of the office. Why, after all, would anyone want a guitar that consisted of little more than a fencepost? The loveliest thing about a guitar was the rich, airy tone that seeped out of its sound holes. To completely eliminate that was ludicrous.

After Les left, the managers chortled among themselves about that crazy guitar player who wanted Gibson to build a broomstick with pickups on it. They would keep chortling for almost another decade.

2.

"HE'S THE REASON YOU CAN HEAR US TONIGHT"

SANTA MONICA, 1946

He stood almost perfectly still as the maelstrom swirled around him, left hand tucked under his right elbow, eyes trained on the stage, ears scanning. Leo Fender was the only still body in the blur of pressed uniforms and evening dresses, the only serious face. Two thousand young couples filled a dance hall thrust aloft over the crashing waves of the Pacific, most of the revelers swaying and jitterbugging, smoking cigarettes and sneaking pulls from hidden flasks. It was Friday night at the Aragon Ballroom on Lick Pier, the Second World War was over, and Bob Wills and His Texas Playboys were playing. From everywhere there seemed to emanate a giddiness, men and women finding unencumbered joy after the long years of the war. Everywhere, that is, but around Leo Fender. For him, this was work.

Standing there in his drab repairman's clothes, his thin mustache crinkling with concern, Leo studied the musicians. They were a cowboy retinue, swaying in white shirts, red ties, and ten-gallon hats. Bob Wills, the bandleader, cawed out into the smoky expanse, tucked his fiddle against his neck, and began to saw a twanging melody into the microphone. Behind him, the bass, piano, and drums came in with a rollicking thump: *boom-slap, boom-slap, boom-slap.*

Out in the ballroom, men brushed back sweaty strands of their hair, took their ladies' arms, and glided out onto the parquet floor for another fast two-step. *Boom-slap, boom-slap.* The bandleader finished a melodic phrase, and Leo Fender saw him thrust his violin bow toward a ruddy-faced sack of a man sitting on the far side of the bandstand, strumming a white guitar.

It was Junior Barnard's turn. The guitarist flipped a switch on his instrument, and its sound became instantly bladelike and brittle. Louder. Barnard's guitar was plugged into a wooden speaker box, and tones began to flow out of it in hot, sticky ribbons. The guitarist slid into a main chord of the song, and his notes seemed to grind out from the amplifier, dark and thick, louder still.

"Get low, Junior!" the bandleader shouted, and the fat guitarist flashed a mischievous smile to himself. His fingers danced across the neck. He unfurled a mellifluous run—all a blur, the individual notes lost inside a thrilling cascade—and punctuated the phrase with one cutting chord, then another, louder. He dashed up to a single note and bent the string, yanking its pitch upward, holding it up there, the note ringing— but then it curdled into something else. Barnard tried to keep going, but a metallic wail rose out of that note, flooded over the band, and spilled out into the room: *YOOOOOOOOOWWWWL.*

Shouts of complaint filled the air as the dancers stopped to plug their ears. The bandleader scowled from the far side of the stage. Barnard fiddled with the knobs and switches on his guitar, trying to make the wailing stop, finally choking off the feedback by splaying his fingers flat across his guitar strings.

Down in the crowd, Leo Fender grimaced. The overeager guitarist had killed the song, infuriated his listeners and bandmates, by trying to take his solo too loud. Junior Barnard *always* wanted to play loud. Of course, it was one of Leo's amps that had fed back, but the amp itself wasn't the problem. That awful screech had been the fault of Junior Barnard's white Epiphone Emperor, and the big hollow box that made up the body of it. Leo had worked on that guitar, had hot-rodded the pickups for more bite, like Junior asked. But no matter what he did to the electronics, Leo knew there was a limit. He knew that a guitar made from a hollow box, prone as it was to producing feedback, was never going to let Junior Barnard play as loud as he wanted to.

Knowing how gadgets worked—what they could do, what they couldn't—had always been Leo Fender's specialty. Anyone who'd met him since about the age of fifteen knew that he had a gift when it came to circuits and schematics, wires and knobs. His parents had seen his technical abilities for the first time one bright afternoon back in 1919, when Leo was just ten years old.

The bouncing jalopy had turned off the main road and sputtered down the dirt driveway toward the Fender family ranch, skidding to a halt in front of the barn where, ten years before, on August 10, 1909, Clarence Leonidas Fender had been born. This was one of the first automobiles anyone had seen around the farm towns of Fullerton and Anaheim in the year after World War I's end, now sitting still while the Southern California sun burned its reflection into the hood. The car immediately drew Clarence and Harriet Fender's son over for a look. For young Leo, the vehicle was an object of endless curiosity: a smoking, bouncing, fussy testament to human ingenuity and restlessness.

The boy walked around the car in a hurried circle. Then he got on his back, squirmed underneath the chassis, and lay there in the dirt, studying the underside of this machine. All of it was caked in dust and grease, but he could still make out distinct parts. He saw the iron block of the engine bolted to a funnel-shaped transmission, which shot a rod of steel—the driveshaft—back to the rear axle. Thin black leaves held the two axles to the body. Skinny rubber tires hunched at every corner.

Leo lay there, taking mental pictures for what seemed like a long time. Then he shimmied back out into the sunlight, clothes painted in dust, thoughts racing, and went back into his parents' little ranch house. A while later, after the car had puttered away, Leo emerged with a drawing he took straight to his mother. Harriet Fender started when she saw it. Her ten-year-old son had sketched the car's underside in perfect detail, capturing not just the appearance of the various components, but their function and interaction with one another. All those complex parts neatly arranged in order. Young Leo had not merely seen the underbelly of this mechanical contraption—he'd understood it.

Cars would forever fascinate him, but not long after he made that drawing, Leo discovered the technology that would lead to his life's work. It lived inside the precious wooden cabinet his parents used to bring country singer Jimmie Rodgers and swing bandleader Benny Goodman into their home and out onto the fields where they grew vegetables. It gathered music and voices out of thin air, as if by magic. It was radio.

Leo's obsession began in 1922, when an uncle demonstrated a machine that received radio signals and amplified them enough to carry over a whole town. Radio was still known as "wireless" then, still so hampered by static that it was mainly used for transmitting Morse code. Yet from the moment he'd witnessed radio's possibilities, Leo Fender was fascinated. He soon built his own crystal set, a simple radio with an earphone instead of a speaker. When the handful of early commercial stations in Southern California would shut down for the night, he'd listen to the maritime communications between Catalina Island and harbors on the mainland.

By high school, Fender had a license to broadcast on amateur frequencies and a radio station set up high in his parents' barn, where he'd built an antenna that captured signals from Arizona and New Mexico. He was known by schoolmates for his ability to fix any broken radio, and for his long, detailed mechanical diagnoses. Decades later, Leo would date the establishment of his radio repair business to 1922, the year he turned thirteen.

It was as if he spoke the language of electricity, or electricity spoke to him. Leo Fender would never receive any formal training in electronics or engineering; rather, it seems he naturally understood them, perhaps *needed* to understand them, and achieved this understanding on his own. This technological world offered a chance to demonstrate his worth, to excel. At first glance, Leo Fender may have looked as capable as any other young man: healthy, from a stable family, a regular attendee at schools in Fullerton. But finding a realm in which he could thrive wasn't so easy, for reasons he would tell almost no one.

Certainly, performing wasn't going to be his specialty. Leo loved music and the sound of instruments, but "he couldn't keep a beat," one classmate told the guitar historian Richard Smith. He built a crude acoustic guitar in high school, yet he never learned to play or even tune the thing, seeing it largely as a technical object, a tool for producing vibrations. Leo Fender would never learn to play the guitar. Later, he'd explain that his enjoyment of the instrument stemmed from the precise pattern of harmonics produced by its strings. Where others heard music, Leo Fender heard physics.

In Santa Monica on that Friday evening after the war, Leo watched as the returned servicemen and their dates jaunted around the ballroom, refusing to let Junior Barnard's storm of feedback ruin the occasion. Like so many white audiences in the West, these couples were elated just to be in the room with Bob Wills and His Texas Playboys, rather than listening over the radio as usual. During the war, Wills had become a folk hero, a western demigod, for bringing the sound of home to the thousands of Texans, Oklahomans, and Arkansans who'd come to work or serve in the Golden State. His style of music, known as "western swing," was a curious combination of hillbilly tunes layered over a rollicking jazz beat: white American melody and black American rhythm. It was music for dancing, and as its popularity grew—whole towns from Amarillo to Fresno would now come out to see Wills play—it needed to get louder. Which is how Bob Wills came to rely on Leo Fender.

As Leo watched the Playboys on the bandstand, he might have briefly let his affection for this music and these musicians distract him. Wills stood up there, with his kindly brown eyes and indefatigable smile, winking at the ladies, while his twelve-piece band kept the rhythm rocking. The bandleader's belly seemed to bulge a little more every time the Playboys' bus rolled up to Leo's radio repair shop in Fullerton. The players would stumble out of the bus, stinking of stale air, booze, reefer, other things Leo did his best to ignore. A few of them would address the balding thirty-something in the plain blue shirt who was never without his belted leather tool pouch. Whatever horrors the road had inflicted on their amplifiers, whatever complaints the musicians had about volume or tone, Leo would fix them. He'd started building electric instruments in the back of his radio shop during the war, because the established guitar and amplifier companies had converted to making bomb gyroscopes or toothbrush handles. By that evening in Santa Monica, about two years later, the most popular band west of the Mississippi would use nothing but his equipment.

Watching the Playboys at the Aragon Ballroom that evening, with all the gleaming smiles and throbbing ranch-dance songs, Leo understood the reasons for his success in this business so far. He knew how to make amplifiers and public address systems sound good. He knew how to make them durable. He adored the electric steel guitar—the flat tabletop guitar that wove such gorgeous, golden ribbons through Wills's western swing music. Steel guitars were built of solid blocks of wood and played by sliding a metal bar across the strings. Leo's versions, played through his own amplifiers, emitted his ideal tone: heavy treble, heavy bass, light midrange to keep from getting muddy. It was a sound like "lemonade," he'd later explain—clear, bright, and punchy.

Leo looked at Noel Boggs, seated on the bandstand behind the electric steel guitar that had come from his radio shop. With its electric volume almost unlimited, its cascades of sound so liquid and fluent, the steel guitar made a star out of Boggs or any capable player in a western band. Standard guitarists, even hotshots like Junior Barnard, sat off to the side of the group, usually strumming their hollow-bodied instruments in near-anonymity. Steel guitarists, like Boggs, played riveting solos and often sat up front.

Leo lingered on a far side of the ballroom, listening carefully. He cocked his head to one side, hearing something strange. Curious, he pushed through the twirling couples toward the center of the room, where he could hear more clearly, and glared at Noel Boggs's steel guitar amplifier. Then, as if a switch had flipped, Leo took off.

He charged toward the bandstand, oblivious to the dancers all around. He dodged spinning shoulders in uniform, tripped over feet, incited a few angry words, but soon he reached the edge of the stage. Wills and his musicians were still pounding away, oblivious, the bandleader's eyes teasing the crowd. A couple of female adorers stood at Wills's boots, mesmerized, one running her hand up his trousers. Her eyes searched up for an approving glance, though Wills was long past the years when he might have given her one.

The Playboys hit the middle of the song, and this time the pianist took a solo. Leo, now at the foot of the stage, reached down to feel the tool belt on his waist. Then he set his palms on the edge of the bandstand, hoisted his body up, and plopped himself onto the stage.

A few dancers gasped. A few more stopped moving, pointed and stared.

"What's he doing up there?"

"Is this some kind of prank?"

It was obvious from everything about Leo Fender that he was not part of the band. His clothes were plain and rumpled. His back was turned. His hair was mussed. His hand seemed to be pulling something out of the pouch on his waist—a screwdriver.

A few of the Playboys rolled their eyes. Leo shuffled over to the wooden box next to Noel Boggs and began probing the back of it with his tool. Boggs just grinned and shook his head. This wasn't the first time he'd seen it happen.

More dancers started to stare and gasp. Murmurs issued through the ballroom. *The hell's this fella doing?*

Bob Wills saw the commotion and leaned into the microphone. "That's our friend Leo Fender, everybody, from Fender Electric," he said, in a Panhandle drawl warm enough to stop wars. "He's the reason you can hear us tonight."

The dancers shook their heads and turned back to their partners. And soon, his tweak made, Leo scurried back to the edge of the bandstand, hopped back down onto the dance floor, and disappeared into the crowd as if nothing had happened.

He'd been up there only a few moments. But after he returned to his post at the far side of the room, Bob Wills and Noel Boggs both noticed something. Boggs's electric steel guitar now came out a little clearer, a little more crisp. The difference was subtle, but both men could hear it. The thing just sounded better.

3.

"THAT'S NOT LES PAUL"

She pulled up to the house around dusk one evening, probably wondering if she was making a mistake. The newspapers were filled with stories of would-be starlets who'd taken such chances, only to meet some unspeakable end. This was a city soon to be terrified by the brutal Black Dahlia murder and captivated by Bugsy Siegel's gangland execution, a city transforming through the wartime influx of servicemen and defense workers into the third-largest metropolis in the United States. Only a decade before, the City of Angels had been little more than a pleasant provincial capital. It was now a chaotic behemoth hobbled by industrial smog and inadequate roads, a place of random violence, dashed hopes, and surging racial tensions.

But Colleen Summers was from Pasadena, and she knew that this troubled place could be a city of dreams. Most of those who'd come to LA during the war now wanted to stay, not just for the pleasant weather

21

and sprouting suburban neighborhoods, but out of a sense that, for all its faults, this was where the future was being created. Even in such a modest place as the bungalow where Summers had pulled up at 1514 North Curson Avenue in Hollywood—a small green house with a curved roof over the entryway and, in the front yard, two palm trees standing like a giant's skinny legs—even there, a glimpse of radical new possibilities might be seen.

Or rather, heard. For the man who'd asked Colleen Summers to come over that evening had claimed over the phone to be a famous guitar player, her favorite. It was a chance the twenty-two-year-old strummer and singer couldn't turn down.

In front of the house, Summers found a gardener mowing the lawn in a dirty work shirt and army boots. He told her to go to the garage and wait for Les Paul, who would meet her shortly. Summers walked down the driveway toward the detached building, slowly growing aware of male voices and music coming from inside. She noticed a little patio in the backyard, with a few orange trees and an outdoor fireplace. The main garage door was sealed shut, but some of the men inside saw her through a window and helped her climb in.

Immediately upon squirming inside, Summers could see that this wasn't a garage in any normal sense. The walls were paneled in white acoustic tile, and a piano dominated the central space. Microphones dangled from shiny stands like lush metal fruit, and disassembled guitars leaned listlessly against the walls. One side of the room had been cordoned off into a booth and filled with what Colleen recognized as recording equipment. This was apparently some kind of studio.

Soon the window slammed open again, and the gardener wriggled in. He was an unshaven man of about thirty in a straw hat, several inches shy of six feet, with a potbelly. As he entered, Colleen could smell the beer on his breath.

"There's Les now," one of the men said.

Colleen gasped. "That's not Les Paul, that's the gardener!" she said.

This had to be a prank. There was no way this wormy figure could be the man who elicited such elegant lines from the guitar. But then the gardener stuck out a dirty hand, smiled, and introduced himself as Les. Colleen was certain she was being mocked and refused to believe that the tall, sophisticated jazzman she'd so long envisioned could be really this schlub. Finally, the gardener picked up a guitar and plucked out a few runs in a fast, frisky style she couldn't help but recognize.

So this was him: the man whose records had filled her family phonograph cabinet back in Pasadena, the artist she'd praised for so many years without ever seeing his picture. Les Paul had invited Summers over to audition for a spot on his new radio show, and she'd thought it would be a great opportunity. Now she must have begun to wonder.

Summers's disappointment with Les Paul wasn't reciprocated. Climbing through the window into the garage that evening, Les saw a gifted young woman whose expectant brown eyes and leveling smile had broken the hearts of more than a few hometown suitors. She sang in a warm, quiet, conversational style—not with any operatic flair or jazzy mystique, but with a clarity and sweetness that were undeniably appealing. Summers had been playing guitar and singing on church stages around Southern California since she was in junior high, and was now leading the Sunshine Girls, a trio within Gene Autry's radio retinue, building a following around Southern California.

With that voice and experience, Les thought Summers would make a perfect foil for a hillbilly radio show he was planning. Despite her disappointment in his physical presentation, she agreed that night to be on it. Les would play the crass country rube, and she'd be the decorous ingenue, shrieking and laughing when he set her script papers on fire, acting genuinely scandalized when he appeared in the studio wearing nothing but his underwear. In between, they'd sing songs. Colleen had been playing guitar since childhood and was a worthier match on the instrument than Les wanted to admit. Even at that first encounter, with his wife, Virginia, and his two young sons resting not thirty feet away inside the house, he began to get ideas about this woman that went far beyond music and a radio show.

Les had come to Hollywood from Chicago back in 1943, hoping to get close to Bing Crosby, America's most popular singer and the person who, to him, symbolized the top of the music world. Almost as soon as Les had arrived in LA, the army had drafted him, but as usual, he managed to schmooze his way into a plum assignment producing discs for Armed Forces Radio. Between a job working with stars and evening club gigs playing jazz for them, Les befriended half of Hollywood. After a single year, he'd talked his way out of the army and, through another bit of conniving, had finally encountered and charmed the great Bing Crosby.

In July 1945, as the United States had prepared to either bomb or invade Japan, the two musicians had recorded a languid ballad called "It's Been a Long Long Time." Bing's voice, a fatherly bass-baritone completely unshaded by worry or doubt, had drifted through the lyrics: "You'll never know how many dreams I dreamed about you, or just how empty they all seemed without you," he sang, before turning over the entire middle of the song—sixteen bars—to Les for a solo. Given space to roam, Les's round, raspy electric guitar went fast and busy, then soft and sweet, deepening the song's feeling of a long, contented sigh. At thirty years old, running on little sleep, Les delivered what might have been the best solo of his life.

Decca Records had released "It's Been a Long Long Time" the following October, two months after Japan's surrender brought the end of World War II. The song's lyrics made not a single mention of the conflict, of the men returning home from all around the globe, of the ecstatic families being reunited, the great baby boom beginning. They didn't have to. The dreamy ballad perfectly captured the national mood and became a hit for the ages, riding the charts through the fall and winter of 1945–46. Les Paul had instantly gained a national reputation. In the wake of that wildly successful first collaboration, a grateful Crosby had helped persuade Les to convert his garage into a private recording studio, and spread the word about the brilliant guitarist with a talent for making vivid recordings.

After Crosby's endorsement, Les received an unending stream of visitors in his backyard, including such talents as singing cowboy Gene Autry, comedian W. C. Fields, and jazz great Art Tatum. They all came for one reason. In 1940s Hollywood, commercial recording studios were run by stodgy, bureaucratic corporations. Any time booked in them was extremely expensive and tightly controlled. Recording itself was done by the book, in a way Les (who by then had accumulated years of experience in radio studios) thought antiquated. So a private studio in a casual backyard—a place where anyone could make a recording, at any time of day, for free (at least at first)—was a revelation. There, musicians could experiment, fool around, show up drunk at midnight. And tireless Les, with his novel ideas about microphone placement and noise reduction, would make them sound good.

During the day, Les played on the radio with his jazz trio and on the short-lived hillbilly show for which he'd auditioned Colleen Summers. He soon couldn't resist trying to charm the young woman, but Summers sharply turned him down, according to biographer Mary Shaughnessy. She didn't find Les attractive, and of course, she had no lack of suitors. Ever since she'd turned sixteen, the local boys had pursued Summers intensely, and she enjoyed their attention. At twenty-two, she'd already been married twice, though the first nuptials were almost instantly annulled, and the second ended in divorce after she refused to stop performing. When she met Les, Colleen had been focusing her attention—intensely, it was thought—on a Pasadena boy named Foy Willing. But then something started to happen.

Like Les, Colleen lived for music. Like Les, she was a creature of the nighttime. She was young and unencumbered, and Les lived as if he were. His wife, Virginia, though married to him for most of a decade, seems to have had little presence in his life, perhaps because she remained outside music. Soon, Les was inviting Colleen out to see his trio perform at Club Rounders, where they entertained such Hollywood stars as Crosby, Groucho Marx, and Bette Davis. As a background singer with Gene Autry, Summers had been in a distant orbit around these people. But now, going out to see Les play, making eyes at him over a cocktail, enjoying the endless introductions he gave her—Les knew everybody—she found herself laughing among them.

In Colleen, Les saw a beautiful young woman who innately understood his obsession with music and who shared his raucous sense of humor. If she couldn't quite match his boundless energy—no one could—she came very close. So the older jazz jokester and the young country singer soon began to fall intensely in love with each other. To distinguish her character on his radio show from the Colleen Summers who sang with Gene Autry, Paul rechristened his twenty-two-year-old costar "Mary Lou." After the initial shows were finished, their relationship turned entirely romantic.

But their professional lives and Les's marriage to Virginia made that relationship tricky.

Everyone in Hollywood knew Les Paul was married, since so many had visited his house to record. Appearances mattered enough that Paul had to be careful who saw him canoodling with another woman in public, so he and Colleen would often just drive off into the night together, listening to after-hours jazz broadcasts, stopping at hotels in the daytime to rest.

While Les and Colleen carried on their secret affair, he went on tour with the Andrews Sisters, a popular vocal group. When the tour hit Chicago, his mother, Evelyn, came down from Wisconsin for a visit, as Les recalled in his autobiography. She'd heard him on the radio that week, she said, and he sounded great. Evelyn didn't give praise by default, and Les would've liked to accept the compliment. But there was a problem. Les and the Andrews Sisters had been performing seven live shows a day, a typical theater engagement for 1947. He hadn't *been* on the radio that week. Les told his mother she must have heard someone else.

"Well, whoever it was, you should sue them," Evelyn said. "When you plug that thing"—that electric guitar—"into a wall, you all sound alike."

Les was hurt. He was dismayed. He thought about it for a few days. And then he realized that his mother was right. Although he'd become a great guitar player, a worthy companion to a top singer like Bing Crosby, Les Paul was still just a guitar player—a sideman.

Singers could never completely be copied, but who besides other musicians knew one trumpeter from another, one drummer, one pianist? Who could tell them apart just by their sound? Les had done nothing so far that couldn't be copied by some eager usurper—and the imitators were already on his tail. There loomed in the near future a reality in which any distinctiveness he had would be completely lost.

Les took this realization not as an annoyance or fact of life, but as an emergency. To become what he wanted, Les knew he needed to stand apart. He needed the same inimitable character that a singer had. And he'd need to create it with the electric guitar.

So Les quit the Andrews Sisters tour in a huff, relinquishing all the money and attention it brought. Then he raced back to his little bungalow in Hollywood, to find a sound no one else could match.

4.

"I'M GONNA DO SOMETHING ABOUT IT"

It was the most unusual instrument to come out of Leo Fender's workshop, and no one could buy it. The little black guitar was not part of the Fender product line, that array of amplifiers and electric steel guitars that drew musicians from around Southern California to Fullerton. It had no name. It was an experiment.

Leo had made it back in 1943, with his friend Clayton "Doc" Kauffman, a fellow tinkerer who'd shifted his interest and ambition from radios to electric guitars and amplifiers. Late one night in the back of the radio shop, Leo and Doc had hastily fashioned this odd little thing from an oak plank. They'd envisioned it simply as a test bed for a pickup, which is why they made the body so small—only three or four inches wide. They thought no one would really use it. Then the locals heard it.

Four years later, Fullerton's cowboy pickers would still roar through that proud little downtown on their motorcycles, pull up to Leo's shop three doors down from the main intersection, breeze past the shelves of records and radios for sale, and ask for that black guitar. There was only one. It was too shoddily built to sell. But Leo would rent it out, and some months it was gone every weekend.

Instead of building that test bed as an electric *steel* guitar—the type played flat like a table, by running a metal bar over the strings, useful mainly for country and Hawaiian music—Leo and Doc had made it a standard, or "Spanish," guitar: the type fingered with bare hands, held against the chest, and played far more widely. However amateurish it looked, it was an electric guitar. Yet unlike every other electric guitar, this one had no hollow acoustic body. It was just a solid plank of wood, with strings and an electric pickup, slathered in glossy black paint. Leo and Doc hadn't intended this design to be radical; they'd built it from solid wood because, back then, they'd known only how to build steel guitars, and steel guitars were solid. Essentially by accident, they'd wound up creating something players loved, a misfit stepchild of a guitar that extended creative expression past what any other standard model allowed. With its solid body, the black radio shop guitar could be cranked up as loud as anyone wanted, loud enough to plunk out over a band, and it wouldn't feed back.

No wonder Leo had been so eager to trade the steady, dull business of repairing radios for the novel, unpredictable one of making electric instruments. At first, even his accidents, like that radio shop guitar, became successes. But nearly two years into running the Fender Electric Instrument Company, by 1947, the situation had drastically changed. Now when Leo looked around the workshop where his namesake instruments were built, he felt not pride, nor confidence, but fear. Doc Kauffman had left their happy partnership early the previous year, scared of taking on debt to build a company. Leo now wondered if incurring new financial obligations had been smart. Though it had barely started, his outfit stood on the precipice of ruin. And if this enterprise went under, Leo knew that everything else he'd amassed in his thirty-eight years— his modest success of a radio shop, his self-respect, perhaps even his marriage—would go with it.

Leo's wife, Esther, had already endured years of sacrifice while he established the radio shop, and with his now running both the shop and the instrument company, the two of them lived as near-ascetics. Esther contributed the salary she earned as a telephone operator to his businesses while adhering to a strict household budget. A lively, unpretentious farm girl—dark-haired, pretty, and at least as odd as Leo—Esther financed her husband's projects, tolerated his absence (with frequent rolling of the eyes), and retorted with a sharp word or two when he went too far. Thirteen years into their marriage, the Fenders rented a house in Fullerton instead of owning one, and plowed all of their earnings back into Leo's businesses. They'd decided not to have children. Leo felt that he didn't have time or money to raise a family, that he couldn't bear any distraction from his work.

The headquarters of the Fender company consisted of two corrugated steel sheds sitting a few steps from the railroad tracks that carried Fullerton's oranges and lemons to the world. Sunlight shone into the sheds' raw interiors, but over the first winter there, Leo had discovered that their roofs let rain leak in. In one shed, wood saws buzzed constantly; in another, metal presses stamped out parts with an ominous, incessant clanging. There was no bathroom, so Leo and his half-dozen employees had to walk down to the train station to relieve themselves. The workers used acetate to finish the steel guitars and kept the highly flammable liquid warm in the most risky way possible: near an open, gas-fed flame. When the fire inspector visited, he was so terrified by this arrangement that he ran off and called from a pay phone. Leo, of course, knew that his factory wasn't a safe environment: one employee had seen his guitar-playing career ended when a punch press sliced off four fingers, and another mishandled a table saw and sent a shard of wood straight into his groin. But right now, there were bigger problems.

To get his instruments into stores, Leo depended on a pair of new partners: Francis Carey (F. C.) Hall and Don Randall, the owner and manager, respectively, of a radio parts wholesaler in Santa Ana, some half hour's drive south of Fullerton. Under the arrangement made with Hall—an upright businessman, pious churchgoer, and rather cold-blooded finance whiz—Leo designed and built Fender electric instruments while Hall's Radio and Television Equipment Co., known as Radio-Tel, marketed and sold them. Instead of handling the Fender line himself, though, Hall had assigned it to Don Randall, an ambitious twenty-eight-year-old former clerk. Leo had been a little surprised at seeing this Randall kid made his coequal in charge of sales and marketing. He could never have imagined how long they'd work together.

To fill Hall's initial order of five thousand steel guitar and amplifier sets, Leo had purchased a boxcar full of walnut originally destined to become rifle stocks. The boards languished as his workers slowly assembled them into steel guitar bodies and amplifier cabinets, and they'd become infested with termites. The wood was ruined, and so were dozens of products. One of Randall's salesmen had been demonstrating a shiny new Fender steel guitar inside a music store, hoping to land a customer, when a termite came boring out of the guitar body in plain sight.

Bugs were only the beginning of the quality problems. Steel guitars left Fullerton without magnets in their pickups; amplifiers would arrive in stores plagued by mysterious hums and buzzes; players would purchase new equipment only to find corroded electronics and cracked finishes—the telltale signs of moist wood. It wasn't in Leo Fender's nature to believe that there was anything he couldn't accomplish. But he now ran a factory producing wooden instruments without having any real experience in either manufacturing or woodwork. He was still just a radio repairman—and it showed.

When Fender amps and steel guitars did come out at top quality, musicians like Bob Wills and the country-western players of Los Angeles raved about them. Leo spent his nights dragging amplifiers and steel guitars to honky-tonks and dance halls around the region, converting one musician at a time with the clear sound and durable design of his instruments. But popularity among pros didn't quickly translate into mass sales. Just getting Fender products into music stores around the country, as Hall and Randall had promised to do, had proven far more difficult than anyone expected.

With orders lagging, Leo had had no choice but to hide from his creditors and intermittently close down the factory. When it did operate, it was normal for workers to rush to the bank on Friday afternoons to cash their checks before the company funds ran out. (The money covering them was usually Esther's pay from the phone company, deposited just in time.) Leo had already taken out two loans from F. C. Hall to stay afloat, humiliating himself in front of his chief investor. Now he was desperate. He'd made every conceivable move to keep the factory from failing, thus ensuring that if it *did* fail, he'd be completely wiped out. So when a slick salesman came through Fullerton one day that year with a big, bright idea, Leo was probably as irritated as he was intrigued.

Of the half-dozen traveling salesmen Don Randall had hired to get Fender products into music stores, none was more effective than Charlie Hayes. The tall, slender Texan could walk up to a crowd of strangers and return a few minutes later having befriended all. "He could sell you a set of false teeth you'd need when you were fifty, if you were twenty-four," a colleague remembered. For Hayes, life was a party, and so was selling musical instruments. Clad in cowboy boots of which he was inordinately proud, and fine, shiny suits finished with a bow tie, Hayes cruised around the Southwest in a Cadillac, selling Fender equipment out of his trunk. He wasn't a musician. He was a schmoozer and a prankster in an era when setting a friend's golf bag on fire made for a good practical joke.

Though his sales territory stretched to Texas and Oklahoma, Hayes kept an apartment in Santa Ana, across the street from Radio-Tel. He enjoyed close relationships with both Don Randall—a boss who was at least as much a friend—and Leo, who shared his love of practical jokes. Hayes served as a bridge between the two men, and a link to the outside world of everyday dealers and players, from which he gathered vital intelligence.

That intelligence—and, most likely, knowledge of Leo's experimental black guitar—informed a request Charlie Hayes made to Leo one day, likely in 1947 or early 1948. He asked Leo to produce a standard (or as it was then called, "Spanish") electric guitar—an ideal complement, he thought, to Fender's line of electric steel guitars and amplifiers.

Hayes was a born salesman, and Leo wouldn't have been hard to sway. He'd seen players visit his radio shop to rent the black guitar. He'd seen the struggles that players like Junior Barnard faced when trying to pull off searing solos on their hollow-body electrics. He knew by then that the electric guitar needed a radical redesign, that music was pushing past what an acoustic body would allow.

But at that moment, with his business sliding toward insolvency, and with his factory unable to build its current products to consistent quality, there was not a whole lot that Leo Fender could do about it.

UP IN HOLLYWOOD, Les Paul wrestled with the knowledge that even being a virtuoso on the guitar would not bring the fame he craved. His own mother had told him she couldn't tell if it was him playing on the radio or someone else, and any new guitar feats Les mastered were quickly copied by others. So he began to think differently. Instead of an end in itself, Les now began to see his guitar playing as one element in a larger project: a whole new sound that would combine his brilliant musicianship, the pure electric guitar tone he wanted, and radical new recording techniques he envisioned.

Les had long been intrigued by the idea of what he called "sound-on-sound"—the layering of several different recordings, or tracks, on top of one another. Technology in 1947 made it possible to layer performances only through the slow, arduous process of recording a track onto one black plastic disc, then recording that disc onto another disc while simultaneously performing the next layer. If even the slightest mistake appeared, everything had to be started over. A multilayered recording was thus mind-bendingly difficult and expensive to make, given the precision and studio time required. But when executed flawlessly, it opened up a world of possibilities. And Les now had his own studio.

As he struggled to conceive this project, the garage studio drew musicians: singers and jazzmen and members of the loose group who sometimes called themselves the Hollywood Hillbillies. These were sidemen in the innumerable cowboy and western swing bands gigging around Los

Angeles—some elite, some barely working. One elite was a steel guitar genius named Joaquin Murphy, who came to Les's backyard one Sunday afternoon that year with an older man, an acquaintance who'd built him an unusually good amplifier. While the cowboy jazzmen milled around the studio and drained cans of beer in the backyard, Les shook hands with a quiet man, six years his senior, with a balding pate and exacting enunciation, who introduced himself as Leo Fender. They soon realized they had a lot to talk about.

Both men loved music; both were onetime radio geeks; both were uniquely preoccupied with the nature of amplified sound. Leo, the private, plainspoken tinkerer, cared for nothing but the immediate technical problem on his mind. He relished engineering not necessarily because it might bring wealth or fame, but because it simply fascinated him: he liked to improve electronic devices more than he liked to do just about anything. If anyone could understand that depth of obsession, it was Les Paul. And yet Les's experimentation had a different aim than Leo's. Les's electronics projects thrilled him on their own, but they had the ultimate goal of helping him achieve his personal sound, the unique style that would take him where he'd wanted to be since childhood: the top. While Leo Fender followed his nose from one intriguing problem to the next, happy to dwell for hours in his private workshop, Les Paul pursued a type of achievement that was intrinsically public.

It's not hard to picture the two of them together, hanging with a group around the Hollywood garage: Les probably overacting, performing the role of host, asserting his place as the alpha while oozing false humility. And Leo, most likely glued to his chair or bent over to inspect some mechanism or circuit, occasionally and impolitely breaking his silence to exclaim either admiration or disdain. Paul, though charming as hell, would've made sure his dominance was clear. Fender would have been largely oblivious to the contest of egos in the room. They must have amused each other—so similar were they, yet so different. If not for their overlapping fascination with amplification and musical instruments, they might never have become friends. Their personalities and worlds were as far apart as any in music could be: one's arena was primarily the stage, the other's, the workbench; one talked and the other listened. Paul hesitated to drop his showman persona and show his technical knowledge, wary of boring his audience. Fender offered detailed, dulling disquisitions to anyone.

Each man clearly developed a sharp assessment of the other. "He talks a lot," Fender mused about Paul, "but he doesn't say much." And Paul would later recall Fender as utterly determined despite the humbleness of his situation—a portrait both admiring and a little condescending. "Leo was a person [who] learned what to do by listening to the person [who was] playing, which is a wise thing to do," Les Paul said years later. "When Leo came over to the house . . . he could listen to his guitar amplifier and ask the musician what he would like to have changed on it. Does he like it? If he doesn't like it, what does he not like about it? Well, he was doing the same thing with the guitar."

And that was where their friendship turned competitive. Soon Leo Fender and Les Paul were focused on—even obsessed with, as only people like the two of them could be—the challenges of electric guitars. They met on Les's patio on Sunday afternoons to listen to the players and discuss ideas. Les had built his Log; Leo had constructed his black radio shop instrument. Both knew there was a major advance on the horizon for the electric guitar, that the present limits on its volume and tone would somehow have to be overcome. They were chasing the sound of music's future. "Fender was in my backyard looking at that guitar"—the Log—"for years," Paul recalled. "And he says, 'I'm gonna do something about it.'"

Soon, though, they met another man, as different from each of them as they were from each other, who was looking to transform the electric guitar, too.

5.

"YOU SAY YOU CAN MAKE *ANYTHING*. RIGHT?"

It was Leo Fender who brought him over, likely one Sunday afternoon that year. Les Paul must have chuckled when he saw the two of them walking down the driveway toward the garage: Leo, dressed as always like a janitor, his engineer's body unremarkable in every way, his expression distracted, as usual. And next to him, this other man, grinning behind a cigarette, a decade older and perhaps half a foot taller, booming with confidence. Booming, literally—it was said that Paul Adelbert Bigsby didn't need much help from the microphone when he called motorcycle races at the local speedway.

Les felt a tension between Paul Bigsby and Leo Fender almost from the start, and he soon learned why. In workshops only about twenty miles apart, both men built steel guitars for the country musicians of Southern California. It didn't matter that their business philosophies were as dissimilar as their appearance and demeanor, that they'd come from vastly different backgrounds. Bigsby and Fender made and sold the same thing. Each believed in the superiority of his designs and regarded the other's warily, at best. Leo never outwardly evinced any disdain for Bigsby—it had been his idea to bring Bigsby to Les Paul's house that afternoon, to include him in the fascinating conversations taking place there. But even in those days, Bigsby sometimes preferred not to be reminded of Leo Fender's existence.

Born in Illinois in 1899, Paul Bigsby had a decade on Leo and fifteen years on Les, and, consequently, a different view of life. He'd spent a wayward youth racing motorcycles through the deserts of California and Mexico, picking up trophies and stories along the way. In Los Angeles, Bigsby had learned the versatile trade of pattern-making. A pattern-maker carved wood into precise shapes—gears, engine parts, even pieces of battleships—that were used to make a mold from which a metal part was fashioned. Not all pattern-makers engineered the pieces they cut, but Bigsby did. Since he could both design detailed mechanical parts *and* create them, he liked to brag that he could build "any damn thing," and he wasn't exaggerating.

Around the end of the war, Bigsby had grown indignant over what he thought were inadequate tools then available to his musician friends. Soon, his last name appeared on the most expensive electric steel guitars in Los Angeles, which he designed and built entirely on his own at a home workshop in the industrial suburb of Downey. Obsessed with traditional craftsmanship, with the neatness of joints and the finish of panels, Bigsby measured his success in the immaculate quality of his final product, not the numbers sold. While Fender offered a complete product line—electric steel guitars and amplifiers—to what he hoped would become a mass market, Bigsby custom-built steel guitars that only established pros could afford. Each one took him a month or more. In 1947, he quoted a price of $750 for one complex model, half the cost of a brand-new Chevrolet then, and about $8,000 today.

Hanging around Les Paul's Hollywood garage on that first afternoon was a group of country-western sidemen, some of them well-known. For all three tinkerers, watching these pros rehearse, record, even just fool around, was almost a sacred rite. To be in the presence of these drawling musicians was an edifying joy, and furthering their music—the common-man songs that had raised them all—was a dear cause. So Les Paul, Leo Fender, and Paul Bigsby listened carefully, noting the way the steel and standard guitarists would tweak the knobs on their primitive amplifiers, how they'd arrange the microphones, what sound they aimed to get. Then they'd pepper the musicians with questions: *How's that tone for ya? What if we give this a try? Does the amp need more bite? More growl? Maybe a bit more chime? Does it got enough hair on its chest?*

When recording had finished for the day, the three men would retire to the patio and take seats around Les's outdoor fireplace, under the orange tree. Sipping on beers—or, for teetotaling Leo, lemonade—they got into the real intricacies, the stuff only sound engineers cared about: frequency equalization, speaker type, cabinet size. What kinds of magnets to use in pickups, where to install the pickups on a guitar, how such details would change the instrument's tone.

It was an obsession the three men shared with rare intensity. Each knew there was a breakthrough on the horizon for electric instruments. None could have foreseen the arrival of rock 'n' roll, but it was clear that music was growing louder and more driving, challenging the limits of acoustic instruments. The electric steel guitar was the star of the western band—so somehow, there had to be a way to get more volume out of the standard electric guitar, too. Yet even apart from one specific instrument, there was a sense among these men that the potential for electric amplification in music hadn't yet been realized, that there was still a lot of power waiting to be harnessed, incredible new tools waiting to be built.

Did Les Paul, Leo Fender, and Paul Bigsby gather the importance of their proximity to one of the first home recording studios in the country? Did they know that western swing in the style of Bob Wills, so popular in Southern California, was driving music toward a louder future? Could they see that their backyard group made up a kind of avant-garde?

Most likely not. This was not Bell Labs or MIT; though these people ached to improve music technology, their improvements were initially aimed at a very tight circle, rather than at the larger public. There was no way they could foresee the wide-ranging consequences that the development of better electric instruments would have. The question in their minds was more immediate: which one of them would perfect a new design first?

Almost as soon as these three had started talking, a competition had been outlined, a race, a challenge—one to which each man brought a different strength. Les was the only expert guitarist. Leo excelled at electronics. Bigsby was a master craftsman. What each stood to gain from the project varied, but for all three, building a better electric instrument would fulfill the promise each saw within himself. And so on Les Paul's citrus-shaded patio, the three most important men in the development of the modern electric guitar began to gather regularly, starting a race that would define the sound of sixty years of popular music.

Bigsby fired off the opening salvo. It was a new pickup—a gray metal oval with a balanced, punchy sound—that he brought to Les Paul, who installed it on one of his main guitars. Storytellers and bullshitters, Paul and Bigsby were both social people, despite their consuming interests, and quickly formed a collaborative relationship. Les liked the sound of Bigsby's pickup so much that he tried to keep it a secret; whenever someone pulled out a camera, he'd hide it behind his right hand. Not that it worked. A popular country player named Merle Travis asked Bigsby about it. Chet Atkins, another gifted country guitarist, saw Bigsby's creation and requested one, too. As players listened to the tinkerers' conversations in the backyard and reaped the fruits of their experiments, the race between the three men accelerated.

It took a decisive turn one weekday morning that year. Merle Travis was strumming his Martin acoustic at the Pasadena studios of KXLA, a booster of local cowboy musicians that would soon become the first all-country radio station in the United States. In rushed Paul Bigsby—an oak of a man and a regular visitor to musician friends playing live at the station. Bigsby and Travis were close buddies, having bonded over their love of motorcycles and music, and they liked to give each other a hard time. Travis would sometimes bait Bigsby's ego by asking him to build wild new devices for the guitar, challenges the older man would accept but not always pull off. On this particular morning, after Travis's radio show had ended, Travis strolled up to Bigsby in the control room and popped a question.

"You say you can make *anything*," Travis said in his distinctive Kentucky drawl. "Right?"

"Any damn thing," Bigsby bellowed.

"Can you build me a guitar like I draw the picture of?"

"Sure! Draw it!"

So Travis grabbed a roll of KXLA script paper and sketched out his design for a new instrument. As a standard guitar player, Travis was sick of all the attention electric steel players got just because their instrument was louder. He'd been toying with an idea: why not build a standard guitar just like a steel, with a solid body shaped to be held against the player's chest, and a neck shaped to be fretted with fingers? In a region then saturated with country music, and in love with the electric guitar, such an instrument, as radical as it would have been back east, just seemed to make sense.

Travis fancied himself an amateur cartoonist, and he drew a detailed sketch with a pencil. He wanted an electric guitar whose body had almost the same width and height as a standard acoustic, but far less depth. That body was to be made like a steel guitar—virtually solid, with no acoustic sound holes—and only about an inch and a half thick. It would be finished with a single electric pickup and an ornate, violin-style tail piece, along with other fancy details.

In handing Bigsby the sketch, Travis may have been jesting, tossing a problem at his friend that he knew would be brow furrowing. But Paul Bigsby didn't hesitate to pick up the gauntlet: he took the roll of paper back to his workshop.

6.

"ALL HELL BROKE LOOSE"

Late at night in the Hollywood garage, Les Paul recorded himself. He was trying to capture the sound he heard in his head, a futuristic style that couldn't be copied. Excited by his talks with Fender and Bigsby, he'd mostly stopped using the Log guitar he'd built back in New York and was using newer experimental instruments, some more conventional and some rather bizarre. Les's workhorses were three modified Epiphone hollow-bodies, each of which had a factory-cut hole in the back that let him easily swap out pickups and other components. These "clunkers," as Les called them, had bolts popping out of their bodies, black tape covering their sound holes to fight feedback, and metal plates set under their strings to limit acoustic vibrations. Next to another project of his, though, they looked downright plain.

Les fashioned the "headless monster" out of a sheet of aluminum and an old guitar neck. He bent the aluminum into a kind of amoeba-like blob to form the body of the guitar and bolted the neck to it. He ran the strings down the neck in the opposite of the usual direction, so the guitar didn't have a headstock with tuners—its neck simply ended. The result was a headless electric guitar with one pickup, a body made out of sheet metal, and no acoustic properties whatsoever. "It was like something from Mars," one friend remembered. And it sounded great. Jim Atkins, Les's former bandmate, called it the "undisputed finest, clearest tone quality instrument that was ever devised" (presumably, he meant by Les). "It looked like a frying pan with strings on it." The headless monster worked well in the studio, but it had to stay there: Les discovered that heat from stage lights would expand its aluminum body and push the strings out of tune, making the guitar tremendously unreliable. He'd taken another bold step in reimagining the electric guitar with this instrument, proving that a guitar didn't even need a wood body—but just as with the Log, he hadn't found quite the guitar he wanted.

By late 1947, though, another wild experiment of Les's was yielding more promising results. It had taken him about five hundred tries, he claimed—five hundred acetate discs cut, ruined, and thrown away—but he'd finally made one recording that showed off all the features of the new sound he envisioned. It was a completely reimagined, instrumental version of "Lover," a sentimental Rodgers and Hart tune originally written for the 1932 musical film *Love Me Tonight*. After so many hours of listening only to himself, Paul wasn't sure what effect the recording would have, so he brought the disc to a party one night at the home of a well-known publicist. The room was filled with his Hollywood friends, famous musicians and show-business people, all drinking and enjoying themselves. "Mary," as Les now referred to Colleen Summers, came, too. After they arrived, Paul snuck over to the turntable, slapped on the disc, and stepped away to watch the crowd react.

It began with layers of bright electric guitar runs racing over each other, some tracks mechanically sped up, their pitch raised, so that the strings seemed to twinkle. One guitar strummed the outlining chords in a standard pitch while countless sped-up layers drizzled out the lead melody, letting it rain down in sparkling little notes. At a minute and six seconds, the music seemed to subside, pausing briefly, only to leap into an even faster tempo, with more twinkling electric guitars playing intricate runs that soon cascaded and collided into each other, forming a dizzying eddy of sound.

"All hell broke loose. No one knew what it was and who was doing it, and questions were flying," Paul recalled in his autobiography. "But Mary knew immediately, even though she hadn't heard it before. She said, 'I know who that is!' "

Les Paul had remade the Rodgers and Hart song into something unrecognizable. Using just his garage studio and his modified guitars, Les had given "Lover" an electric renovation, outfitted Old Hollywood in the sound of science fiction. He'd created something that no other recording studio could then produce, and dazzled everyone at the party.

Given this reaction to "Lover," Les knew the record had to be released. Decca Records, with which he'd been associated, deemed the production too wild, so Les decided to try Capitol Records, an LA upstart that in only five years had become one of the biggest labels in the country. He showed up late one Friday afternoon to the office of A & R man Jim Conkling, who was packing for a flight. Conkling told Les they'd meet when he returned, but Les once again snuck "Lover" onto the turntable. Conkling listened in amazement as the waves of sped-up electric guitars crashed over one another and agreed right then to release the song. The two of them wrote out the basic conditions of a contract, including the stipulation that Les could work out of his garage studio and deliver the master recordings he made himself to Capitol.

And with that, Les Paul was no longer just a sideman. He now had his own solo record deal as an artist. Capitol would release "Lover" in early 1948, and Les felt sure it would be a hit. The driving force behind this achievement, just as Les had envisioned, was his pioneering recording techniques paired with a pure electric guitar sound—as pure as he could then get.

That winter, Les took Mary home to Wisconsin for a celebration. His father and older brother had bought a tavern in Waukesha called

Club 400 and planned a grand-opening party over three days in early January. With a recording contract at Capitol, a revolutionary new single on the way, and a young woman in his life whom he deeply loved, Les had reason to celebrate, too. On the drive east, though, he picked up a fever. Sweating in the high-altitude Arizona mountains during the dead of winter, he began to worry that he was seriously ill.

Les returned home to find his father furious at him for traveling and sleeping with a twenty-three-year-old singer while still married to another woman. George Polsfuss had been notoriously unfaithful to Les's mother, and their marriage had collapsed in a bitter divorce when Les was eight. But George was now a converted Presbyterian and a remarried man, and he didn't think his son should be with a homewrecker. Evelyn, who usually disapproved of her son's female companions, decided that she liked this Mary Lou.

Club 400 was no rough-hewn roadhouse but an elegant saloon just across from a train depot, with a sweeping art-deco bar, Formica tables, long curtains, and patterned wallpaper, as if half diner and half living room. Les spent several days there jamming with his hometown buddies and bragging about the record Capitol was about to release. By the time the festivities ended, George Polsfuss's opposition to Mary had started to soften. He told his son, however, that this young lady was too nice for him—that a "roughneck" like Les would end up hurting her.

Meanwhile, Les's flu showed no sign of abating. As they headed south out of Waukesha, intending to stop in Chicago before driving home, the illness grew worse. Paul was perspiring in the brittle Midwestern cold, delirious. He couldn't stop to see friends in Chicago. As he and Mary cruised down Route 66 into Missouri, he asked her to take the wheel of their Buick convertible and lay down in the passenger seat to rest. Voices on the radio warned about a winter storm about to slam into Oklahoma, exactly where they were headed.

Paul was curled up in the car, half-asleep, when he heard Mary scream. He bolted up to see the big Buick sliding sideways over an icy bridge. He grabbed the wheel and kicked Mary's foot off the brake, straightening out the car for a moment. But he couldn't keep the heavy vehicle from skidding on the ice. The two of them watched, terrified, as the Buick plowed through the wooden guardrail, slipped off the overpass, and plunged some twenty feet into the ravine below. Les threw his arm in front of Mary to protect her face. Neither of them were wearing seat belts, so when a speaker in the backseat tore open the car's convertible top, they fell out with it. The Buick landed upside down on the frozen river. Les and Mary landed beside it, alongside their guitars and equipment. There they lay amid the snow and ice, fifty miles from Oklahoma City, waiting for someone to find them. Because of the storm, there was no traffic on the road that January Monday.

Finally, a telephone operator noticed that a line had been cut somewhere between the towns of Davenport and Chandler, Oklahoma. Only because the accident severed the line did authorities find the scene. Doctors at a local hospital determined that Mary had been lucky—she'd suffered only a cracked pelvis and a few scratches. Les, however, had punctured his spleen, broken his nose, and cracked his collarbone, six ribs, and his pelvis. After lying in the snow all those hours, his fever had turned into full-scale pneumonia.

The worst, though, was his right arm—his strumming arm. It was shattered in three places, including his elbow. Doctors believed it might have to be amputated from the shoulder down. Only days earlier, Les Paul had seemed on the cusp of stardom, with a thrilling single ready for release. Now, suddenly, no one knew whether he'd ever play the guitar again.

7.

A "NEWFANGLED GUITAR"

American Legion Post No. 277 stood off a country road near the town of Placentia, just east of Fullerton. The barnlike building was a former citrus packing house that looked like it had risen right up out of the orange groves, an island of shingled civilization amid Placentia's oil derricks and dust. On Saturday nights in 1948 a band of western musicians convened there, many of them regulars on a popular local radio show. Their agenda was the usual: to get the folks dancing.

Leo Fender was a regular at these gatherings. He showed up not to cut loose but to handle the sound system for the performers—to ensure they could be heard over the increasingly boisterous din of the legion hall's increasingly large audiences. One evening late that spring, Leo was wandering around the building in his dusty work clothes. Slowly, carefully, he set up his hand-built plywood public address system and arranged a set of his amplifiers on the stage. In walked Merle Travis, the country guitarist who'd formed a friendship with Paul Bigsby and given the big man a sketch, challenging him to create a different kind of guitar.

Tonight Travis showed up with an oddly thin guitar case.

Travis stepped onstage and opened the case, and what he pulled out of it riveted Leo's attention. It was a standard guitar—the kind you fret with your fingers, not a steel—but like nothing Leo had ever seen. Its body was impossibly, absurdly, beautifully thin: an inch and a half, perhaps, from the back to the front. This body had the same height and width as a standard acoustic, but with no thickness and no sound holes. Its top was all solid wood. Solid bird's-eye maple, in fact, so the entire thing, its usual hourglass guitar-body shape, gleamed as if gilded, and appeared to be spotted with rivulets of darker wood: the so-called bird's eyes in the maple. The accent pieces around the bridge were intricate, even florid. The headstock was a flowing, avian shape with all its tuners arranged on top, to be within easy reach of the player.

A single magnetic pickup sat under the strings, which—it occurred to Leo as he took in this instrument—meant that the only way to get any sound out of it was to plug it into an amplifier. This instrument was not acoustic. It was a totally electric guitar. A hunk of wood, basically, with a neck and strings. There were knobs for volume and tone, and a switch to alter the sound of the pickup. But there were no holes to emit acoustic sound—or capture feedback.

As soon as he had a chance, Leo Fender approached Merle Travis and asked about this "newfangled guitar." Gushing over his new accessory, Travis reeled off the instrument's strengths: it was loud, it was beautiful, it was thin and easy to play. Its mostly solid-wood body kept the strings ringing like those on a steel guitar. The headstock wore the name "Bigsby" in elegant script.

Fender couldn't have missed this last detail, but he was too fascinated to be polite. Here, suddenly, was proof that his black radio shop experiment—a standard guitar built like a steel, with a solid-wood body—had shown the way forward all along. The only way standard guitars could get much louder was by going completely electric, jettisoning sound holes and large acoustic cavities—by throwing out much of what had made a guitar a guitar. Bigsby was apparently already building such a radical instrument. But how well did it work?

Leo asked if he could borrow Merle Travis's new trophy and return it at next Saturday night's western dance. Amazingly, Travis agreed. (Nice guy.) At the end of the show, the player handed his gorgeous new guitar over to Fender, who—although he would deny these events for the rest of his life—drove back to Fullerton that night with its thin case laid out on the bench seat of his sedan.

Leo had abstractly envisioned adding a standard guitar to the Fender line, and had listened when his salesman Charlie Hayes suggested it. Now he knew he *had* to do it—and soon. Travis's Bigsby guitar was getting all kinds of attention: from onlookers who'd never seen such a skinny six-string, from players who'd never heard anything like the sweet electric patter it emitted through an amplifier. That Bigsby guitar was alluring—for Leo, dangerously so. It was beautiful; it was a breakthrough. It must have sent his mind racing with thoughts about the future, the possibilities of volume, of tone, of expression. He was dying to get the guitar back to his workbench, to run its signal through his oscilloscope. But Leo must also have dwelled on the fact that Merle Travis's new electric guitar was custom made, a one-off, expensive. Because he was already envisioning another way to do it.

The quality crisis that had threatened to drag Fender into ruin was now starting to let up, but the company was still far from stable. If Leo truly wanted to design his own standard electric guitar, he'd have to work on it at night, after his daily production run had been completed. Only by constantly churning out new merchandise—and praying that Don Randall and his team could sell it—could he keep his struggling outfit afloat.

Luckily, Leo now had help in both production and design. He'd recently hired a wiry Arkansan named George Fullerton to be his all-around assistant, shop foreman, and companion through endless desolate nights in the workshop. Fourteen years younger than Leo, and a skilled guitarist, Fullerton had to be cajoled into coming on board. But for Leo, his presence was worth swallowing a little pride.

The men had first become friends when George Fullerton moved to California just before the war. Both were music and radio enthusiasts, but when George opened a rival electronics shop almost across the street from Leo's, the older man was angered and hurt. Their relationship turned cold. But even in a town of some thirteen thousand, Leo couldn't get away from George, especially not while running sound for the country gigs George's band played.

The passage of two years and the worsening fortunes of the instrument company seem to have overridden Leo's bruised ego. Soon, he viewed George Fullerton as the perfect man to rescue Fender. A hard early life in the Ozarks had taught George a panoply of skills: he knew electronics, mechanics, and woodworking; he was an illustrator and a painter; he could play guitars and build them. After months of persuading, Leo convinced the younger man to come work in his dangerous factory part-time, in the evenings, and they began to make steady progress toward rebuilding the hundreds of Fender steel guitars and amplifiers that had been returned under warranty. When they finally finished these repairs, in the late winter of 1948, Leo and George set fire to the heap of discarded steel guitar bodies and amp cabinets behind the plant, burning to ashes all the evidence of Fender's near-failure.

George expected to return to his job wiring fuselages at the Lockheed plant. But Leo knew that if the company didn't have someone with this man's talents, he would end up right back in the same mess. The chances of convincing George to stay weren't good: he'd made it clear that building steel guitars and amps in a stifling workshop wasn't his idea of a great career, and he didn't even play the steel guitars Fender made—only standard guitar.

Searching for a sales pitch, something that would convince a young father to give up a steady aerospace job in that uncertain period after the war, Leo shared with George his nascent vision for a new electric standard guitar. A guitar that could be—*should* be—revolutionary. Like most of American manufacturing, the musical instrument industry had been virtually erased by the war effort. Now normal life was resuming, and Fender's competition was moving slowly. Leo told George that this little company could have a major impact with the new type of standard guitar he had in mind. But he could only make such an instrument with a skilled guitarist and woodworker on board.

Leo's pitch worked. That day, Fender gained a huge asset, a man even more important than Doc Kauffman, the partner who'd first gotten Leo interested in electric instruments. George Fullerton would spend the next forty-three years working alongside Leo Fender—building, designing, and testing, as well as serving as Leo's chief interface with the rest of humankind.

Over chilly nights together in the factory, Leo and George now confronted the most basic of questions: What should an electric guitar be? If the instrument truly didn't need an acoustic body, as Bigsby's Merle Travis guitar seemed to have proven, what *did* it need? What could it allow a player to do that current instruments did not?

To answer these questions, the two men haunted dance halls and honky-tonks around Southern California, pressing up against stages to ask lanky cowboy players what they liked and didn't like about their instruments. Leo gathered vital intelligence and ideas from the Sunday afternoon sessions at Les Paul's house—doubtlessly, noting the mess of experimental guitars scattered around his garage—and closely studied Bigsby's Merle Travis guitar for the week that he borrowed it that spring.

Obviously, the new instrument had to solve the core problem created by putting an electric pickup in an acoustic guitar: feedback. Leo and George's chief goal was to let players turn up loud without creating ruinous screeches and howls.

But the drawbacks of hollow-bodied guitars didn't end there. These instruments were painstakingly assembled out of dozens of thin wooden panels and had necks that were carefully glued to the body, which meant that if any part of the guitar was broken or damaged, the entire thing had to be sent away for a lengthy and expensive repair. Meanwhile, the player, who usually owned only one guitar, would be out of work.

At the time, life on the road for a western sideman was extremely rough: bands crammed six or more players and their equipment into station wagons, or piled larger ensembles into hard-sprung tour buses. However wholesome country music could appear, its lifers witnessed every vice and crime imaginable: alcoholism and drug addiction (Benzedrine and reefer were big), gambling and prostitution, regular brawls and the occasional murder. As accessories to this life, delicate wooden guitars were bound to get smashed or shattered. Leo and George wanted their guitar to be durable, but they also knew it must be easy to repair when, inevitably, some part of it broke.

Naturally, the thing had to be affordable. A giant firm like Gibson could offer a broad line of instruments, with plain models at the low end and opulent creations at the top, but Leo wanted to sell the Fender guitar for a price the average semiprofessional could manage, to maximize its accessibility and, hopefully, its sales.

So: loud, durable, and cheap. Leo and George had come up with a set of specs no electric guitar on the planet then fulfilled. And there was still another. Their new instrument *had* to sound gorgeous; otherwise, what would be the point? Yet achieving sonic brilliance was probably the challenge Leo perspired least over. He knew he possessed one great skill, a core ability that meant everything here: From the maze of an electric circuit—from the countless possibilities of resistors and capacitors and potentiometers and magnets and wiring and power supplies and schematics—Leo Fender could conjure whatever lush and evocative sounds he desired. He could make human tones arise from a tangle of matter. That wizardry seems to have formed the bedrock of his identity—and likely his sense of self-worth.

From almost the moment he'd encountered the world of radio electronics as a thirteen-year-old, Leo Fender had wanted to excel in it. Perhaps some part of him understood, even back then, that these machines offered him a unique opportunity for mastery and success. He certainly came to see this later, after his parents chose to send his younger sister to a four-year college instead of him, depriving him of any formal education in engineering or electronics, and after he'd tried selling ice (which he hated) and working as a government bookkeeper (where he was laid off after four years). Radio work was something—perhaps the only thing—he knew he could do well. Because of what had happened to him as a child, the list of endeavors at which Leo Fender could likely succeed was unusually short.

In 1917, Leo's family grew vegetables on their ten-acre plot in Orange County, selling them every Saturday at a market on the coast. To earn extra money, Clarence Monte Fender, Leo's burly, pipe-smoking father, would arise long before dawn and get to the stockyards outside Los Angeles, where he'd load up his wagon with manure and bring it back to Fullerton to sell as fertilizer. Monte had started his own working life on a Kansas dairy at age twelve, and taught his son that being a man meant working tirelessly—that work made you who you were.

One evening that year, after a Saturday trip to sell vegetables, Leo arrived home with his father. He was seven or eight years old, and it was his job then to clean out the wagon bed—to sweep or wash out the residues of the day's haul. He was up there that evening in the high perch of the farm wagon, scrubbing, sweeping, tossing out buckets of water over the worn wooden planks, working like his father taught him . . . when, suddenly, he lost his balance.

Leo tried to steady himself, but he couldn't. Instead, he pitched over the side of the wagon and tumbled down onto a fence post, landing hard on his face. The fall battered Leo's body and smashed his right eye. He cried out for help, and his parents carried him inside. But while the bruise slowly dissipated, Leo's right eye refused to heal. Then it became infected. Monte and Harriet Fender were frontier-hardened farmers, and they waited a long time before seeking a doctor to look at their son's eye. By the time a physician finally saw the wounded child, there was nothing to do but remove the eye altogether.

So Leo Fender, not ten years old, was now without his binocular vision. He would wear a glass eye for the rest of life.

Having a glass eye meant that Leo would never excel at boyhood pursuits like football or—his father's favorite—wrestling. It meant he would never get called up to serve in the military. As a kid he'd felt ashamed, embarrassed by the droop on one side of his face caused by the glass orb. Naturally taciturn, he reacted to the handicap by retreating further into himself.

But although Leo couldn't see as well as other people, he loathed the idea that he was any less capable.

Five years after the accident, an uncle introduced him to radio electronics, opening up a world in which he could show his abilities. And almost thirty years later, fortified with the knowledge of his expertise, Leo decided to give up running his successful radio shop and train his focus on another challenge: creating a completely new type of standard electric guitar, like Bigsby had for Merle Travis, but in his own way.

Leo could now look at a machine and see instantly its strengths and weaknesses. Just as he had borrowed and examined the Bigsby creation, Leo helped himself to what he believed were the best ideas in current electric instruments, whether they came from local competitors like LA's Rickenbacker—which had been the first to offer a commercial electric guitar in 1932, and which even sold a compact solid-body guitar made out of an early plastic in the mid-thirties—or elite giants like Gibson, or his own electric steel guitars. Instead of gluing the new neck to the guitar body, as a typical guitar maker would do, Leo borrowed Rickenbacker's method and simply bolted the neck and body together. This took minimal effort, and if the neck ever had to be replaced, the player could do it themselves in five minutes. The fact that this method ran counter to prevailing aesthetics did not bother Leo, since it was eminently practical.

There were dozens of other decisions to be made, about wood types, body sizing, string spacing, and the arrangement of electronics. George Fullerton, who unlike Leo knew how a standard guitar should feel to a player, sketched outlines of a body, cutting blocks of wood in various shapes to ensure proper sizing and balance. He and Leo first designed a body that had hollow but sealed-off resonating chambers inside, rather than one made of solid wood. For the neck material, Leo settled on hard rock maple, the same material used in bowling pins, as it was so strong a full-grown man could stand on the neck without breaking it.

Working day and night amid the clatter of the factory's saws and presses, George soon learned one reason Leo's former partner, Doc Kauffman, had left the business: Leo Fender labored seven days a week, starting early in the morning and continuing—fueled by endless cans of Planters peanuts—until two or three a.m. On the coolest nights that spring, he hooked up a gas hose to a steel drum, lit a spark, and let the lambent, cherry-red barrel radiate heat. The room still didn't get very warm.

8.

"POINT IT TOWARD MY BELLY BUTTON, SO I CAN PLAY"

Lying in a hospital bed in Oklahoma City, Les Paul wavered close to death. The gossip columnist Walter Winchell had written about the car crash and suggested that Les wouldn't survive. Wracked by pneumonia, injured seemingly everywhere, Les coughed until he screamed. After hours of surgery, the doctor at Oklahoma City's Wesley Hospital, who turned out to be an old friend, finally made some progress toward reassembling the right arm. The patient would live, it now seemed, but perhaps without the ability to play guitar.

By then, Les was alone in the hospital. Mary had recovered within weeks and was out on the road singing with Gene Autry. While Les waited to see how well he'd heal, on February 23, 1948, Capitol released his "Lover" single with a similarly futuristic instrumental called "Brazil" on its B-side. Just as he'd witnessed at the party, it stunned almost everyone who heard it. Critics at the jazz and pop magazines raved. "Paul goes one-man guitar band. Six guitars recorded individually then dubbed together," *Billboard* wrote. "Effect awesome but brilliant." And that was about "Brazil." Of "Lover" itself, the magazine gushed, "Man, this is gone . . . technique so good it's ridiculous." DJs around the country began playing the songs several times a day. "Lover" hit the charts and rose to no. 21, with "Brazil" reaching no. 22—impressive performances for instrumental songs. Les's doctor even brought in a radio and placed it at his bedside, so the patient could hear his hit song and the excited listeners and DJs.

But it all meant nothing to Les. Bound to the hospital bed, alternately coughing and screaming, his right arm only tenuously held together, Lester Polsfuss could barely eat or sleep. He was miserable—his life, once so carefully constructed, had shattered in several places, just like his playing arm. He had no idea whether his fingers would ever again fly across a guitar fretboard. He didn't know how Capitol Records would treat him during what was sure to be a long recovery. His career had plunged into deep uncertainty, and the medical bills were piling up. Newspapers had reported widely on the crash, and although they'd kept Mary's real name hidden—Les was reported to be with a certain "Iris Watson," twenty-three years old, at the time of the accident—the illusion of his having a stable private life had been cracked wide open. There was so much doubt, and so much pain, now and in the foreseeable future. Even if he got lucky, there'd be difficult mending and relearning. Les Paul had finally become popular on his own as a performer, and he couldn't enjoy it at all.

After two months in Oklahoma, he was flown to a hospital in Los Angeles, where doctors finally found the cause of his lingering fever and began treating it. The question remained what to do about his shattered arm. Lying in his hospital bed one day, Les heard two doctors arguing about it in the hallway. One wanted to amputate the arm completely, eliminating any chance of his ever playing guitar. Another argued that after all the man was a *guitar player*—shouldn't they try to fix the arm before giving up? The two doctors came into Les's room and presented

him with the options: a dicey bid to reconstruct the elbow, or an operation to take off his right arm altogether. Les recalled himself as having a
ready quip: "I'll tell you what. Let's not say we can't save the arm until we
prove we can't. Okay?"

The optimistic plan was to rebuild the elbow with a slice of bone
grafted from his right leg and a metal plate attached by seven screws.
Once the doctors set the arm in position, Les would never again bend
his elbow, but he might regain flexibility in his shoulder and fingers. This
was the best-case scenario.

Before the surgery, the doctors asked at what angle Les wanted his
arm screwed together. "Just point it toward my belly button, so I can
play," he told them.

Les emerged from the surgery looking like the most miserable man
ever to wear a toga. A white cast surrounded his torso from one shoulder
down to his hips. The broken arm was now bent permanently at ninety
degrees, and was anchored to his body with a broom handle. Bruises and
swelling covered his right arm, and the merest feeling tingled in his fingers. He began to wriggle the digits on both hands, trying to get sensa-
tion and dexterity back. Slowly, he grew hopeful that he might one day
resume playing the guitar. And with that, his old sense of humor began
to return. "I finally got so ornery they threw me out," he wrote that year,
in a form letter to the many DJs who'd spun his first release.

> I'm back home now lying on my back thinking about how you jokers
> came through for me when I really needed it. "Lover" and "Brazil" are
> number 6 in the Big *Variety* as I write so maybe your efforts (and what
> plugs they were) will help get me out of hock with the docs (a poet
> yet!). Seriously, though, I don't know how to thank you. But the next
> time I drive across country I promise to take more time and drop in
> to see you instead of trying to crash that disc jockey show that old St.
> Peter's running. That's where I made my big mistake. Well, right now I
> look like Mr. Plaster of Paris. They've got me in a plaster straight jacket
> that won't quit, but it won't be long now. I'm going to do a Houdini any
> day, and see whether the busted wing will work.

With much healing ahead of him, and a bit more optimism, Les started to take advantage of the forced pause in his career. He'd done a great deal by then, and yet he knew—even after the reception of "Lover"—that he was a long way from where he wanted to be, a long way from what his mother would call "the top." Lying in bed, he read electronics manuals and books on philosophy, drifting deep into thought. This was a recharge, a chance to stop, assess where he was going, and perhaps refocus himself and his efforts. Les remembered his childhood years playing hillbilly music, his passionate leap into jazz in the 1930s, his tours with pop singers after the war. Thinking about all he'd seen and done, especially the time spent with the Andrews Sisters and Bing Crosby, Les began to feel that playing jazz—despite all he loved about it—was not going to get him the large audience he craved. "When my trio and I would come out and play our jazzy stuff, the audience would applaud like, 'That's good. That's very nice,'" he recalled in his autobiography. "Then the Andrews girls would start singing, and the crowd would go nuts. They were connecting with the audience by giving them what they wanted to see and hear, and I got the message."

Though the futurism of "Lover" had dazzled the public, Les also suspected that the novelty of his flashy guitar playing and sound-on-sound recording techniques would wear off someday. He thought about adding yet another dimension to his sound—and remembered the hillbilly radio shows he'd first done with Mary Lou. A man and a woman performing together, and playing off each other, naturally gave an audience a lot to relate to. But Les didn't consider Mary a serious musical partner then. He thought of her as a hillbilly singer, a "lightweight," he told his biographer. He wanted to pursue a more powerful female vocalist, someone like Rosemary Clooney, Doris Day, or Kay Starr.

As feeling came back to his fingers, he retaught himself the guitar. He'd done it once already, after the electric shock in Queens, but this time would be a much greater challenge. The huge ring of plaster surrounding his chest kept him from even holding the instrument close to his body, so he set it on top of a modified guitar stand. Before too long, it seems, Paul Bigsby came over with something to make the effort a little easier.

What Bigsby brought to the Hollywood garage one day was a curious and forgotten milestone in the development of the guitar: a solid-body electric with a miniature body and a full-size neck. It was built of exquisite wood and with full electronics, like Bigsby's Merle Travis guitar—but with a body small enough to fit around Les's cast.

Les would long after deny any knowledge of this instrument, since the existence of a Bigsby guitar built for him deeply complicated the story of his long and profitable relationship with Gibson. But Bigsby left players' names on the patterns he made for their guitars, and a team of researchers discovered the pattern for this one decades later, while cleaning out an old instrument factory. When Bigsby biographer Andy Babiuk confronted Les with the pattern bearing his name, apparently in Paul's own handwriting—a pattern that perfectly matched a strange Bigsby guitar that had been sold at a garage sale only a few miles from Les's longtime home—Les finally acknowledged it. "Bigsby brought over this little guitar that he'd made up," he told Babiuk. "We fooled around with it and I threw it in my pile of guitars. It was so small that it was hard to play."

However little use it saw, the instrument shows how fluid things were in those Hollywood days. Les Paul, a name long associated with Gibson and his own experiments, worked with Paul Bigsby on a radical solid-body electric guitar—a vital step toward what the instrument would soon become.

As the nimbleness returned to Les's fingers, and as Les adjusted to having his right elbow at a permanent bend, he managed to record a few new discs. Capitol wanted a follow-up to "Lover," and Les desperately needed the money; medical bills from his accident had nearly bankrupted him. While still encased in plaster, he recorded the jazz standard "Caravan," "What Is This Thing Called Love?," and a few others. Meanwhile, the outward appearance of his personal life began to adjust to its furtive reality.

A friend who visited Les and his wife, Virginia, at home that summer remembered that when their conversation ended, Les walked him to the corner outside. When they got there, Les suggested they head to a nearby tavern, where, to the friend's surprise, Mary Lou was waiting. Les went off with her for the rest of the evening. Not long after that encounter, Virginia finally gave up on being married to a largely indifferent husband and moved with their two children back to Chicago. Les didn't even protest; he later claimed that he'd known marrying Virginia was a mistake. "I let myself be talked into it," he wrote in his autobiography. "I knew my first love was always going to be the guitar, and that first love is very selfish." Others saw the continuation of a pattern in which Les charged toward his own goals and jettisoned any impediments—human or otherwise—that slowed his progress.

With Virginia now gone, Les moved Mary into the Hollywood bungalow. The friend who'd seen Les and Mary rendezvous at the bar was shocked at how quickly the change occurred. "Four weeks later," he told Les's biographer, "I got back to his house and there [Mary] is, washing his clothes, scrubbing the floors. I look at Les and he doesn't say anything. He just laughs."

9.

"WE PERFORM LIKE WE'RE SINGING IN THE BATHTUB"

SUMMER–WINTER 1949

In the summer of 1949, more than a year after the crash, Les and Mary drove to the Mayo Clinic, in Ohio, to have his cast removed, and decided to stop for a few days in Waukesha. Les hadn't performed live since the accident and thought the tavern owned by his father and brother would make a friendly, low-stakes place for his shaky fingers to debut.

Inside Club 400, he got an old friend to play bass, set down a chair against a mirrored wall, and, with a clunker guitar under his still-healing right arm, proceeded to joke and jam for the hometown crowd. Something about the arrangement didn't suit him. Perhaps the sound was too thin, or perhaps Les had been expecting a rhythm player who didn't show up. Different versions of the story abound, but for whatever reason, Les soon pulled Mary out of the crowd, thrust a guitar into her hands, and—ignoring her obvious reluctance—coaxed her to not only strum but sing. Mary normally sang country, not pop or jazz, and other than a brief run of radio shows at the start of their relationship, the two had never performed together. She didn't know the words or chord changes to Les's songs, so she stumbled, prompting Les to correct her.

But Les could see immediately that the crowd adored Mary. The two of them, wildly in love, had a natural spark, and they tossed out the kind of affectionate banter that's hard to fake. Les realized before the set ended that the female singer he wanted, the onstage companion he'd been mulling since the accident, had been with him all along. He hadn't considered it—he'd thought Mary's unadorned voice wasn't suited for pop or jazz—but Les, of all people, knew that a crowd's reaction doesn't lie. There was no question: this "Mary Lou," the girlfriend for whom he'd jettisoned his wife and children, should *also* be his costar, joining him onstage and on recordings, adding her sweet, familiar voice to the circus of sounds from his guitar. Colleen Summers was up for it, too—maybe sensing that by combining their talents, these two longtime accompanists could make a strong claim for center stage.

Rehearsals started the following day in Les's mother's basement. Next, the couple set up at a jazz club in Milwaukee to practice in front of an audience, hoping to ease Mary's lingering stage fright—all the worse now since, as the lead vocalist, she was the center of attention. While preparing for those gigs, Les flipped through a local phone book, seeking a new stage name for his singer. He'd always called her Mary, or, on the radio, Mary Lou. Now, he decided, she would be known as Mary Ford. When they returned to Hollywood a little later, Les cajoled NBC into giving him a radio show on which Mary also sang and performed. They were paid $150 per weekly, fifteen-minute episode, just enough to keep them afloat.

One day that summer, Les's old friend Bing Crosby pulled up to the Hollywood bungalow with a gift in the trunk of his car. It was an Ampex Model 300 recording machine, an early version of a piece of equipment that would become standard in recording studios for decades to come. Using magnetic-tape technology developed in Germany and copied after World War II, the Ampex provided vastly improved sound quality over acetate discs, and though it was large—a silvery mass inside a suitcase, with two reels that held spools of tape—it was ostensibly portable. Crosby had adopted the technology almost as soon as he'd heard about it, since its high fidelity allowed him to prerecord his radio shows. Les could never have afforded the machine himself, but the gift from Crosby would spur a major change in his life—and with it, the future of recording. Les quickly realized that he could simply add a second recording head to the Ampex's original one to allow for multitrack recording, or "sound-on-sound." It would no longer be necessary to laboriously bounce songs from one platter to the next. The tape machine could do it all, and its portability would allow Les and Mary to record their weekly NBC show from the road. Immediately after receiving Bing's gift, they loaded up the trunk of their Cadillac and headed for Chicago.

Les had wanted to play at the Blue Note ever since "Lover" had first tantalized the public more than a year earlier, but the accident had kept him from making it to the stage of this elite jazz club. Finally at the Blue Note as part of a duo with Mary, he produced as much uproar over his clothes as his music. In an era in which pop and jazz musicians performed in fine suits or tuxedoes, *Newsweek* wrote that patrons at the club were "all but stunned" by the couple's debut. "In sport shirt, unpressed pants, Argyle socks, and loafers, Les was as relaxed as his clothing as he gave out with his extraordinary guitar style . . . Mary Ford, an attractive blonde who sings and plays second guitar, was almost as casually attired." But the review, headlined "Paul's Comeback," was unmistakably positive. In keeping with their low-key attire, Les and Mary and their electric guitars possessed a familial, slightly mischievous appeal that won over every crowd that saw them. "We perform like we're singing in the bathtub," he told the charmed *Newsweek* reporter.

Soon the couple hunkered down in Les's old neighborhood of Jackson Heights, on the edge of New York City. They still owned the bungalow in Hollywood and were recording shows for NBC in Los Angeles, but events in the East kept occupying them. In October, Les's father died, and the couple returned to Waukesha; at the end of the year, they were hired for another club engagement in Milwaukee. Back in the vicinity of home, Les remembered how his father had disapproved of his living and traveling with Mary without being married to her. George Polsfuss had warned his son not to make this sweet girl part of his hectic performer's life, believing Les would wear her out. But Les's and Mary's careers were growing ever more intertwined. They loved each other, and they were hopeful about the future.

So on December 29, 1949, at the Milwaukee County courthouse, the man born Lester Polsfuss and the woman born Colleen Summers married, with two friends as witnesses. Neither Les's mother, Evelyn, nor his brother, Ralph, who both lived less than twenty miles away, attended the ceremony. A few hours later, in a move that would foretell much about their marriage, Les and Mary picked up their guitars and strode onstage for another gig.

10.

"IF LEO MISSES THE BOAT NOW I WILL NEVER FORGIVE HIM"

SOUTHERN CALIFORNIA,
FALL 1949–SUMMER 1950

After closing down the factory one evening in the fall of 1949, Leo Fender and George Fullerton drove up Highway 101 to a sprawling dance hall on the north side of Los Angeles called the Riverside Rancho. Billing itself as "the Home of Western Music," the Rancho was the most prominent country-western venue in town, offering live music nearly every night. Its interior was slathered in frontier kitsch, with Spanish tiles topping false eaves, whitewash trim around the stage, and walls that sagged with weathered wooden boards and wagon wheels. Performing that night was Nashville's Little Jimmy Dickens, a grinning, soon-to-be-famous country singer who stood four foot eleven on the Rancho's broad stage.

As Dickens played, Leo and George strode through the smoky dimness to a corner near the bandstand, carrying a prototype of their new solid-body electric guitar. The room was filled with white Angeleno men in crisp slacks and shirts, twirling grinning ladies in long dresses. The stench of stale beer pervaded the venue. Back in the dark, male voices were swelling with whiskey.

Leo and George were waiting for the band to take a break, hoping to talk to the guitarist, when a young man walked in, noticed them sitting there with a strange-looking instrument on the table, and sidled over. His greasy hair, which was parted to one side, framed a dashing young face with dark features. The man asked about the guitar in a thick Georgia accent. Leo held up the prototype and must have beamed.

The white-enameled body of the instrument looked almost alien it was so thin, with a single cutaway on the lower side to allow players' fingers to reach the highest frets. A small black pickguard curled up next to the strings like an artful tattoo. One black electric pickup—the heart of the machine— sat in a gleaming metal tray under the strings. At the base of the thin body, two knobs protruding from a steel plate allowed for adjustments to volume and tone. Here was radio technology, screwed into a wood-shop project.

"Well, could I try it?" the stranger drawled.

And so Leo handed it over. The young man took the guitar and sat down on an edge of the stage, far from where Jimmy Dickens was warbling with the band. He started running his fingers over the thing, unplugged, nearly silent. Leo Fender and George Fullerton watched from their table, having no idea who this man was.

"Live it up" was his philosophy, "money green" his favorite color. Jimmy Bryant, then known as Buddy Bryant, held regular gigs at the Fargo Club on Skid Row and was rising quickly in the LA country scene. The handsome guitarist fancied himself a jazzman, almost a bebopper, a pure artist—and the blur of his fingers put jaws on the floor wherever he played. Maybe it was the Purple Heart he'd been awarded for fighting Germans in the war, or the abusive childhood that had encouraged him to pick up the fiddle, or the drinking habit, or the metal plate in his head from a combat injury, but Bryant never lacked for self-confidence. When Dickens's band took a break, the guitarist asked if he could plug into one of their amplifiers, and the band members agreed.

Right then, Leo and George discovered whom they'd been talking to. Cranking the amp to a biting volume, Bryant began to unfurl fluid runs up and down the Fender guitar's thin neck. The first thing everyone noticed was his speed—a lightning quickness that he'd picked up from playing fiddle breakdowns. But Bryant wasn't only fast. As with some of LA's best country pickers, the foundation of his style was jazz, which let him conjure a vast range of moods. Bryant wrung humor out of his flurries, tapping out voices that addressed and answered one another as if an entire horn section were conversing through a single guitar solo. The Fender's thin neck let him reach preposterous speed, and the sharpness of the guitar's tone gave his phrases clear punctuation. In contrast to the warm, often muddy-sounding hollow-bodies of the day, the Fender issued bright and crisp, with emphasis on the bass and treble and a thin midrange. It cut through the smoky room with the presence of an electric steel guitar, just as Leo had intended.

A crowd of dancers gathered around as Bryant, still sitting on the edge of the stage, sent flutters of notes out from the strange contraption in his hands. Even the band members stood wide-eyed, watching him play. Bryant and this prototype guitar soon became the evening's main entertainment, regaling the Riverside Rancho for more than an hour, as George Fullerton remembered. No matter how complex or quick his runs became, Bryant simply sat there, still but for his fingers, wearing a devious grin while casting sprays of electric sound out of this incredible machine. Little Jimmy Dickens never retook the stage.

That evening gave Leo and George tremendous new confidence in the ideas they'd pursued over so many late nights. Bryant's vivid playing and the reception it got validated Leo's notion that an electric guitar could indeed be solid, simple, and plain so long as it supplied powerful volume and good tone. It seemed the audience at the Rancho had been enthralled as much by the strange look of the guitar as its sound. The thin shape and graceful curves of the Fender prototype exuded a sense of modernity and newness, while its sharp, metallic tone struck virgin ears as fresh, even futuristic—the aural equivalent of a gleaming patch of chrome.

As Leo showed the Fender prototype around Southern California, close observers noticed its similarity to the guitar Paul Bigsby had made for Merle Travis. Both bodies filled nearly the same dimensions; both had one electric pickup near the metal plate that secured the strings to the body, known as the bridge; and both had a section of the body cut away to allow access to the upper frets. Some felt that Leo had simply copied his competitor's work. "I designed the Fender guitar, you know, and Bigsby built the first one," Merle Travis said years later. Indeed, signs that Leo had learned from Bigsby would continue to reappear.

But while Bigsby's work embodied old-world craftsmanship, Leo's prototype embraced the age of mass production. The pattern-maker had toiled over the smallest details, from fretboard inlays shaped like the suits of playing cards to a neck joint that he spent hours shaping by hand. The radio repairman, on the other hand, glued together two blocks of pine, rounded off the edges, and bolted on a neck cut from a slab of maple before finishing the guitar in chrome and plastic. This was the leap from classical design to modernism; from the age of walnut to the age of celluloid; from the America of brick-and-iron cities to the America of stucco-and-glass suburbs.

Though the Fender prototype did look toward the future, it remained—like Leo himself—stubbornly modest. Bigsby's Merle Travis guitar was one exceedingly fine tool for an expert, the Rolls-Royce of six-strings. Leo had instead built a Volkswagen. He knew that an everyman guitar would sell better than an elite one, and he needed it to sell. But he simply wasn't the craftsman Bigsby was; he wasn't an artisan who invested his ego in the smoothness of a neck joint. Rather, Leo was a technician: a man who judged himself by the clarity of a signal, the logic of a circuit—and now, the easy replacement of a guitar neck.

After that night at the Riverside Rancho, Jimmy Bryant soon demanded his own Fender electric standard guitar, and in exchange he agreed to publicly endorse Fender instruments. Leo was thrilled. His ostensible rival was not.

On October 7, 1949, Paul Bigsby completed a new standard guitar, a custom job that had been ordered by none other than Jimmy Bryant. Another bird's-eye-maple beauty inspired by the Merle Travis creation, this instrument at first had Bryant's name inlaid in black letters on the top of its body. When Bigsby called to say that the guitar was done, Bryant backed out, explaining that he'd just made a deal with Leo Fender and no longer wanted it. Paul Bigsby was enraged. He hadn't spent a month or more making a single instrument so that some mouthy guitar player could reject it. In a fit of spite, Bigsby cut out every bit of Bryant's name and filled in the cuts with wood. Then he covered over the entire section with a black pick guard and sold the guitar off to another player.

So far, there hadn't been much sense of direct competition between Leo Fender's instruments and Paul Bigsby's. But with Leo now developing his own standard electric guitar, that was starting to change.

While Leo showed the new guitar off to players, Don Randall, the man tasked with trying to sell Fender instruments to the world, found he couldn't get an example of it out of Leo's hands. He desperately wanted to have a standard guitar ready for the industry trade shows of 1949, only to have Leo refuse. "I have done everything I know to convince Leo of the importance of having this material ready for the show," Radio-Tel owner F. C. Hall had written that year to Randall, who was then on the road. "Still he states that it is impossible to deliver these items in time." The demands of the business were banging at his door, but Leo, still stung by all those early warranty returns, wouldn't release a prototype until he was sure he'd gotten it right.

As Randall tried to sell the new standard guitar to dealers sight unseen, Leo made dramatic changes to the design. In late 1949, he decided that the guitar should have a solid-wood body instead of one with hollow chambers. It would be a board, basically; heavier but nearly foolproof to build. Leo also designed a headstock—the panel at the far end of the neck where the strings end—that arranged all the tuning pegs on the upper side, to be within easy reach of the player. Merle Travis had asked Paul Bigsby for this feature, and Bigsby had achieved it by ingeniously modifying the tuning machines to make them fit in one row of six, rather than the typical two opposing rows of three. On his second prototype, Leo used exactly the same tuners, modified in exactly the same way, and fitted them to a vaguely similar headstock. He later would insist that he'd come to this idea independently. He even denied borrowing the Bigsby guitar—but in light of the evidence, these denials are ludicrous. Leo Fender was simply doing what he'd always done: adopting a good idea.

By the summer of 1950, Don Randall was dying to show Leo's creation to the world, eager to see how it would be received at the major trade shows. The musical instrument industry was then a chummy club of white men, whose trade magazines ran briefs on which executive had just married or which had returned from a Hawaiian vacation. Well before long-distance phone service, widespread television, the fax machine, and the Internet, trade shows were where all the action (including the cocktail-swilling and back-slapping) happened. Every significant dealer attended to find out what their stores should be stocking. Getting a standard—or as it was then called, "Spanish"—electric prototype on display would make a major statement about Fender and the future of the guitar.

At thirty-two, Don Randall still found traveling around the country on business a thrill. He'd slept in a hotel for the first time only a couple of years earlier, and in letters to F. C. Hall he'd express feeling guilty about the exorbitant cost of his staying in Chicago and New York on business. Straightforward and likable in that small-town American way— "definitely the high moral type," as Hall once described him—Randall was frugal by habit, having come from a family of poor Idaho farmers who'd migrated to Orange County to seek a better life. Although he'd wanted to be a doctor, and probably had the brains for it, his parents couldn't afford the education. Instead, Randall had taught himself electronics, earned a commercial radio operator's license, and picked up some German and Spanish. In high school, he'd captained the basketball team, had his photo—strong square jaw and unflappable brown eyes— in the paper. During the war, he'd worked for the Army Signal Corps, its communications division, at an air base in Santa Ana. So while avoiding combat, and staying close to his wife, Jean, and their young son, Randall had felt the ennui of a new father staring down a long working life— especially after Hall requested his discharge from the service in order to get him back hawking radio parts.

Thank God, then, for the Fender line. Randall was now selling products he found fascinating, even if he couldn't play them, products that required hanging out with colorful musicians and traveling to trade shows. That summer of 1950, while Leo was fussing over the design, Randall and his salesman pal Charlie Hayes finally unveiled Fender's newest product at the National Association of Music Merchants convention in Chicago.

Randall had branded the guitar "the Esquire" in a catalog that spring, boasting that it could be played at "extreme volume." In Chicago, the instrument made its in-person debut—sparking notice as a wild creation from what was then a minor outfit in the far West. The Fender Esquire was the first solid-body standard electric guitar most industry insiders had ever seen, and the first intended to be mass-produced for everyday musicians. The guitar was easy to play, durable, and repairable, and could get very loud without feeding back.

Competitors overlooked all that. Most mocked the Esquire as a "canoe paddle" or a "toilet seat with strings." Fred Gretsch, whose New York firm made guitars and other instruments, told a colleague, "That thing'll never sell." The Fender looked like it came from a different universe than the hollow-bodied instruments of Gibson, Gretsch, and Epiphone—and it did. Those Eastern and Midwestern companies worked in fealty to the European tradition of guitar-making, in which artisans known as luthiers hand-built stringed instruments according to long-established standards. Except for their pickups, F-holes, and steel strings, the elite hollow-body electric guitars of 1950 weren't so different from the acoustics made in Spain in 1850. To a traditional luthier, the idea of bolting a neck to a wooden board and calling the result a guitar, as this tiny California firm had done, was heresy. It was mass production, not artisanship.

Musicians to whom Don Randall showed the Esquire found it exciting, even revelatory. Yet serious problems with the design emerged. At the trade show, the Esquire's single, bright bridge pickup seemed lonely and impoverished next to competitors' two- and three-pickup guitars. "It really looks hot, but it still isn't a very good instrument for rhythm," Randall explained to Hall. The Fender pickup just sounded too sharp for playing background chords, an essential part of any guitarist's duty.

A friend also warned Randall that the Esquire's unreinforced maple neck was vulnerable to bowing as the guitar's tightly wound strings exerted pressure on it. Leo seems to have believed that the maple neck was strong enough on its own, but Randall was already having to apologize for his demonstration model. At the show, he learned that Gibson had invented a way to forestall bowing by adding an adjustable metal rod to the inside of the neck—and that Gibson's patent on this design had just run out. "I really believe that this should be carefully considered," Randall told Hall. "We could do ourselves a lot of harm by putting out a weak product."

Even as the most established companies mocked Fender's solid-body design, others raced to copy it. Randall had revealed Leo's ideas to the world in Chicago, thereby starting the clock on any advantage of surprise Fender had. The few Esquires that had been released to musicians so far were coming back with problems: dented pine bodies, shorted-out pickups, warped necks. Time was growing short to get the product into worthy shape and out to dealers. Though Radio-Tel had announced the guitar, marketed it, displayed it—and had even started taking orders for it the previous fall—Leo was still meddling with the design.

And Randall was growing desperate. "Francis," he wrote to Hall that summer of 1950, "I don't believe you realize the gravity of the Spanish guitar situation. If something isn't done soon we will have a very bad name. The complaints are terrific already and if you could talk to some of these people who have been made so many promises you would understand better what I mean."

Out on the road with players and dealers, Randall worried that only *he* truly saw Fender's opportunity: "We have the beginning of a very fine product in our Spanish guitar. Nothing has been produced, in the past, by anyone that has created the excitement and speculation among dealers, players and even our competitors as has this instrument. Now if we don't flood the market with our product you can bet your life our competitors will be right behind us with the same instrument only better and much fancier. The idea in our guitar has made a hit and believe me we better get on the ball—every day is precious. . . . If Leo misses the boat now I will never forgive him."

Randall knew that Fender had an instrument that might change not just the fortunes of their company but music itself. Everything now depended on getting Leo to relent on his obsession with improvement.

11.

"THE TIME WHEN IT WILL BE DELIVERED IS INDEFINITE"

CALIFORNIA, SUMMER 1950–SPRING 1951

On June 28, 1950, the handsome, cocky guitarist Jimmy Bryant arrived in the studio for his first recording session with Capitol Records. This was the label of Les Paul and the leading LA country singers, and Bryant was thrilled to be recording there—though he would have been more thrilled if he were the star. Instead, he and the steel guitarist Speedy West had been hired as session players to back a deep-voiced country boy named Tennessee Ernie Ford and a pop singer named Kay Starr on a couple of duets.

Jimmy and Speedy had been building their reputation on a popular local country music TV show and were now getting featured segments that earned them even more notice. The men would sit at each other's elbow and race through a jaunty instrumental while flashing conspiratorial grins: Speedy pricking the strings of his Bigsby steel guitar, making them sparkle; Bryant flying around the fretboard of his prototype Fender Esquire. Both played so fast that together they earned the nickname "Flaming Guitars."

Their job that June day wasn't playing on a local TV show or hinterland square dance, however. It was a major recording date at one of the most important labels in the country. And, it would turn out, the very first recording session to capture Leo Fender's new electric guitar.

From the moment the musicians started into the ballad "I'll Never Be Free," something new began to happen. As Tennessee Ernie Ford and Kay Starr entangled their voices and a jazzy piano twinkled far in the background, the two electric guitars dueled in sci-fi tones—Speedy West slapping notes out of his steel, Jimmy Bryant issuing bright, liquid phrases on his Fender. "Each time I hold somebody new, my arms go cold aching for you," Starr and Ford sang lushly. Behind them, Bryant played a pattern taken from the rhythm and blues bands popular on the south side of Los Angeles. When the singers paused, Bryant or West leapt out of the background, playing a twitchy little run or dribbling out a quick flurry of notes. But when the solo break came, Speedy West got the spotlight for all of it, a producer's call that must have left Bryant frustrated.

Though marketed as country, "I'll Never Be Free" came out as rhythm and blues played by heartsick white people—it was based on a classic old blues called "Sitting on Top of the World." The presence of electric guitars reinforcing an R & B groove pushed the record past old-style western swing and hillbilly, and toward a harder, simpler style of country that would become known as "honky-tonk," after the rough halls in which it was played. And the electric tones of Jimmy Bryant and Speedy West would be essential to the song's appeal. By the fall of 1950, "I'll Never Be Free" sat at no. 2 on the national country charts and no. 3 on the pop charts—an astounding success. Its B-side, an up-tempo Ford and Starr duet entitled "Ain't Nobody's Business but My Own," on which Bryant's virtuosity was given more space to roam, hit no. 5 in country and no. 22 in pop. People sure seemed to like the gleaming, sharp voice of that Fender electric guitar. But even by the time Jimmy Bryant used it on a couple of national hits, most listeners still couldn't buy one.

"I HOPE THEY start shipping the Spanish guitar soon," Dave Driver, the Fender salesman who handled the Pacific Northwest, wrote to F. C. Hall on August 15, 1950. "I had built quite a lot of interest in it. In many places they had fellows come in to see it, and I also went out to show it at their request. Now when I call, they ride me." Driver and the other Fender salesmen were deeply frustrated: their customers wanted an Esquire guitar, but they couldn't get one. Leo Fender wasn't yet satisfied with the design, so the Fullerton factory wasn't producing the instrument in significant numbers.

A few examples did find their way into the world. Leo allowed Dale Hyatt, a longtime employee who now ran his old radio shop, to sell what Leo claimed were "seconds"—flawed models unsuitable for the regular channels of business but likely to bring in some much-needed cash.

In the summer of 1950, Hyatt drove a truckload of Fender equipment north through California's Central Valley, stopping off at bars and honky-tonks along the way. He pulled over in Manteca, a farming town in Northern California where his brother lived, and that night went into a bar where a country band was playing. Hyatt had several Esquires with him, and took one inside to show the band, hoping to make a sale. The guitarist liked it and started playing it onstage. After a few minutes, though, the guitar suddenly quit working—its pickup just stopped sending out any signal. Hyatt had no idea what had gone wrong, but he went out to his truck and brought back another Esquire. Thirty minutes later, this one cut out, too, with the band onstage, in the middle of a song. The crowd was growing restless, and Hyatt was embarrassed. "[The crowd] started saying, 'There he goes again, ladies and gentlemen, wonder how many he's got?'" Hyatt told author Tony Bacon.

Luckily, the third Esquire Hyatt brought in lasted for the rest of the evening. The player was impressed—and apparently unfazed by the Esquire's dubious reliability. The next morning, he came to Hyatt's brother's house and asked to trade his son's train set for a Fender guitar.

When Leo heard this story, he made sure that if the Esquire's wiring shorted, the signal would only be diminished, not completely cut. With the help of Jimmy Bryant, he also worked on a second pickup to give the Esquire a tone besides the sole strident one produced by the pickup near its bridge. Bryant considered himself a cowboy jazzman, and like most jazz players, he appreciated elegant hollow-body guitars, especially Gibsons, for the warm, mellow tone that issued from pickups mounted near their necks. As Leo experimented with his own neck pickup, Bryant encouraged him to try to match the sound of Gibson's grandest hollow-body, the Super 400. Creating that airiness and warmth with the Esquire was impossible, but Leo imitated it by designing a chrome-plated metal cover for the neck pickup that cut the high signals it captured. The mellower sound from this second pickup added a whole new character to the Fender guitar, and in recording sessions and live dates that year, Bryant made good use of it.

One day, Leo Fender looked at his Esquire prototype and realized that its neck was bending upward, succumbing to pressure from the strings. This was the bowing problem Don Randall had been warned about in Chicago, and it was a catastrophe. Any imprecision in the location of the frets would lead to inaccurate notes, and making the instrument comfortable to play required controlling the narrow gap between the strings and the frets. Leo had thought the guitar didn't need a reinforcing rod, and he'd been utterly wrong. "I believe that Leo is very much concerned about the Spanish guitar neck," F. C. Hall wrote that summer of 1950 to Don Randall. "However, he hates to admit the situation." Hall said that Leo would have to design a whole new neck to fix the problem, delaying release even further. "The time when it will be delivered," he wrote, "is indefinite."

Leo and his factory employees spent much of that fall designing a so-called truss rod and devising a way to install it. George Fullerton's wiry father, Fred—who'd joined the company two weeks after his son—

developed a method in which a channel was cut in the back of the neck, the rod was inserted, and then it was covered over with a narrow strip of walnut. The Fender guitar thus acquired another quintessential visual feature: the so-called "skunk stripe" of brown wood running up the back of its yellow maple neck.

By the start of 1951, Leo was finally satisfied with his electric standard guitar. With two pickups, a striking asymmetrical headstock with all the tuning pegs on one side, and gleaming chrome components, the Fender Esquire had evolved dramatically. This slab of wood transformed into a guitar had become a professional-quality instrument, and Don Randall felt it needed a new name to distinguish it from the more primitive item he'd shown the previous year. As Fender was surrounded in Southern California by the industry of mass communication, working with players like Jimmy Bryant who earned their living on the radio, Randall decided to call it the "Broadcaster." If the model were to succeed, after all, it would do so largely over the airwaves.

A full-page insert ran in the February 1951 issue of *Musical Merchandise*: "New Fender Electric Standard," the headline proclaimed. Detailed illustrations, based on photos that Leo took himself, pointed out the guitar's features: a "modern cut-away body," an adjustable bridge, a switch that selected between the two pickups. The early Esquires were painted black, but these drawings showed a Broadcaster with a translucent blond finish capped by a black plastic pickguard, giving striking contrast to a design that was otherwise radically plain.

Orders had poured in to Radio-Tel ever since the fall of 1949, but now, Leo didn't want to make the single-pickup Esquire for which the early orders called. His factory began producing the newer two-pickup Broadcaster. Leo didn't care that he was about to ship a guitar other than what the buyers had asked for, that the difference in names and specs would confuse many. He wanted to put the best example of his creation out into the world first. One way or another, he assumed, the back orders, many of which had been languishing in Radio-Tel's files for nearly eighteen months, would get filled.

But among those who noticed the announcement of the Broadcaster were executives at the Fred Gretsch company in Brooklyn, makers of guitars and drums. On the morning of February 20, 1951, Don Randall received a telegram:

> YOUR USE OF TRADEMARK BROADKASTER ON YOUR ELEC-TRIC GUITAR IS INFRINGEMENT OF OUR TRADEMARK BROADKASTER U.S. PATENT OFFICE REGISTRATION 347503 OF 29 JUNE 1937. WE REQUEST IMMEDIATE ASSURANCE THAT YOU ARE ABANDONING THE USE OF THIS NAME—THE FRED GRETSCH MFG CO

Fender spelled the name of its guitar with a "C," but that didn't matter. In the universe of musical instruments, "Broadkaster" belonged to Gretsch, as a moniker for its flagship drum line. The Fender salesman on the East Coast was already encountering dealers confused by the coexistence of the Broadcaster guitar and Broadkaster drums.

Here was an embarrassing and frustrating setback—one more delay after so many, and this one coming just when it looked like Fender had finished its standard guitar. Randall wrote to his salesmen, admitting a major mistake but striking his usual upbeat tone: "It is a shame that our efforts in both selling and advertising are lost, but I am sure we can change over with little or any detrimental effects." He asked for other name ideas, too. But Gretsch's complaint was not going to keep Fender from getting its instrument out. After the telegram, someone in Fullerton, probably Leo himself, simply cut the "Broadcaster" lettering off the headstock decals, and guitars were shipped from the factory bearing no model name at all, just "Fender" in thin cursive.

Three days after the bad news, Randall had an idea. The revolutionary technology of the day was television—a device similar to radio, but with a screen that showed moving pictures along with sound. It was already a hit with American consumers; some twelve million televisions flickered in the nation's homes by 1951. Leo's old radio shop now had a television and a speaker hanging in its front window that lured passersby to stand and watch. The Fender electric guitar would enter a world in which Americans didn't just listen to their news and entertainment but *watched* them in real time. People would hear this electric guitar with their eyes.

So Randall coined the name "Telecaster." It sounded newer, fresher, and sharper than "Broadcaster," more in line with the times, perhaps even vaguely telepathic, hinting at supernatural ease of play. *Telephone, television, Telecaster*: Instruments of communication. Ways to be heard and seen. Powerful new technologies.

It took a month for Randall's patent attorney to clear the name. Leo's factory would use the "Fender"-only decals until August, probably because Leo didn't want to waste them. But by the spring of 1951, the instrument was in full production in Fullerton and for sale everywhere Randall's salesmen could get it. Two pickups, a body of solid wood, a thin neck that allowed for fast movement. "This guitar can be played at extreme volume without the danger of feedback," the catalog touted. Now it had a name that announced it as belonging to the second half of the twentieth century. The Fender Telecaster had finally arrived.

12.

"GUESS I SHOULDN'T HAVE FOUGHT YOU
SO LONG ABOUT RELEASING THIS"

HOLLYWOOD AND NEW YORK CITY,
WINTER 1950–SUMMER 1951

After "Lover," Les Paul released a string of singles, and only one—"Nola"—matched the success of the first. Critics were grumbling that his "new sound" had grown tiresome. Les felt enthusiastic about the music he was making with Mary, but Capitol Records didn't. The label turned down their initial recorded collaboration, and their first real release together, "Until I Hold You Again," did nothing exciting on the charts.

In late 1950, the singer Patti Page released "The Tennessee Waltz," a lovelorn ballad that became a blockbuster hit. The recording featured multitracked layers of her voice—a technique Les felt was borrowed, or stolen, from him. Les and Mary quickly released their own version, and it reached no. 6 on the pop charts early in 1951. Their release almost certainly confused buyers who were seeking Page's record, but this was a common route to success in the cutthroat music industry. Les didn't care—he ached to reach the top of the charts, stubbornly aware that even with his reputation as a guitarist and Mary's beautiful voice, the couple was still considered a second-tier act at best.

To rise up a rung, Les persuaded Mary to record a song she hated. Their next big release, in January 1951, was the cloying jingle "Mockin' Bird Hill," a tune Mary had dismissed as soon as she heard it. But Capitol had suggested it as a potential hit, and Les agreed, suspecting that its bouncy, singsong melody would glue itself into listeners' ears. The label and Les were right: the couple's "Mockin' Bird Hill" went to no. 2 and stayed there for five weeks, despite complaints from critics that "ditto vocals"—meaning sound-on-sound recordings—"have been milked for all they are worth."

With this success, Les felt emboldened to press Capitol to release a recording it had been sitting on for months. He thought the song and production were stupendous—perhaps the wildest sound-on-sound job he'd ever done, with Mary or without. But Jim Conkling, Les and Mary's A & R man at Capitol, steadfastly refused to release it. Record shops already had dozens of different copies of this tune by various artists, Conkling said, and none had sold well. He believed there was no way stores would stock one more version. To Les, this must have sounded similar to the rejection Gibson had given his Log guitar eight years earlier.

Ever since they'd started performing together, Les Paul and Mary Ford had toyed with "How High the Moon," a standard sometimes called the "national anthem of jazz." They tried out different tempos and arrangements, carefully noting which versions received the most applause. One night, they recorded it on the Ampex tape machine in the tiny apartment they kept in Queens, New York. Their "How High" raced along, with Les cutting out bright, busy lines on one of his clunker guitars and Mary's singing layered into an anodyne sheen.

As sung by, say, Ella Fitzgerald, who kept it in her live show for years, "How High the Moon" was a tune about longing for a distant lover, its mood wistful but not devastated: classic fare for the lounge era. Les and Mary's interpretation was R & B–like in its blistering tempo and otherworldly sonics. Les's harried, single-note runs screamed despite the lack of any distortion on his guitar, and Mary's vocals conveyed warmth and coldness simultaneously, a soaring melody made slightly nauseous by so many disembodied layers of electronic voice. Their song was no personal demonstration of feeling, no revelation of longing, but a canvas for brilliant new sounds and textures. It was a production in which tonality mattered more than the tune itself—an utterly modern recording.

Les was desperate to put it out, and finally, in early 1951, the couple caught a break. Jim Conkling was leaving to become president of Columbia Records, and with one foot out the door, he relented on "How High the Moon"—since, if the disc sold badly, it would no longer be his problem. On March 26, 1951, Capitol issued Les Paul and Mary Ford's stylized take on the jazz standard. Reactions from the press came immediately. One critic at the *St. Louis Post-Dispatch* called it the "most unusual side of the week." He also noted it among the bestsellers.

Les and Mary had made some solid hits, but it soon became clear that "How High the Moon" was succeeding on a different scale than anything they'd ever done. In less than a month, the recording hit no. 1 on the all-important *Billboard* pop chart, a spot it held for nine weeks. It became ubiquitous on radio and jukeboxes. It also found appeal outside the pop market, becoming the first single by a white act to reach the higher echelons of the rhythm and blues charts, rising to no. 2 on the jukebox list in May. All in all, the song would stay on *Billboard*'s popular tally for twenty-five weeks that year. Its appeal, as a jazz standard transformed into a revelatory piece of recorded pop-art, was tremendous. Virtually from the moment of its release, Les's and Mary's lives changed forever.

By November, the couple could claim sales of more than four million records in six months. Their total for the year 1951 would reach six million wax platters sold. For even as "How High the Moon" grabbed the no. 1 slot, their earlier release, "Mockin' Bird Hill," held strong just below it. Observers in the press were flabbergasted by what seemed like an overnight success. "So far this year, Paul and Ford have turned out about one bestseller a month," *Time* magazine wrote in October. *Cash Box*, a jukebox trade magazine, noted in August that the duo had "risen to the top of the ladder in just a few short months, and [were] still going strong." Their "How High the Moon" had officially gone blockbuster—and even Jim Conkling had to admit it. In early September, Conkling, now the head of Columbia, sent a telegram to the Hollywood bungalow: "Dear Les and Mary congratulations for having the No. 1 record of the year according to *Billboard* Disc Jockey poll. Guess I shouldn't have fought you so long about releasing this."

To those just taking notice, the couple seemed to have come upon a surefire formula for making hits. And in a sense, they had. Over years of performing with the guitar, Les had learned how to dazzle audiences with his instrument, but he'd also learned that virtuosity alone wasn't enough. Even setting off electric fireworks in between verses from a beautiful singer wasn't a reliable crowd-pleaser. Les and Mary's trick was to put all their tricks together—the crisp, modern sound of his electric guitar; the sweet, vaguely hillbilly flavor of her voice; and the multivalent textures of his sound-on-sound recording techniques. They gave audiences a shock of the modern, but crucially, they didn't alter the hummable core of a song. "This 'New Sound' Mary and I do doesn't fool around with the melody," Les once explained to a reporter. "It leaves the tune alone and puts the filigrees around it. The tune is there; it's just got a new and fancy frame."

A lot of behind-the-scenes work helped capitalize on Les and Mary's newfound popularity. Within weeks of the release of "How High the Moon," the couple were doing everything they could to make the song ubiquitous, traveling around the country to meet DJs, appearing on radio and television shows, and performing live. In less than three months, they visited some fifteen hundred disc jockeys and record stores in thirty cities. Les loved driving around and doing publicity; he almost never turned down an appearance, and by the end of 1951 these efforts helped bring him and Mary to the peak of national fame. Their hits continued. In late August, *Billboard* announced that Les Paul and Mary Ford held four spots on its Best Selling Pop Singles chart simultaneously. They were the only artists in history to do so.

13.

"IF YOU DON'T DO SOMETHING, FENDER IS GOING TO RULE THE WORLD"

CALIFORNIA, MICHIGAN, AND
PENNSYLVANIA, SUMMER–FALL 1951

Hunching over his desk at the Radio-Tel offices in Santa Ana, Don Randall watched orders pour in for Fender's new Spanish electric guitar. In March, he reported working three or four nights every week until ten thirty p.m. and still falling behind. Exhausted and thrilled by May, before guitars had even left the factory bearing the new Telecaster name, Randall crowed about the order deluge in letters to his salesmen. Then he pushed them for more. "Our Spanish guitar is selling in quantity that surprises even us, but we still aren't doing a good job," he told one. Some dealers had ordered the Fender electric so long ago that they were surprised by its arrival, but most moaned about not getting guitars fast enough.

At $189.50, plus $39.95 for a hard case, the Telecaster was a relative bargain, and Fender was setting new sales records every month. Randall still thought the company could do better. He remembered what it had been like to walk the floors of the trade shows and be laughed at by Fender's larger rivals in the East, to see his firm casually dismissed for even dreaming up a solid-body guitar. There was one thing, he knew, that would shut those naysayers up for good.

That spring of 1951, there would have been no better endorser for the new Fender guitar than Les Paul, the most popular electric guitarist in the country. Getting a Fender Telecaster in Paul's pop-star hands would virtually guarantee massive sales and acceptance around the country—not just in California and the Southwest, where Fender was already popular. It would be a coup, nabbing this famous player from established firms like Gibson and Epiphone, whose instruments he'd always preferred. Don Randall knew that Leo and Les were friendly, and both Don and Leo desperately wanted Les to adopt the Telecaster. So one evening in the middle of June, Randall went to try to make it happen.

"I was up in Los Angeles Saturday night, and talked to Les Paul," Randall wrote to a colleague on June 21, 1951. "[I] left him a guitar and amplifier to try this week, and he is going to give them a good workout and let me know his opinion. You probably know he has been using one of our Super Amps for a long time. In fact, it looks like he must have had it for a hundred years or more. This week, he is trying a Pro Amp and Telecaster guitar and his comments should be very interesting."

To Les, Randall gave a translucent blond, two-pickup Telecaster with no name decal, its neck inscribed with the date 5-10-51. Les apparently thought the guitar was a prototype rather than a production model, more or less confirming Randall's impression that he couldn't be bothered to pay too much attention to either the guitar or the man delivering it. "This was the first occasion I had to meet Les and to watch him perform in person, and believe me, he is really a fine instrumentalist," Randall wrote. "However, he appears to be somewhat self-centered. Mary Ford is a very gracious person and very talented. She sings beautifully and plays the guitar better than nine-tenths of the people playing today." Self-centered or not, Les Paul mattered enough that Randall eagerly awaited his verdict.

Les later recalled that there with the Telecaster was a note from Leo, asking him "to look at [the guitar] and think about it." Here was an instrument that embodied the ideas Les had long championed, a solid-body guitar that showed the way to the future. Leo wanted Les's endorsement, but business may not have been his only motive. Leo would've wanted to show his friendly rival what he'd been up to—to brag, just a little, in the quiet, matter-of-fact way he did everything. The advances that Les, Leo, and Paul Bigsby had talked about on those afternoons in Les's backyard were reflected neatly and powerfully in the Telecaster. What had been just wild notions, near-hunches, were now a commercial product, modestly priced, practically designed, and available in music stores all around the country. They'd all been working on the same problem, and Leo believed he'd solved it—not just for a few well-heeled professionals, as Bigsby had, but for guitar players everywhere.

"This is where I'm going," Leo told Les around this time, as Les recalled. "Would you like to come and be a part of it?"

Les thought joining with Fender might be smart. Leo had shown the ability to realize a radical and controversial idea. The Telecaster was now a guitar that regular working musicians could buy, one strikingly different from anything else hanging in a music store. A partnership with Leo "first hit me as a swell idea," Les recalled.

Then he started to consider his long, on-and-off relationship with Gibson, whose guitars he'd loved since childhood. The Fullerton operation, though it had a revolutionary new product, was still tiny. "There was no Fender then," Les told an interviewer—which, while incorrect, suggests the meagerness of Fender's national impact. "There was just Leo planning to do this."

Gibson had turned down Les's idea for the Log a decade earlier, and Les now played mostly Epiphones he'd modified himself, but he still felt a connection with the prestigious Michigan company. Crucially, Les also decided that he didn't really like Leo's Telecaster very much. The sound of it was too bright and sharp for him. The design was too plain, too straightforward, too unlovely. The Fender was a common man's guitar, and Les had always viewed himself as exceptional.

When Leo came to ask what Les thought of the instrument, and brought up the possibility of an endorsement, Les had bad news. "I told Leo, 'Geez, you know, I've had a great relationship with Gibson all these years, and it's part of the biggest instrument company in the world, and I'd like to take another shot at doing a guitar with them before I make a move.'" Les just wasn't ready to give up on Gibson, even though Gibson had laughed at his last big idea. In his autobiography, Les claimed that Leo understood this decision. "He was okay with me not wanting to abruptly jump into something new."

But Les didn't just decline the endorsement. He decided to use Leo's breakthrough in a way that would change their relationship forever. In Les's telling, he tried to wield the Fender solid-body as leverage to get Gibson to make the kind of instrument *he* wanted. After taking a close look at the Telecaster, Les claims he called Maurice H. Berlin, president of Gibson's parent company, and told him about it. At a subsequent meeting, according to Les, Berlin asked him what he thought of the Telecaster. Les tried to put a bug in the executive's ear: "I believe the solid-body guitar is going to be very important," he told Berlin. "And if you don't do something, Fender is going to rule the world."

UNBEKNOWNST TO LES, Gibson was already working on an instrument to compete with the Fullerton creation. After seeing the Esquire on display at a 1950 trade show, M. H. Berlin and Ted McCarty, the president of Gibson, had ordered their staff to begin developing a rival solid-body electric guitar immediately.

The Gibson company still occupied the Kalamazoo factory it had moved into in 1917, after rising high on the success of founder Orville Gibson's exacting designs for mandolins and guitars. As one of the most respected American makers of stringed instruments, Gibson employed a staff of experienced artisans, many first- and second-generation Americans, still with German or Dutch names and accents, who practiced the fine art of luthiery. One man might develop a specialty—carving a body cutaway or shaping a neck block—and spend decades doing nothing but that single painstaking task. Builders tuned the company's guitars by tapping their hollow bodies, listening to the resonances, and shaving or sanding wood until they got the precise sound they wanted, using skills that took years to perfect. Naturally, then, the fact that some unknown California outfit had bolted together a guitar out of boards—and that Gibson would have to compete with such a monstrosity—inspired some disgust in Kalamazoo. "We didn't think it took a lot of skill to build a plank of wood that made a shrill sound," remembered Ted McCarty. If Gibson was going to build a solid-body guitar, it would do so while meeting Gibson standards.

Designers had nearly a year to work on the instrument while Fender's operation fussed and delayed in getting its Telecaster to market. They realized quickly that a solid-body shaped like Gibson's large jazz guitars would be uncomfortably heavy—and a small shape would work well. In 1951, they settled on a prototype with a solid mahogany body roughly three-quarters the size of a standard Gibson, and a single, sharp-pointed cutaway. A thin layer of maple was glued to the top of the body to brighten the tone. This maple panel was also contoured, or "carved," giving the top of the guitar a curvaceous shape that offered several advantages. For one, it followed the design of Gibson's carved-top hollow-body guitars, which were inspired by the rounded shape of a violin and had been a key innovation of company founder Orville Gibson. McCarty also believed the curves would distinguish—and dignify—Gibson's solid-body contender. "I said, 'Look, if we are going to make a guitar, we are going to make one that will be different than anything Leo was making,'" McCarty told the guitar historian Robb Lawrence. Gibson's president knew that Fender didn't have the equipment or craftsmen to make a carved-top guitar. It was a feature his biggest competitor couldn't copy.

Ted McCarty later said that given its position, Gibson "needed an excuse" to release a solid-body—a way to reconcile the avant-garde idea of the instrument with the august image of Gibson. To find one, he and M. H. Berlin had to look no further than the *Billboard* charts of 1951, or the reader's poll in that year's *DownBeat* magazine. At the top of both was the man who'd first brought them that broomstick with pickups, who'd been urging Gibson to make a solid-body guitar since the early 1940s, who'd turned the metallic gleam of his home-built instruments into a sound that was both popular and respectable. The endorsement of that player would give Gibson a great excuse.

So in the fall of 1951, only a few months after Don Randall and Leo Fender had sought Les Paul's endorsement for their new solid-body guitar, McCarty flew from Kalamazoo to New York City for the very same purpose. McCarty met with Phil Braunstein, Les's financial adviser, and the two drove some ninety miles out of town to try to find Les and Mary, who were holed up in a hunting lodge near the Delaware Water Gap, in a mountain retreat owned by the bandleader Ben Selvin. The couple had set up their equipment in Selvin's living room and planned to record nonstop, day after day—or rather, night after night: their habit. Upon hearing that they'd have a surprise visitor, Les sent his brother-in-law, Wally Kamin, to find the party at a nearby diner and guide them up the twisty, narrow roads to the top of the mountain. When McCarty and Braunstein finally arrived at the lodge late that night, heavy rain poured out of a pitch-black sky.

Inside, after a warming cup of coffee and a few minutes of small talk, McCarty unveiled the prototype his designers had so carefully labored over. Here was Gibson's version of a solid-body guitar: A classic rounded shape with a single cutaway. Inarguably elegant. Two single-coil pickups of the kind found on the firm's hollow-body electrics. A thick mahogany body capped with a carved maple top. A mahogany neck that had been carefully glued—not bolted—to the body. Plugged into an amplifier, the guitar produced a rich, powerful sound, with a response that could vary from warm and round to bright and clear with the adjustment of its pickup switch and tone knobs.

Though entirely the creation of Gibson designers, not Les himself, the prototype solid-body shared profound similarities with Les Paul. Both stood as conservative radicals within their historical moment, pursuing new ideas without violating current standards of respectability. The sonic advances Les had achieved were tremendous, but he innovated within the established order of the music industry, according to what he knew would please a large, grown-up audience. Gibson luthiers had struck a similar balance. A solid-bodied, purely electric design stood as intrinsically radical in 1951. Yet this prototype strove in every way to meet the standards of respectability long established by Gibson's acoustic models, from its familiar body shape to a carved top that suggested fine, old-world craftsmanship.

Even the guitar's sound was conservative, mimicking the mellow tones that hollow-body electric guitars employed in jazz. A Fender Telecaster might scream or twang or even howl; it could certainly offend some ears. As envisioned by its creators in 1951, this Gibson model was almost incapable of producing an ugly or unbalanced sound. It was a solid-body electric with none of the raffishness or bellicosity of the Fender; a guitar for tuxedos and velvet-curtained theaters rather than ten-gallon hats and dusty honky-tonks.

Inside the airy, wood-paneled hunting lodge, Les plucked out runs on the Gibson prototype. As Mary puttered about upstairs, he called up to her, delighted. "They're getting awfully close to us," he said—by which he meant that this instrument nearly matched the sound of their homebuilt clunkers. "I think we should join them."

As with most activities involving Les, negotiating the details took place through the night, fueled by pots of coffee that Mary brewed and poured. By the time she was cooking them breakfast, Les, Ted McCarty, and Les's financial adviser had a deal written out by hand on a page and a half of plain paper.

In the entire history of Gibson guitars, going back to the late 1800s, only two players had been given signature models. Lester Polsfuss would be the third. Gibson would call its first solid-body electric guitar the Les Paul Model, paying Les a royalty for every instrument sold. Even better, the company would claim that Les himself had designed the guitar, capitalizing on his reputation for technological innovation.

In return, Les would offer his insights and feedback to Gibson, suggesting a few tweaks to the prototype. He would also not be seen in public using any other maker's guitar, or risk losing his earnings. The executives were so serious about this last point that they sent Les a supply of Gibson nameplates to stick on his clunkers, covering up their Epiphone badges, while the new instrument was readied for production. The nameplates wouldn't be needed for long. Gibson planned to offer the new guitar—featuring Les Paul's signature emblazoned in gold on the headstock—the very next year.

14.

"LIKE A SURGING UNDERTOW"

CALIFORNIA AND CHICAGO, 1950–1952

The guitar players who hung around the Fender factory all moaned about the same problems. Leo couldn't fix the trouble with their wives or mistresses, or the old heaps they drove around on the terrible LA roads—but one of their complaints did get his mind humming. The guitarists would hear of gigs playing upright bass for a night, but they couldn't take them, because the upright bass was unusually difficult to play. On the "doghouse," as musicians called it, you had to just know where to put your fingers to find a note—there were no frets to show which points on the neck corresponded with which pitches. Holding down those eighth-inch-thick strings was challenging on its own. String bass players were thus difficult to find, leaving bands incomplete. Listening to these complaints, Leo mused that if any of his guitar-playing friends could quickly adjust to a bass, they'd have another source of rent money.

The plight of impoverished musicians aside, it really was too bad the doghouse was so hard to play, since the instrument was all but essential to most music. On a standard eighty-eight-key piano, there are nineteen keys, representing nearly two octaves, below the lowest E note of a standard guitar. The guitar bottoms out at eighty-two hertz, but human hearing goes down to about twenty hertz. These sonic depths are where notes solidify into percussive thumps, and they give music a particular power. Listening to a mezzo-soprano sing a beautiful aria won't get the folks dancing, but a bass's simple, deep, repetitive rhythm will.

As Leo continued his pondering, he saw how outdated the double bass really was. Like an acoustic guitar, it couldn't stand out among the saxophones and trumpets in popular bands. Bass players couldn't even hear *themselves*—Leo would see them leaning over to put their ears against their instruments, soaking up the vibrations through their skulls. He also knew the difficulty and loneliness that an upright bass could cause its player. Even a "three-quarters size" model stretched to nearly six feet in length and could barely fit in a car. Usually players put their instrument in a canvas bag and tied it to a car roof, hoping it wouldn't rain, hoping that the huge thing wouldn't fall off while they were driving, which it often did. Or the player drove alone, their wooden burden taking up the entire passenger cabin, while everyone else in the band yukked it up in another car.

These problems bounced around in Leo's mind while he was developing the Telecaster, and they came to a head one night while he was at a Mexican restaurant. Leo gave few details about this revelation, but it's easy enough to picture.

A warm evening in 1950. It was time to go home, but Leo's mind was still buzzing after his day at the workbench—a day perhaps spent tweaking the neck pickup on his new electric guitar, or fending off calls from Don Randall for more product. He clicked off the lamp over his bench, walked out of his steel factory building, and made the five-minute drive in his '49 Ford sedan to the rented duplex where he and Esther lived. Then they took off for a rare dinner out.

At the Mexican restaurant, Leo's mind was still occupied by work, but eventually, his attention drifted over to the mariachi band performing inside the dining room—a common sight in Fullerton, where many, including some of Leo's earliest and most loyal employees, were of Mexican descent. The mariachis had a couple of acoustic guitar players, and, to accompany them, one man strumming what looked like a huge, bulbous guitar. This instrument had six strings pulled across an acoustic body—a body the size of a large man's chest and as deep as a washtub. Its low notes wafted through the restaurant like heavy whispers as the musicians walked through, serenading different tables. Leo watched the mariachis perform, saying nothing at all to Esther, the wheels of his mind turning while his beef enchiladas (or whatever they were) cooled on the table. He was usually quiet—but it would have been clear from his penetrating gaze that a big idea was forming in his head.

Nearly all stringed bass instruments in Western music, like the double bass and the cello, are played vertically. The wooden bathtub the mariachis were using was a *guitarrón*, a bass instrument played horizontally, like a guitar. Watching the mariachis, Leo realized what his competitors hadn't: that building a bass in the same shape as a guitar would solve a lot of problems. A horizontal design would make an easy adjustment for guitarists, of course, and would free up the player to dance and move around. If Leo built a bass just like his new electric guitar—with a solid, feedback-resistant body—it wouldn't even need a massive acoustic chamber like a *guitarrón*; it could be thin and light and still get as loud as the player wanted. Some previous designer had sought a booming, portable bass instrument, and their decades-old solution led Leo to an idea that made perfect sense: just build a bass like a deeper-pitched electric guitar.

Not two years later, the fruit of this idea showed up on the other side of the country.

One evening in the late spring or early summer of 1952, a jazz critic named Leonard Feather scanned the players on the stage before him, trying to make sense of what he was hearing. There were the usual dozen or so members of Lionel Hampton's big band. The leader and vibraphonist had stationed himself out front, nodding and grinning as he pattered over the tiles of his instrument, clearly pleased with the thick, limber swell of the groove. Hampton's music was pure pleasure—swing jazz, agile and humorous, with a beat that bore the muscle of rhythm and blues. Hampton's players looked every bit the urbane professionals they were: their fine dark suits and freshly shined shoes set off the gleaming brass of the horns and the chrome accents on the drum kit and guitar.

The *guitar*—that was what struck Feather, a friend of Hampton's and a longtime critic for the magazine *DownBeat*. There were two guitars up onstage, which was strange. And there was something else, "something wrong with the band," a usual character missing from its instrumental lineup: the hulking brown silhouette of the upright double bass. Feather scanned the battery of players onstage and didn't see its outline. As large as a man, maybe larger, the acoustic bass shouldn't have been hard to find. "And yet," Feather recalled later, "we heard a bass." Hampton's orchestra seemed to glide along on a wave of low-end might, sounding a little weightier in the bass register than usual.

Feather looked at the two guitars again. One was a standard, hollow-body jazz model. The other appeared like something out of a science-fiction comic book. Its "peculiarly shaped body" had two horns—there was nothing else to call them—and a yellow finish with a modish black blob on one side. Its neck stretched past the length of a standard guitar's and ended in a strange asymmetrical headstock, with all the tuning pegs lined up on one side. Other details stood out on the lower half of the body: two "electric controls and a wire running to a speaker."

Feather had never seen anything like this before. He was so curious that he approached the bandleader during the next set break and asked about it.

"That's our electric bass," Hampton told the critic with customary enthusiasm. "We've had it for months!"

Feather had never heard of such a thing, and he looked the instrument over as Hampton and his bass player, Roy Johnson, walked him through its details. As a jazz writer, and a friend to musicians, Feather was well aware of the burden bass players endured in playing and transporting their gigantic instruments. Compared to an upright, this yellow, bloblike bass was tiny—a broom instead of a bathtub. Roy Johnson said it was so easy to play that he'd used it on a gig the first night he'd gotten it.

Feather spent the next set listening carefully, noting the "deep, booming quality of the instrument's tone," nearly as warm and mellow as an upright's. To make a doghouse louder, all you could do was slap the strings harder, and that just made a sharp popping sound. With this, when you turned up the volume knob, the bass notes actually got louder. The result, Feather noted approvingly, "cut through the whole bottom of the band like a surging undertow."

By the time he left the club that night, Leonard Feather was buzzing with the same excitement that had caught Hampton and Johnson. A while later, in a July 1952 feature story for *DownBeat*, he declared that this thin electric bass could be a "sensational instrumental innovation." But quite a few jazz players—and leaders in almost every other realm of music—wouldn't be so sure.

The previous fall, Don Randall had written to Fender salesmen about the new electric bass the company was developing: "The neck is fretted like a guitar, and it is simply one of the most sensational products to hit the market," he told East Coast salesman Mike Cole. "We have several out being checked by big time operators . . . The reports are simply astounding."

The instrument would be called the Precision Bass, a name chosen by Leo "due to the fact that it is fretted and leaves no guess work as to where the notes fall." Players could press down in the same place as on a guitar for the same pitch, just one octave lower. "It may be hard for you to get used to the idea of a bass being played like a guitar, but the performers are really going for it in a big way," Randall wrote. "It can be played on the down beat rather than having to use the regular bass motion of grabbing at the strings. It also produces full volume output with a minimum amount of effort, which means they can develop a very fine, fast finger style of playing. It has allowed these bass men to improve their technique far beyond anything that anyone ever imagined."

Back then, Randall was right about one thing: it was hard for people to get used to the idea of a bass played like a guitar. The following summer, in 1952, he and his salesmen unveiled the Precision Bass at the major trade show in Chicago, and were met with no small amount of derision. "Portable String Bass Really New," mused the headline in *Musical Merchandise*, with a story far more skeptical than the usual promotional blurb: "Obviously, the new bass is a big departure from the standard type of bass, as it is only one-sixth the size and is played in the same position as a guitar."

The Precision Bass looked different from any instrument on the market, weirder even than the boardlike Telecaster. Leo had wanted its weight to balance horizontally on a player's lap or shoulders, and to achieve this, he and George created a body that had two horns curving far out over the neck, like the fingers of flames painted on the side of a hot rod. The shape struck some as incredibly ugly, others as terrifically provocative—but it came from Leo's obsession with practicality.

Other details, like the chrome knobs and bridge cover, the translucent yellow finish and black pickguard, were taken straight from the Telecaster. Putting them together into an instrument for which there were no existing dimensions to copy, nor any usable strings to buy and test on prototypes, had put Leo and George through another year of headaches and lost sleep. The result was Fender's most original creation yet—and its most controversial.

At the trade show, a photographer captured salesman Mike Cole trying to hand a floor model to one wary-looking music dealer from Connecticut. "Yes, it IS a bass," a caption writer would quip. Salesman Charlie Hayes, who was also present, would later recall that "those who were not sure if Leo was crazy when he brought out the solid-body guitar were darn sure he was crazy now, since he came up with an electric bass. They were convinced that a person would have to be out of their mind to play that thing."

Leonard Feather's excited reaction in *DownBeat* had been an exception. In 1952, most people had a hard time seeing what this skinny electric Fender bass would be good for.

DOWN THE HALLWAY at the same Chicago trade show, "dealers really rushed the guitar room" where Gibson was introducing its new solid-body electric. "Those who played it . . . said that all traces of feed-back and over-tone have been eliminated in the Les Paul Model Gibson," one report went. "Those hearing it agree that it produced a wealth of contrasting tonal effects, from brilliant treble to full, deep bass, with a good solid in-between voice for rhythm."

Everything about the Gibson Les Paul suggested privilege and status. The instrument's long list of features—a body made with two types of wood, volume and tone knobs for each pickup, faux mother-of-pearl inlays—paled next to its most striking aspect: a metallic gold finish. In 1952, guitars came in black or shades of stained wood, not bright hues. The gold finish both distinguished this instrument and, of course, exuded opulence. If Leo Fender had built a Volkswagen with his Telecaster, the Gibson Les Paul was a Cadillac: mannered, smooth, and striving for elegance in every detail. On its traditional headstock curled the signature of the man himself, in flaky gold lettering as large as the Gibson logo.

Les, of course, had had almost nothing to do with the development of the instrument, adding only a bridge he'd developed (which, because of a production error, hampered the earliest models) and insisting on the gold finish. But he'd let the claim stand. For decades, it would help buttress the wildly incorrect statement (which Les also never quite denied) that he "invented" the solid-body electric guitar, an instrument that simply can't be attributed to one single person.

By 1952, in the wake of the Telecaster, a handful of competing solid-body models had reached the market. Only Gibson offered one that tried to improve on the Fender and sold for a higher price. The most respected American guitar maker had given its imprimatur to the idea of a fully electric six-string—and after realizing this in Chicago, its competitors were livid. "Ted, how could you do this?" Fred Gretsch complained to Gibson's Ted McCarty. "Now anybody with a band saw and a router can make a guitar. That's the sort of thing that Fender is selling." Gretsch insisted to McCarty that if the rest of the companies hadn't followed Leo Fender's lead by making a solid-body guitar, the trend would've died out.

But McCarty saw that a fully electric design had undeniable advantages. As music grew louder, fighting feedback would only become more important. The solid-body electric wasn't going away, even if companies like Gibson and Gretsch ignored it. The only option was to answer Fullerton with something better.

"He's cutting into the market," McCarty said of Leo Fender. "And we're going to give him a run for his money."

15.

"DIM LIGHTS, THICK SMOKE, AND LOUD, LOUD MUSIC"

CHICAGO, MEMPHIS, AND
BAKERSFIELD, 1948–1952

Three miles from where Don Randall and Ted McCarty were unveiling their new solid-bodied electric instruments, in a black neighborhood in Chicago, a revolution was beginning. This revolution would determine the future of Fender and Gibson, Randall and McCarty, Leo Fender and Les Paul—and alter the sounds musicians made across the world. It first gathered force when a style of music born decades earlier, in the fields of the South, came to the city. One of the men who'd brought it was an obscure black sharecropper born McKinley Morganfield, an almost invisible presence in the United States but for the songs he sang as Muddy Waters.

Days after Muddy Waters stepped off the train from Mississippi, in 1943, his sister had told him: "They don't listen to that kind of old blues you're doing now, don't nobody listen to that, not in Chicago." The popular sound then was slick, up-tempo swing jazz, led by saxophones and pianos. Muddy was thirty years old and had spent almost his entire life on a cotton plantation near Clarksdale, venturing north to make money in a factory, not pursue a career in music. But in Chicago he kept meeting older bluesmen he knew from down south, folks like Big Bill Broonzy, who introduced him around as a good blues singer. Muddy just had a look about him, a fineness that seemed to mark him as special. His straightened hair was slicked back around the sides of his head and combed neatly, making him look younger than his years. High cheekbones framed huge brown eyes whose initial mirth hid an innate wariness—and hid it well. The magazines would call him "Dreamy Eyes."

Muddy's uncle had laughed at the simple acoustic guitar his nephew brought to the city. That thing might do in the South, where the night was silent, but not in Chicago, with the automobiles and the street cars and the clatter that a liquor-fueled party made in even a small room. So the uncle gave Muddy his first electric guitar, a cheap hollow-body with a pickup. Muddy and another friend started jamming in the four-room apartment he rented on the West Side, getting a few songs together, and soon they were playing parties. There was a tavern a half block from Muddy's place where he'd go to drink and sometimes eat. Back then "he was almost like a bum off the street," the tavern owner told biographer Robert Gordon. But when Muddy asked the proprietor of the Club Zanzibar to let him and his boys take over the bandstand one evening, she agreed.

Here was where the revolution really began, as far back as 1948: a small room with stools at a half-circular bar, Formica tables capped with black plastic ashtrays, boxes of bottled beer stacked against the wall. A room filled on weekend nights with men in crisp slacks and pressed shirts and women smiling from under fur hats, all trying to forget the hours they spent stamping out paychecks at the mill or the stockyard. No white faces, but that was no surprise in this part of Chicago. The surprise was the music, which hit like a wall.

Muddy would sit in a chair at the front of the tiny stage, caressing his electric guitar. A suitcase-shaped amplifier lay in front of his legs, aimed out at the gyrating ladies and the men chewing pigs' feet and corned beef sandwiches. There were only three other musicians up there with him—another guitarist, a drummer, and a harmonica player—and not a single sax or horn. The core of the music was vocals, rhythm, and electric guitar. Yet it overwhelmed the room. Muddy's instrument was cranked up so high it distorted the amplifier, his crackling tone tracing the drummer's slow shuffle. When he finished singing a verse, Muddy slid over his guitar strings with the piece of metal pipe on his pinky, sending out a wailing, moaning sound. His slide seemed to jab toward a resolution that would never quite come, mirroring the ache in his words, scraping the song toward its climax. And when the solo ended, Muddy slammed his dreamy eyes shut and let a hoarse tremble surface in his voice, as if he could barely get the next lines out:

Minutes seemed like hours, and hours gon' to seem like days
Seems like my baby would stop her old evil ways
Minutes seemed like hours, and hours seemed like days
Well now, seems like my baby child, well child would stop her low down ways

The people gyrating near the bandstand writhed in joy to this exquisite portrait of longing—a personal longing, of course, but in some ways a public one. The song was called "I Feel Like Going Home," once a classic country blues, now an electric lamentation for a black community that had recently left the South to find a better life in this noisy and chaotic Northern city.

One gig turned into more. Muddy's band would visit other clubs, ask to sit in with the bands, and then blow them off the stage with the power and intensity of their amplified music. They called themselves the Headhunters, slashing their way into more and more gigs around town with their electric instruments.

A while later, Muddy found himself inside a downtown recording studio, where the people in charge, a well-to-do white lady and a foul-mouthed Jewish man, asked him to do a song or two of his own. Muddy agreed. With his amp turned up so loud that his strings crackled through its speaker, Muddy sang that old slow blues from the Mississippi Delta.

He gave himself over to the words, conjuring the distraught tremble that killed in a club: "Well, brooks run into the ocean, and the ocean run into the sea / If I don't find my baby, somebody gon' sure bury me."

"What's he saying? What's he saying?" said the Jewish man in the control room, a club owner named Leonard Chess. Here was just a singer and an electric guitar, backed by an upright bass. Chess was laughing skeptically, shaking his head. "Who the fuck is going to buy that?"

Chess's partner, Evelyn Aron, hadn't heard this music before, either. But she liked it. "You'd be surprised who'd buy that," she told him.

Aristocrat Records pressed up three thousand copies of release 1305, "I Can't Be Satisfied" backed with "I Feel Like Going Home," performed by Muddy Waters. The ten-inch, 78 RPM platters went out to corner stores and beauty parlors around Chicago one Friday. By the next afternoon, every one of them was gone. People snapped them up so quickly that Muddy could find only a single copy.

A critic for *Billboard* heard the record. "Poor recording distorts vocal and steel guitar backing," was the assessment. But it wasn't the recording that had distorted the guitar—it was the overdriven amplifier that gave it that thick, worried tone. Muddy's electric guitar and amplifier had begun to transform the Mississippi Delta blues, the country blues, into the electric blues. "I Feel Like Going Home" reached no. 11 on the national *Billboard* charts—a feat that neither Muddy Waters nor Leonard Chess would have dreamed of.

In the club, performing with another guitar, a harmonica, and drums, Muddy's music reached its full power. Yet Chess (who soon assumed total control over Aristocrat and renamed it Chess Records) refused to bring Muddy's full group into the studio, seeing no reason to mess with a successful formula. Muddy, seeing the reactions of crowds in clubs night after night, hankered to capture the potency of his new electric blues, though, and finally went renegade to do it.

In a covert session for the Regal label, Muddy Waters and his band made an astounding document. "Ludella" featured the front line of his club band—Muddy on lead guitar, Jimmy Rogers on vocals and guitar, and their harp player, the explosive genius Little Walter, filling in. Drums and bass came in behind the three of them, laying down a heavy, rolling, medium-tempo beat. From the very start, Muddy was all over his guitar, bending notes in ecstatic agony, keeping his overdriven amplifier growling. While Little Walter cried through his harmonica, Rogers moaned about a woman sneaking around, a woman who "just won't get along." The intensity, the sheer heaviness of the performance, was devastating. It was 1949. "Rock 'n' roll" as such was still years away. But there is no other word for it: the song absolutely rocked.

More hits came, and by the early fifties, Muddy's electric music had a hold on Chicago. "They even named it the Muddy Waters blues," a contemporary remembered. Muddy hadn't been the first to play blues songs on an electrified guitar, of course, but his band was "the first to use amplification to make their ensemble music rawer, more ferocious, more physical, instead of simply making it a little louder," the critic Robert Palmer would later write. Muddy was taking music to new realms of expression and power through the electric guitar. One of his bigger hits was a song called "Rollin' Stone." The revolution was under way.

IN THE SPRING of 1951, another young black musician from Clarksdale, Mississippi, was preparing for a rare opportunity. Ike Turner played piano and led a band called the Kings of Rhythm, and a white man had asked to record his group at a studio in Memphis. The Kings of Rhythm were a cover band and didn't have any original songs of their own, but that wasn't going to hold them up. While driving up Highway 61 toward Memphis, Turner's sax player, Jackie Brenston, rewrote the lyrics to an up-tempo rhythm and blues hit called "Cadillac Boogie." He ostensibly named his song after an engine that Oldsmobile had just introduced, called the Rocket 88, but there was no missing the undertones: this was a song about sexual power. The Kings of Rhythm showed up at the Memphis Recording Service with the song still unfinished and, with the help of the studio's owner, a man named Sam Phillips, worked out the arrangement right there.

They had one problem. When they'd pulled over to change a flat, Willie Kizart's guitar amplifier had fallen out of the trunk of the car, busting its speaker cone. There was no way to get it fixed. Phillips, though, liked to record musicians as they presented themselves, without polish. He didn't want to tell these teenagers that their gear wasn't good enough to record, so instead he came up with a cheap solution: stuffing a wad of paper up against the rupture in the speaker cone. It was free, and, surprisingly, the electric guitar sounded pretty good coming through it—buzzing and distorted, bristling with emotion.

On that early March day, the group cut Brenston's "Rocket 88": Willie Kizart's electric hollow-body blaring, its raspy tone like a saxophone ripping through hell; Ike Turner pounding a groove on the piano keys; Brenston boasting about riding in style—"everyone likes my Rocket 88"—as the whole ensemble tore through what was essentially a standard R & B boogie but seemed to everyone who later heard it like something else, something altogether new: a joyous explosion of young energy, yoked to a surging and infectious rhythm. Muddy Waters's electric music evoked the past; this record spoke to right now.

Released by Chess Records and spun incessantly by a friend of Sam Phillips at the white Memphis radio station WHBQ, "Rocket 88"—credited not to Ike Turner or the Kings of Rhythm but Jackie Brenston and His Delta Cats, much to Turner's irritation—amazingly shot to no. 1 on the *Billboard* R & B charts. The song roared past Les Paul and Mary Ford's "How High the Moon," which was then enjoying rare success for a white pop song among black listeners, and the two songs' juxtaposition showed the crossing musical currents of that crucial year.

Les and Mary had hit the charts with careful, polished layers. Ike Turner and Sam Phillips arrived in a miracle of accident and improvisation. Both "How High the Moon" and "Rocket 88" gave unusual prominence to electric guitars, but the latter sound, channeled through Willie Kizart's busted amplifier, came out more distorted and distraught than on any previous hit record. Its sandpaper grit would have infuriated Leo Fender and Les Paul, had they heard it. Yet that distortion was doubtless part of why "Rocket 88" found even more success with white audiences than "How High" had with black ones.

White people simply didn't listen to "race records" or rhythm and blues or whatever this was—then, suddenly, they did. The hipper white teenagers clamored for "Rocket 88" and anything like it, of which there was plenty, since the song was essentially a rewrite. This wasn't the more visible jazz of upwardly mobile black Americans, nor the gospel of good-hearted churchgoers, nor the gutbucket electric blues of Chicago mill-workers; it was the impulsive, erotic, urgent expression of black youth, perhaps the least powerful members of a minority then subject to open segregation in the South and systemic oppression everywhere else. The sound was so powerful that after hearing it, a white Philadelphia DJ and bandleader named Bill Haley decided to change his entire direction, switching from Bob Wills–style western swing to rhythm and blues. And Sam Phillips, who'd captured "Rocket 88" in his Memphis studio, began to get ideas about the magnitude of success a white singer might find with this music.

SOLID-BODY ELECTRIC INSTRUMENTS were so new that they hadn't yet penetrated the musical communities of Chicago and Memphis, even as musicians there started the revolution in which they'd become essential. In California, especially among the country players who were close to Leo Fender and Paul Bigsby, the new tools spread faster. People could see and hear the changes they were ushering in, and the response wasn't always positive.

One night in Bakersfield, 1952. A row of honky-tonks lined the road out of this gritty oil town, and one joint had booked Joe and Rose Lee Maphis, a singing couple who'd moved to Southern California on the recommendation of their friend Merle Travis. The two were scheduled to play at a place called the Blackboard Cafe, a club known as much for its nightly violence as for charging the highest beer prices in Bakersfield—seventy-five cents a bottle, not twenty-five.

Pushing through the double doors into the saloon, Joe and Rose Lee could hardly see through the cigarette smoke. A few lamps cast a wan glow over the mirrored wall behind the bar, the shuffleboard table, and the wooden floor, where patrons, enthused by beer or whiskey, dragged their feet to the music, swaying in each other's arms. It hit Joe and Rose Lee that this airborne din, this atmospheric crackle they were hearing, was in fact *music*. There was a band up on a high stage, five people producing a tremendous racket. The Orange Blossom Playboys had a steel guitar, a piano, a fiddle, and a drummer, who kept the music moving to a steady beat, something Joe and Rose Lee hadn't seen before. In Virginia, decent white people didn't dance to folk music; they didn't need a drummer for it, and, while listening to it, they certainly didn't get drunk and sway in the arms of some barroom lover.

There was also a greasy kid playing lead guitar up there, slicked-back hair, face like a peanut. He was holding a thin little instrument. Every pluck of its strings seemed to puncture the leaden atmosphere in the Blackboard like an ice pick striking a helium balloon. His yellowish guitar sounded *electric*, the brightest thing in there, and seemed to push the imbibers into doing things Joe and Rose Lee had never seen adults do in public.

To these Southerners, the Blackboard was a temple of sin. They didn't know that the peanut-faced lead guitarist's name was Buck Owens, that he'd purchased his Fender Telecaster from a bandmate the previous year for $35, that he and another vice-tainted local named Merle Haggard would come to embody a vital and rough-hewn style of country music named after the city of Bakersfield. Rose Lee and Joe couldn't have dreamed that the Fender Telecaster would one day become as closely identified with country music as a cowboy hat.

They only knew what hit their senses: the gritty environs of the Blackboard, a place where women spoke of the sex act with a frankness unheard anywhere else, where men broke into fights three or four times a night and shrugged off the odd murder. Buck Owens hadn't been the first to discover that the Telecaster's solid body and long, sturdy neck could be handy in a fight.

The Virginians were so stunned by what they saw and heard that later, driving back to Los Angeles, they portrayed it in a song. Their lyrics linked the atmosphere of the Blackboard to many varieties of sin:

> *Dim lights, thick smoke, and loud, loud music*
> *Is the only kind of life you'll ever understand*
> *Dim lights, thick smoke, and loud, loud music*
> *You'll never make a wife to a home-loving man*
>
> *A home and little children mean nothing to you*
> *A house filled with love and a husband so true*
> *You'd rather have a drink with the first guy you meet*
> *In the only home you know, the club down the street*

Thus was the penetrating sound of the Fender guitar first linked to behavior deemed unfit for polite society. Barely a year after it hit the market, as a musical revolution burbled forth around the country, the Telecaster was already starting to change how bands worked and sounded—already carving a gap between those who would give themselves over to the new electric music, and those who heard in it a serious moral danger.

16.

"LES HAS ACTUALLY MADE A NEW INSTRUMENT!"

CHICAGO AND MAHWAH, NEW JERSEY, 1952–1953

As the hollers of the crowd ricocheted off the walls of the Chicago Theatre and reached the ears of Les Paul and Mary Ford, he smiled wider. She tensed. No achievement—not their run up the pop charts, not their well-reviewed stint at the Paramount Theatre in New York—could soothe the stage fright of this pastor's daughter. The crowd tonight would break attendance records for a stage show at the 3,800-seat Chicago Theatre, but as Mary stood there on the boards, receiving applause in a frilly white gown, her insides vibrated with fear.

They'd had an arrival fit for conquering heroes. Les and Mary had been ferried into the city across Lake Michigan on a yacht, as the fireboats escorting them raised up their hoses and sprayed columns of water in celebration. Chicago pols had declared it Les Paul and Mary Ford Day to mark the start of their performances. Outside the theater's towering edifice, dozens of fans had paraded that afternoon, holding signs that read "Vote for Les Paul and Mary Ford, the original Guitarocrats." (It was an election year.) Some wore little pendants with the stars' names emblazoned over the outline of an electric guitar. The major downtown music stores both put up window displays featuring Les Paul and Mary Ford and their new Gibson guitars.

That evening, though, the husband and wife stood alone under the bright lights and faced the challenge that came with every live performance: replicating their complex multitracked songs onstage. Les grinned in his pressed suit, held up his gleaming signature instrument, and put a folksy twang in his voice: *You know, this new Gibson guitar has a special feature called a Les Paulverizer, a device I designed to make it sound like five or ten or fifteen guitars at once,* he would've said. *With this new Les Paulverizer, Mary and I can multiply ourselves onstage just like we do at home. Right, Mary?*

Many in the audience believed him. A few reporters would note that there was an array of electronic equipment backstage, out of sight—and two more people back there helping with the show. Mary's sister Carol lurked with a microphone and a voice virtually indistinguishable from her sister's, while her husband, Wally, played recorded tracks of Les and Mary's guitars to fill out what they performed onstage. There was no special echo device inside Les's Gibson guitar, of course—just a tape machine behind the curtain. But it made for a great illusion. "If people didn't realize it was a hoax, I wasn't going to tell them," Les wrote in his autobiography.

Les and Mary got through a few songs and reached the climax of the set. Les started in on another monologue about how much he loved his new guitar, how he'd adored the instrument since childhood. The couple took up "There's No Place Like Home," a sweet old hillbilly song, and in the middle of it, Les plucked out a fancy little run. But as he basked in the applause, Mary, standing a couple of feet away, copied his playing note for note on her own guitar. The crowd laughed.

Les's smile fell into a frown; he shot his wife a cruel look. Then he played a more complicated passage, his fingers fanning up the fretboard in a blur, a grin on his face—until Mary broke in and played the same lick herself, coolly replicating every bit of what Les had done. Screams of laughter and surprise from the crowd. Hardly anyone knew that pretty little Mary, as they thought of her, was a ferocious guitar talent.

The husband yelped in mock disgust. But Les gathered himself, winked at the crowd, and then set off a flurry of notes, his left hand racing around the neck of his guitar, his right hand furiously striking the strings. The solo ended as Les arrived at the highest notes on his neck, hitting the pinnacle in one sharp, glassy prick. No way up from there. Cheers from out in the dark.

Then Mary started in on the same solo at the same speed, her fingers gliding swiftly and faultlessly up the neck of her own instrument. After she'd gotten just a few notes in, though, Les dashed over and yanked the electric cable out of her guitar. Her efforts were drowned in silence. The crowd roared.

It killed every time, this routine. It was the carefully practiced peak of the show; even critics liked its suggestion of musical rivalry. "It sounds obvious in conception, but in execution it's brilliant," wrote London's *Melody Maker* a few weeks later, when the duo had made their first trip across the pond. "He starts a flashy run; she breaks in to duplicate it. He tries something trickier; she matches. His mock exasperation could have been fatuous, but it's amusing. The fooling is not incidental to his playing . . . He makes it appear that his guitar is backing up his personality."

The dynamic it showed was real. Les's hyperactive guitar style reflected a man who ceaselessly pursued whatever goal was at hand, working eighteen or twenty hours at a stretch, proudly going for days without sleep, and keeping Mary alongside him. But while both husband and wife worked hard, the public gave Les most of the credit. He was the virtuoso and the sound engineer; to most people, she was the girl who sang. Reporters who saw them perform were often shocked to learn that Mary could do more than wear a dress and vocalize. "Gal, incidentally, is a nicely gowned looker, and fact that she also can handle a git-box comes as a surprise to most of the ticket-holders," *Variety* reported of a 1951 performance. Almost no one bothered to note that the woman had been playing guitar all her life.

Performing came like breathing to Les, but no achievement, however rarefied, would let Mary get comfortable. "I still dread going onstage," she told a women's magazine. "My stomach turns into knots, and I wish I were home." Even with her fears, the couple ruled Chicago for those two weeks in August of 1952, breaking all previous attendance records at the downtown theater and taking in more than $37,000 (nearly $350,000 in today's dollars) in the process. They repeated this feat all over the country, as well as in England.

People were simply fascinated by this husband and wife, who, after all, resembled no other figures in public life. Features in *Look*, *Pic*, and *Cosmopolitan* probed the couple's creative domesticity in what was soon its dramatic new setting. In 1952, Les and Mary left the West Coast for good and moved to a sprawling mountainside ranch house in Mahwah, New Jersey, about an hour outside of New York City. Here, they could record all day and night without disturbing any neighbors, and without traffic noise or planes flying overhead. The home would also be the setting for their new television offering, *The Les Paul and Mary Ford Show*, sponsored by Listerine. Just as they recorded for Capitol in their Hollywood garage and living room, they'd tape these five-minute TV segments around their house, emphasizing the normalcy of their lives even as they showed how, with a microphone over the sink, Mary could record her vocals while doing the dishes. Gags abounded, and usually not at Les's expense. Mary played a bewildered spouse who happened to make music while fulfilling her domestic duties—her ability to have this multiple identity courtesy of a genius husband who ran the show.

Les turned the whole New Jersey house into a recording studio, filling it with the finest equipment and effectively guaranteeing that there was no moment during which he and Mary couldn't be working. It made a novel setting for TV, but soon, just as George Polsfuss had feared, living as Les's costar began to wear Mary out. Not only did she find performing in public intrinsically nerve-racking; there were so many events to get through, and each one asked a lot of her. She had to not only sing and laugh and play guitar, but look immaculate in a dress and full makeup for every show—even a radio appearance. All this while traveling frequently on aggressive itineraries, eating badly on the road, and recording constantly with a partner who refused to rest. She began relying on vodka to help her cope with the stress. "[She] kept saying, 'We have more money than we can ever spend. Why don't we take a break and just be us again?'" Les would write later. "And I wanted to do it, but then the phone would ring and there would be something else to do, more people to please, somewhere new to go, and I could never say no to more work."

By 1953, Les and Mary couldn't get away from their reputations even when they wanted to. They were recognized on weekend getaways while dressed in grubby clothes, and discovered and hounded while staying in foreign hotel rooms under fake names. And they were still getting *bigger*. That year they released "I'm Sitting on Top of the World," their thirteenth consecutive hit to sell more than five hundred thousand copies.

With astronomical record sales, the Gibson endorsement deal, earnings from live performances, and a Listerine contract worth $2 million over three years, Les and Mary were becoming fabulously wealthy. Les spent freely on electronics and recording equipment but lashed down the purse strings when it came to other expenses. "He was tighter than the bark on a tree," Gibson's Ted McCarty remembered. He wouldn't hire assistants to help with the driving or the domestic duties, and, to the frustration of their manager, he even resisted buying Mary new clothes to wear onstage or paying to get her hair done.

Still, a seemingly boundless success helped smooth the differences between husband and wife. One evening in the spring of 1953, Les and Mary were resting in a St. Paul hotel room when Les heard a song come on the radio. It was Anita O'Day singing a midtempo version of "Vaya Con Dios," a jazzy lament with heavy string arrangements and western-themed lyrics. Les turned up the radio.

"Mary, how do you like that song?" he asked.

Mary was sitting on the bed, mending a dress. "I love it," she said. "But I don't know what it is."

It was a song Capitol had been begging them to record. On June 1, 1953, the label released Les and Mary's version of "Vaya Con Dios." It shot to no. 1 on the *Billboard* charts and sat there for nearly three straight months, becoming bigger even than "How High the Moon." In contrast to their frantic breakthrough hit, "Vaya Con Dios" was languid, almost deliriously slow and romantic. The couple's hillbilly roots showed right through their pop sparkle.

"Vaya Con Dios" brought Les and Mary's worldwide record sales to more than fifteen million copies and made them inescapable on television, on the radio, in jukeboxes. Les was thrilled and wanted to keep going; Mary was exhausted and desperate for a break. According to Les's biographer, she now privately referred to her husband as a slave driver, and she wasn't alone. At the height of the couple's success, Mary's sister Carol and her husband, Wally, fled New Jersey for California, having tired of living under Les's unrelenting work schedule.

Yet all that work had brought Les exactly what he'd wanted since childhood. He was now the most popular and important electric guitar player in the country—and the world. "What Benny Goodman did for the clarinet, Harry James for the trumpet, Tommy Dorsey for the trombone, and Coleman Hawkins did for the tenor sax, Les Paul has done for the guitar," *Metronome*'s George Simon declared in 1953. "He has brought it into such prominence that it has become an almost newly discovered instrument for many people, as well as one with which musicians can make more sounds and more money than ever before. You only have to hear some of his fantastically successful records to realize this. And it's not only the multiple recording devices that make the Paul guitar sound so different from others. It's that Les has actually made a new instrument!"

Les had given his name to a Gibson model, of course, but he'd also made the guitar far more worthy of the spotlight—and had put it there. His playful, athletic style demanded a hearing from anyone who picked up the instrument. And by helping to pioneer the solid-body electric guitar's bright, metallic tone and almost unlimited volume, Les had helped transform it into a worthy match for the saxophone and trumpet, instruments it could never previously compete with. What had long been a background voice could now stand up front—even if Les was the only one in pop music currently asking it to. (In jazz, it was Les's late friend

Charlie Christian, playing with the Benny Goodman Sextet, who pioneered an electric guitar style similar to that of a brass soloist.)

In part because of this transformation, these years saw a considerable increase in guitar sales. When Les and Mary made promotional visits to small-town Gibson dealers, the stores would be flooded with fans looking for an autograph or a quick jam session. "I am sure more man hours were devoted to the manufacture and assembly of fretted instruments this year than ever before," Gibson president Ted McCarty told a trade association in 1953, with numbers to back him up. Rising sales benefited the whole industry, and just as Les Paul stood first among guitar players, so did Gibson among guitar manufacturers. Fender had been the earliest to release a commercial solid-body electric, but after 1952, many players converting to this design found it difficult to resist the gold-painted Gibson. Everyone knew that Gibson meant quality, that Les Paul meant fame. Together, they made for the most desirable solid-body electric guitar on the market.

17.

"HE DOESN'T LIKE TO GET INVOLVED WITH THINGS THAT ARE UNPLEASANT"

FULLERTON AND MAHWAH, FALL 1952–SUMMER 1954

One day a Fender employee asked Leo why he ate a can of spaghetti for lunch every day, instead of buying a hot sandwich from the food truck like everyone else. "Because for the difference in price between the spaghetti and the sandwich," Leo replied, "I can buy a handful of resistors."

Despite having introduced the first solid-body electric guitar to the market, despite the favor the Telecaster found among country players, despite the steadily rising sales figures it drove, Leo Fender still worried about affording even the smallest components of his amplifiers. His factory employed thirty-three people by Christmas of 1952, and had expanded from its original steel sheds into a squat new cement building with more space and, at last, a company restroom. Leo and Esther still lived in a little rental town house in Fullerton. After a two-year whirlwind during which he'd sent the Telecaster and the even more radical

Precision Bass out into the world, Leo's sole indulgence seems to have been a chunky new Dodge sedan.

But no rest had been earned; nothing could be taken for granted. In Fullerton, Leo still designed every product, hired every employee, and oversaw every aspect of production. Thus his fixation on the cost of parts, which he'd calculate out to fractions of a cent, scrawling tallies on pieces of scrap paper. His obsessive mind struggled to oversee so much, and the resulting disorganization, exacerbated by material shortages during the Korean War, made the factory's output terribly erratic. In letters from Santa Ana, Don Randall and F. C. Hall vented frustration about their inability to get Fender products out on time and fretted about the harm it did the company.

Now there was Gibson to contend with. The Telecaster had awakened the fury of the industry leader, and Gibson's competing product could bury Fender if it didn't come up with a proper response. Leo would have to fight against an instrument bearing the name of—and ostensibly designed by—a man who'd once been his friend, a coconspirator in this new realm of solid-bodied electric instruments. Leo's personal feelings about this situation were never recorded. But Les's decision to reject the Telecaster, and to instead endorse an instrument from Fender's largest competitor, seems to have brought an end to any closeness between the two men. What had been a friendship was now a rivalry. Everyone in Fullerton saw the Les Paul Model as an existential threat. Fender had made a Volkswagen, and now, somehow, it would have to answer to Gibson's Cadillac.

Other products were squeezing Fender in different ways. In 1952, Paul Bigsby began selling a bridge for the electric guitar that let players subtly shift the pitch of the strings downward by pressing on a lever. When the player released the lever, the strings returned to standard pitch. With this Bigsby True Vibrato, a standard-guitar player could emulate the wavering sound of a steel guitar, along with many other effects. It was the first reliable version of what would become known as the whammy bar. Les Paul loved Bigsby's vibrato and started using it; Merle Travis also got one, and before long, many players wanted them, including those who hung around the Fender factory. So in 1953, Bigsby introduced a version of his vibrato designed for the Fender Telecaster—a project that took considerable effort, since it had to replace several key parts of the guitar.

The relationship between Bigsby and Fender had been largely friendly. Bigsby didn't seem to care much that Leo had borrowed some of his ideas for the Telecaster. When Bigsby couldn't keep up with demand for his custom solid-body guitars, he'd tell customers to drive over to Fullerton and buy an instrument from Leo Fender. But by creating a vibrato for the Telecaster, Paul Bigsby sparked a new sense of competition between the two outfits. Looking at the Bigsby True Vibrato, Don Randall saw that this other firm had become the best source of a feature that many players wanted and that Fender didn't offer. He told Leo to create a competing vibrato system for Fender's successor to the Telecaster.

Everyone knew Fender would need to improve on its first solid-body. Almost since the moment he'd handed the Esquire prototype to Jimmy Bryant, back in 1950, players had been telling Leo what was wrong with it. Some purported flaws were purely aesthetic, while some were worryingly technical. Bob Wills and his main rhythm guitarist, Eldon Shamblin, complained about the Telecaster's plain, thin body, comparing it to a "two-by-four." Bill Carson, another local country sideman, had received a Telecaster in 1951 in exchange for working part-time for Leo at the factory. But as he got more recording work, Carson started to hear complaints about the tuning of his guitar. The Telecaster offered only limited adjustments for its strings, and it sometimes could not be brought into perfect tune with itself. A note at the far end of the neck might be the same E played by the pianist, but farther up, past the fifth or sixth fret, another supposed E was noticeably off-pitch. If session producers felt someone couldn't play in tune, they wouldn't call them for future work. Carson thus believed the Telecaster's intonation problem threatened his livelihood.

Carson and others also loathed the hard corners of the Telecaster's body. In profile, the guitar really did look like a plank, with flat sides meeting a flat top at nearly ninety degrees. After hours of sitting in a recording studio or standing on a stage, these corners dug painfully into a player's chest. Several complained about this, but Carson was now one of the half-dozen musicians who constituted the Fender "guinea pigs" (as Leo called them), and he decided to act. After getting a second Tele-caster, Carson took a hacksaw to his first, cutting out a section of its body around where it touched his chest, and slicing some wood off the top back corner, where it met his forearm, to make a beveled edge. Then Carson started dicing up the bridge so that each string saddle could be moved back and forth to adjust for intonation. This cut-up guitar "wasn't very pretty," of course, but Carson could use it in the studio. It was com-fortable, and it could be tuned properly. Leo hated that a player had butchered one of his guitars—most people thought of his instruments as his children. But looking at Carson's modifications, he got the point.

In 1952, Leo made plans to expand the Fender factory yet again. A large new site was carved out of the orange groves on the southeast side of Fullerton, in what would become a major industrial park, home to National Cash Register and the Kimberly-Clark paper company. When Fender arrived in 1953, the plant consisted of three white concrete-block buildings, each long and narrow, lined up next to each other with open alleys in between. If the factory needed to expand further, identical new buildings could be added to this row.

Inside, though, "the place looked like a complete mess," Forrest White thought when he saw the new facility for the first time. "It was obvious that no planning had been done before they moved in. There was abso-lutely no evidence of work flow. Amplifier and guitar assembly benches were all mixed together—no separation at all." Nor had there been any consideration of noise. Metal punch-presses, which stamped out ampli-fier chassis and guitar components at ear-shattering volume, were set just outside the uninsulated wall of the main factory office, ensuring that the company's secretaries were drowned in a cacophony all day long.

To White, oversights like the arrangement of machines and the lack of a system for ordering parts were deeply upsetting. A skinny, nervous Ohioan with a personality many saw as cold—even sociopathic—White was an amateur guitarist and industrial manager who'd first met Leo in 1948 and decided almost immediately to worship not just Fender instruments, but the man himself. After joining the company as plant manager, White began to organize the factory operations by any means necessary. He'd post brutally passive-aggressive public memos on company bulletin boards and intimi-date prospective employees by hardly ever smiling. When guitarist Jimmy Bryant stumbled around the factory sipping from a beer can (the backseat of Bryant's car was famous for its mountain of empties), White mercilessly booted the Fender endorser out of the factory, upholding company policy. His intensity was foreign territory for the laid-back Fullerton plant, where veteran employees walked around without shoes (and men without shirts) on hot summer days, and it earned White enemies from the start.

White thought of himself as Leo's number two—but so, since 1948, had George Fullerton. The two clashed immediately, as White recounted in his memoir. When White told Fullerton that he wanted to rearrange the factory floor for better efficiency, Fullerton shot back, "What makes you think you can come in here and after two weeks decide that everything is wrong and needs changing?" After yelling back and forth, Fullerton, normally a soft-spoken fellow, huffed off to complain to Leo. Meanwhile, White skulked in the factory office. Seeing him there, Leo's secretary, Ione, leaned over cheerfully from her desk: "You'll find that he doesn't like to get involved with things that are unpleasant," she told White, refer-ring to Leo. "Welcome aboard!" Much of White's job would turn out to be handling the unpleasantness Leo preferred not to get involved with.

The factory staff had also expanded to include Freddie Tavares, a wiry, gregarious, Hawaiian-born guitarist who'd work as Leo's lab assistant when he wasn't doing recording sessions up in LA. Tavares's recording work had included playing the steel guitar riff in the Looney Tunes theme song, and he would get more high-profile spots in the future. One of his first tasks at Fender was assisting Leo as he designed a competitor to the Gibson Les Paul.

Bill Carson wanted four or five pickups and a bridge that allowed the adjustment of each string's intonation. Don Randall and Charlie Hayes wanted a vibrato unit to compete with Bigsby's. Several guinea pigs wanted a body that had cutouts to reduce pressure on the player's torso. (A body that "fit like a good shirt," in Carson's words.)

Leo wanted the weight of the guitar to balance on the player's lap. George Fullerton wanted a recessed jack for the amp cable, so that the guitar could be rested on the ground without damaging the cable. Don Randall wanted a sunburst finish—yellowish wood grain at the middle, fading to black at the edges of the body—because every other guitar company had one and Fender didn't, and because it looked pretty.

Carson wanted a headstock that looked like the one on Bigsby's Merle Travis guitar, with more swooping curves. Jimmy Bryant wanted the new guitar to be called the Jimmy Bryant Model. Bill Carson would call early prototypes "Carson's guitar."

Don Randall wanted the new instrument ready for display at the trade shows of 1953, one year after Gibson had debuted the Les Paul Model.

So Leo started drawing.

RUMBLINGS OF A new sound were growing louder. In 1953, the hirsute Philly bandleader Bill Haley scored a minor hit called "Crazy Man, Crazy," which some listeners described as "rock 'n' roll music." The next year, a DJ named Alan Freed brought his hugely popular radio show, *Moondog's Rock 'n' roll Party*, from Cleveland to New York City. And that same summer, a white nobody named Elvis Presley entered Sam Phillips's recording studio in Memphis and spat out a record called "That's All Right," which became a regional smash.

Meanwhile that year, news arrived that finally seemed to promise Les Paul and Mary Ford a break from their tireless efforts. The couple announced it with an unusual full-page ad in *Billboard*, featuring a huge drawing of a stork holding a Les Paul guitar in its mouth, and page-crossing type that was meant to look handwritten. It read:

"Mary is taking a little time off to attend to some very special business—Les."

"And Les will probably take all the credit for it—Mary."

After five years of marriage, Les Paul and Mary Ford were about to have their first child. It was the summer of 1954, and Mary was due to give birth in the fall. Neither Mr. and Mrs. Guitar, nor virtually anyone in the gleaming hallways of the recording establishment, could see what revolution lay just around the corner.

18.

"WHY DON'T YOU ASK FOR THE MOON?"

TEXAS, NEW YORK CITY, AND SOUTHERN CALIFORNIA, FALL 1954–SPRING 1955

He picked up the guitar in elementary school, after his brother returned from the war with the habit of plunking out chords. Young Charles Hardin Holley (as his family name was spelled)—Buddy, everyone called him—got his own $15 Harmony six-string at a pawnshop, and from then on, that was how he spent much of his time at home, on the bus to school, and in the long Texas afternoons afterward. The guitar in his hands "was another instrument entirely," Buddy's oldest brother, Larry, told the writer Ellis Amburn. But lots of people in the town of Lubbock played: this was the Panhandle, the land whose emigrants had brought guitar-driven hillbilly music to California, the same ranch country where Bob Wills had perfected western swing. A place where the rows of cotton fanned out toward an endless flat horizon, where apocalyptic dust storms browned out the sun. There was not much else to do besides pick guitar and go to church.

On the white side of town, country music wafted through the air like specks of field dirt. Buddy Holley picked up hillbilly classics like "Footprints in the Snow," picked up the mandolin and the banjo and some Hank Williams tunes, too. By the time he reached high school, his band played regularly on the radio and at venues like the Cotton Club, just over the line from where Lubbock's God-fearing city fathers outlawed the sale of alcohol.

The Cotton Club was one place where Buddy saw Elvis Presley perform. There's a photograph: Elvis shining on the left side of the frame, a twenty-year-old greaser whose fine clothes encase a molten core of sex, his gravity pulling every set of eyes in the room toward him—including those behind the thick glasses orbiting far right. After Buddy's band opened for Elvis a few times, the two became friendly, and the Mississippian's sound, as well as his scandalous sense of freedom, began to rub off. "We'd been hillbillies, but after the Cotton Club we were rockers like Elvis," bandmate Sonny Curtis remembered. Seeing what Elvis got away with unleashed a new energy in Buddy. Instead of standing frozen at the microphone like a country singer, he started shaking and writhing, radiating a little heat of his own. It wasn't the suggestive hip-swaying of the soon-to-be King, but it was still a heady show of vim for a skinny young four-eyes.

Then there was the guitar. In 1954, around the time he began picking up the rhythm and blues music played on the other side of town, and before he saw Elvis ignite hillbilly into rockabilly, Buddy began playing the most modern instrument available: a solid-body electric guitar. A gold-top Gibson Les Paul with matching Gibson amplifier was very nice kit for a teenager from a struggling family to own, even if Buddy feared how the nine-pound guitar would treat his shoulders. His was a 1952 model, made before Gibson started adding serial numbers and before designers fixed the original, flawed bridge. The Gibson was a fine-quality instrument that would have subtly signaled an affection for rhythm and blues—and Buddy was already listening obsessively to Muddy Waters, as well as black vocal groups like the Drifters. Just as Gibson heads Ted McCarty and M. H. Berlin would have hoped, Buddy's love for Les Paul's guitar work also likely influenced his selection of a gold-top.

When Elvis added drums to his live band, equipping himself for a big beat, Buddy and his crew followed. The singer-guitarist showed up to rehearse at drummer Jerry Allison's house with the shiny new Les Paul, and man and instrument grew into a tight unit. Buddy complained about the weight of his new guitar, but that didn't stop him from using it in every gig the group could get: at ice rinks and vocational group meetings and radio stations and of course at the Cotton Club, where the end of a set might be celebrated with a few Falstaff beers. Contrary to some impressions, Buddy was no saint—no stranger to the sway of alcohol or the lure of women or the rush of a fight. He may have looked geeky in his metal-framed glasses, but "he was an average hard-on good ol' American boy," as his friend Jerry Coleman put it.

Elvis's earthquake rise, from regional hotshot in 1954 to national phenomenon in 1955, shook the confidence of the major record labels, who presided over the national musical output like somnolent grandparents. Falling out of their easy chairs at the sound of this rock 'n' roll, their reading glasses tumbling off into alarming articles in *Time* and the *Saturday Evening Post*, company executives realized they needed to answer the popularity of the sneering young buck from Memphis. RCA snatched up Elvis's contract from Sam Phillips for the magnificent sum of $35,000, and the other majors cast about for Presley clones, hoping, on the one hand, to find someone equally compelling, and, on the other, that this rock 'n' roll would prove just a fleeting tremor.

Next to his friend Elvis Presley, Buddy felt his image was too plain. He'd been a western-shirt-and-jeans kind of performer—just a poor schoolboy enjoying a local reputation—but now he decided he needed the best in clothes and equipment. He asked his oldest brother, Larry, for a loan of $1,000. "Why don't you ask for the moon?" Larry replied. But, inspired by Buddy's determination, the older brother scraped together the funds and wrote out a check.

Numerous Holly biographies date these events to the following year, after Decca Records offered "Buddy Holly" a contract (and inadvertently sliced the "E" off his last name). But receipts found by the late Holly expert Bill Griggs put the loan in a different context. Larry apparently made it in 1955, long before Decca Records was paying any attention. This is clear because the first place Buddy took Larry's thousand dollars was B. E. Adair Music, at 1207 Main Street in downtown Lubbock. The store touted that it carried "the famous Gibson and Fender guitars" and was "the only authorized dealer for such within 50 miles." Buddy knew Adair salesman and teacher Clyde Hankin, who'd given him a few lessons.

One day in the spring of 1955, according to receipts, Buddy strolled into Adair's carrying his gold-top Les Paul guitar and matching amplifier, along with Larry's mountain of cash. He'd only owned the Gibson for about a year, but he already wanted to replace it. His problem with the guitar was likely not, as some claimed, that the instrument was too plain—a Les Paul was the most princely solid-body on the market. Rather, Buddy probably decided to trade the guitar because it was too heavy. His thin frame had tired of the clunky, nine-pound Gibson. And Buddy had played another guitar hanging in Adair's that promised to be far more comfortable, a striking, futuristic model that had just come on the market.

THE FIRST SHIPMENT had rolled out of Fullerton in October 1954, only a few months before Buddy Holly bought one in Lubbock. Don Randall named it the Stratocaster, summoning images of space travel, of a rarefied altitude a level or two up from the Telecaster. The guitar was both an upgrade to the Telecaster and Fender's answer to the Gibson Les Paul— yet it looked nothing like either. The sole instrument it resembled was the Fender Precision Bass, from which its two-horned outline was taken.

But only the Stratocaster's body had been, as the ads proclaimed, "comfort contoured": the back side was curved to accommodate a player's chest and belly, and the top back corner was beveled so it wouldn't jut into the player's arm. The two horns on the body formed cutaways that let a hand freely travel up the neck, while helping to balance the guitar's seven pounds across a player's lap or shoulders. These features made the Stratocaster the most comfortable guitar yet produced, an instrument that fit around the human body rather than cutting into it. Once again, a radical design had been born through Leo's obsession with practicality.

Randall seemed to anticipate that shortly after the Stratocaster's release, Americans would become obsessed with space travel through the launch of Sputnik and the rivalry of the Cold War. The Jet Age was already nigh when Fender began advertising the Strat in the spring of 1954, the whooshing curves and jutting roofs of Googie architecture already rising along the boulevards of Southern California. Corporate logos were melting into boomerangs, car trunks were growing fins. Even the first advertisements for this guitar featured the symbol of an atom. Yet neither Randall nor Leo could have foreseen how well their new instrument would fit the aesthetic and social currents of the decade. At a time when faith in and fear of new technologies was peaking—with automatic transmissions and Communist satellites, all-electric kitchens and the hydrogen bomb—the Fender Stratocaster announced itself as an ideal integration of technology and artistry.

When Paul Bigsby saw a picture of the guitar inside his modest white house in Downey, however, he felt not elation, or admiration, but rage. A Fender brochure sat on his dinner table. In his booming voice, Bigsby cursed the name Leo Fender until the walls shook. "That son of a bitch ripped me off!" he yelled, so loud that his daughter would never forget it. When he looked at this new instrument—at the shape that would delight Buddy Holly, the guitar that would change the idea of what a guitar could be—Paul Bigsby felt the sting of betrayal.

Besides its contoured, double-cutaway body, the Stratocaster's most remarkable feature was its "Tremolo Action" lever, which let players lower or slightly raise the pitch of all strings for dramatic effect. "A flick of the wrist means live, tremolo action—perfect pitch!" chirped the magazine ads. It worked better than the True Vibrato Bigsby had first designed, and it came standard on the Stratocaster. Thus, only a year after Bigsby had crafted a nifty add-on for the Telecaster, Leo released a guitar that made Bigsby's work pointless, his Fender-compatible product obsolete. Other firms, like Gibson and Gretsch, regarded Bigsby's vibrato so highly that they began installing it on their guitars at the factory. But Leo and Don

Randall hadn't even considered doing this. Players who wanted a Fender with a whammy bar were simply steered toward a Stratocaster and the tremolo that Leo had designed himself.

Such a series of events might seem standard in business: one company introduces a product, another follows up with a competing version. But in the mid-fifties, the electric guitar industry was small and familiar. Leo Fender and Paul Bigsby were compatriots whose enterprises had so far not seriously conflicted. But while Bigsby was building guitars out of love and pride, Fender was trying to build a national empire. That empire was now pushing against the gates of Bigsby's beautiful little domain.

If Bigsby was miffed that his friend had chosen to create a new, competing vibrato system, he was fully infuriated by another grab of Leo's. Looking at the first Fender brochure on his dinner table, Bigsby saw that the Stratocaster's headstock—the wooden panel at the end of the neck—appeared to be a direct copy of the shape Bigsby had been putting on all his standard guitars since 1948. Its sloping line placed all the tuners on top, with a round knob at the end and a sweeping curve on the lower edge. The Stratocaster had very slightly modified Bigsby's proportions, but the similarity was undeniable.

The headstock was a straight steal, as Bigsby saw it, and therefore grounds for legal action. Bigsby called his lawyer, and, according to his daughter, Mary Bigsby, tried to pursue a lawsuit against Leo Fender for copying the headstock. But while Bigsby had patented his vibrato, he'd apparently not secured a trademark on his headstock shape. There were too many echoes of it in older instruments. Leo Fender later told the writer Tom Wheeler that he'd borrowed the Stratocaster's headstock shape from an old Croatian instrument he saw in the Metropolitan Museum of Art in New York. There were other precedents, too: in the nineteenth century, the celebrated acoustic guitar builder C. F. Martin had arranged a guitar's tuning pegs in a single line and cut a headstock shape similar to the Fender and Bigsby designs. Because of these instruments and the lack of a trademark, Bigsby was told he didn't have a legal claim, according to his daughter. The former motorcycle racer could yell all he wanted, but Fender was free to market its new creation.

For the rest of his life, Leo Fender would deny copying Bigsby. But, though he may have seen an older instrument in a museum at some point, he'd clearly borrowed another one of Bigsby's designs. Fender guinea pig Bill Carson even claimed to have shown Leo the Bigsby shape and asked to have it incorporated into the Telecaster's successor. "I told Leo I wanted a large, fancy headstock like the Bigsby guitars had," Carson wrote in his memoir. "As it turned out, the final shape did indeed have a Bigsby look."

19.

"LET'S TRY THIS AGAIN"

LAS VEGAS AND ELSEWHERE, 1954–1955

Mary Ford leaned over the edge of the balcony and looked out at the lights of Las Vegas glimmering against a backdrop of black desert. Back in the yellow glow of their room, Les was lying on the floor, scrunched up underneath some piece of recording equipment, trying to make a repair. The couple was back out on the road. But it was just the two of them together now that Mary's sister Carol and her husband, Wally, had gone home to California. For Mary, the absence of others, especially her sister, only worsened the almost unbearable misery of this experience.

On November 26, 1954—Thanksgiving Day—Mary Ford had gone into labor at the Valley Hospital in Ridgewood, New Jersey, and given birth to a little girl. Colleen Paul arrived prematurely, weighing only five pounds. Newspapers around the country reported that both mother and daughter "were doing fine," but soon doctors noticed that the little girl wasn't breathing normally. Two days later, the baby was rushed in an incubator from the New Jersey hospital to St. Vincent's in Manhattan. A surgery at first seemed to correct her respiratory distress.

But at one fifteen a.m. on November 30, Les Paul and Mary Ford's first child died. Mary was still at the hospital in New Jersey and wasn't told right away. According to Les's biographer, she learned of the baby's death when the singer Perry Como, a friend of the couple, read the news in the morning paper and called to offer his condolences. Hearing Como's words, straining to understand what had happened, Mary Ford shattered. Grief just broke her apart.

Papers nationwide had reported on the death of little Colleen Paul, even as music columnists still gushed at the amazing success of her parents' recording career. The couple had kept recording until the very day Mary gave birth, hoping to stockpile a few discs for release during their time away. Drinking beer and vodka to cope with stress, staying busier than she probably wanted to, Mary had hardly rested during her pregnancy as she tried to satisfy the demands of being a chart-topping pop singer. Les didn't just encourage their hectic lifestyle; he enforced it. All the activity, the nerves, the drinking, the exhaustion—Mary must have wondered after that tragic Thanksgiving if the way she'd lived had something to do with little Colleen's premature birth, her acute respiratory distress, her untimely end.

After Colleen's passing, Mary Ford had descended into an abyss. The preacher's daughter from Pasadena had hardly laid eyes on the precious child she'd wanted so badly, only to see her torn away. Now she felt a raw, searing pain, an ache from which she thought she might never escape. In the weeks after that awful Thanksgiving, she'd been paralyzed with grief, permanently horizontal, the flood from her eyes unceasing.

Les had thought that taking a trip to Europe would distract Mary from her sadness, and she'd spent the winter there with him hoping it would, too. But in Europe they'd done almost the same thing they did at home: careen through one city after another in search of who knows what. Les had spent a fortune on sound equipment. In Spain, Switzerland, and Sweden, Mary had stared out the window and thought about the daughter she lost. It was a hell of way to spend the longest vacation Les ever gave her.

The calendar read 1955 by the time they came home. Mary ached inside, but her allotted grieving period had ended. It was time to get back to work—to be the person she'd been or pretended to be: smiling and enthusiastic and eager to greet her audience, though the thought of going onstage sent tremors through her still. This reticence now conflicted even more sharply with Les's enthusiasm, his desire to be out there, talking to the fans, playing and recording. On the road, there was no one else around to absorb his energy anymore—no one but Mary to try to slow him down. Les had never been good at taking it easy, but ever since they'd gotten back from Europe, he was just all *go*.

Mary glanced in at her husband lying there on the floor. He was biting his lip in deep concentration, aiming the silvery tip of his soldering iron at some piece of electronic guts. She let out a sigh. The balcony of their room looked out over the hotel pool, and far down there she could make out the frolicking shapes and sounds of Lucille Ball and Frank Fontaine, comedians and fellow guests at the hotel. They weren't working. They were enjoying themselves. The stars' laughter echoed around the pool deck and up off the stucco walls of the building, slipping in through the open balcony door, mocking Mary's sour mood.

"You know, we're up here, and we work so hard," she said out loud, absentmindedly, just as much to herself as to her husband. "And they're down there goofing off. Doing nothing."

Les had just finished the repair and was putting his machine back together. "Yeah, they're goofing off and they're not getting anything done," he said. "Now, come back over here to the microphone, and let's try this again."

Les's response irked her. All she heard was *try it again*, or *one more time*, over and over—so incessantly it drove their hotel neighbors crazy, even the ones who loved the music. From next door the neighbors would rush over at three a.m., pounding on the door, apologizing, saying, *I love you, you're great, but please, stop playing that same thing over and over, I'm so sick and tired of it.*

Well, imagine how tired of it *I* am, Mary wanted to say.

There had been a time when every performance felt like it made a difference, when every stage and every microphone had meant something new. But that feeling was gone. When she and Les had returned from Europe, they'd been shocked at how much music—and the country—had changed in their absence. Looking at the charts, the names they knew, their friends, had disappeared or fallen far below where they'd once stood. In place of Bing Crosby, Frank Sinatra, Patti Page, and Perry Como now rose obscure figures like Elvis Presley, Bill Haley, Ruth Brown, Fats Domino, Little Richard. All singing raucous little numbers about teenage love, it seemed.

Les dismissed them as vulgar impostors, chumps who knew but one tempo and couldn't play an instrument to save their lives. But Mary had noticed that since the arrival of this rock 'n' roll music, their own records faced a stronger headwind than they had in years. The single they'd released that summer of 1955, "Hummingbird," got positive notices in *Billboard* and *Cash Box*, and the couple's DJ friends said nice things about it. But after an initial burst of attention, it had fizzled out, rising to only no. 7 on the pop charts—a disappointment compared to their previous hits. Meanwhile, everyone seemed to be dazzled by some fellow named Chuck Berry, and Bill Haley had spent the summer at no. 1.

Naturally, all the attention given to this kids' music annoyed Les, but it didn't dissuade him. If anything, he felt that the rise of rock 'n' roll made his and Mary's live performances only more important—a chance to show what *skilled* musicians could do. Even while the new music surged to prominence, Les thought there were plenty of places for him and Mary to draw a contrast, to make a stand—so many that Mary found the task of even tallying them exhausting. The couple still had their own television show, sponsored by Listerine. They were scheduled to appear that fall on the first televised broadcast of the *Grand Ole Opry*. The magazines were still calling, asking for cover stories. Also calling was the White House, where the couple had been requested to play for President Eisenhower and Vice President Nixon and their families. Mary shuddered at the thought.

The dry desert wind wafted into their hotel room. Mary put on her headphones and looked over the lyrics sheet for the song they were trying to capture. Thinking of the work ahead depressed her, especially since there'd be even more now, with these challengers. She wanted to lie by the pool and laugh like Lucille Ball, or hole up quietly at home in New Jersey and not worry about performing so much. But whenever she voiced this latter urge, Les just glared at her. He could be so cold sometimes, so indifferent.

The backdrop to Mary's life with Les had always been the couple's shared conviction that their future would be inevitably brighter than their present. Now Mary worried that no amount of work would take them to a better place. How far would Les want to go? How far, she wondered—pulling the balcony doors closed against the desert night and turning toward the microphone—could she stand to go with him?

20.

"WE HAD NO IDEA THAT 'MAYBELLENE' WAS RECORDED BY A NIGGRA MAN"

NEW YORK CITY AND ST. LOUIS, 1955–1957

Ed Sullivan, a glum head on too-narrow shoulders, shrugged in front of the curtain and started to mumble: "Here, from Lubbock, Texas, the Crickets"—he spat out the name with a contemptuous nod—"with one of their hit records." A patter of applause rose invisibly, and then a chord fell brightly down the neck of an electric guitar. Suddenly on-screen there was a delicate young man in a rumpled black suit and bow tie, wearing Elliot-style eyeglasses. He looked up, directly into the camera, and for a moment there was a flash of pure terror in his eyes, a look that seemed to ask just what the hell he was doing here, in this New York City theater, submitting to this grouchy old man, about to play at an intolerably low volume.

In the next moment, the singer and his three companions fired into the number, and when the drums and bass hit, a glimmer of a smile appeared in Buddy Holly's expression. When he looked back into the camera, the light in his brown eyes had brightened from fear to determination. Every passing second seemed to imbue him with confidence. Perhaps he was reinforced by the infectious drive of "That'll Be the Day," by its charming mix of vulnerability and cockiness: "You say you're gonna leave me / You know it's a lie / 'Cause that'll be the day-ay / When I die."

But as Buddy's smile narrowed into a mischievous smirk, it must've discomforted some of Ed Sullivan's eleven million viewers. Here, it must have seemed, was another damn rock 'n' roller. "That'll Be the Day" shuffled and scooted along; it was music to bop to; it was teenager stuff. But then, the Crickets all looked like decent prom dates. Buddy Holly smiled; he wore a bow tie. He was no tramp like that Elvis Presley; if he came for your daughter, you might actually let her leave with him. On the other hand, he did sway suspiciously, and the way his voice cracked and warbled with desperation—"You gave me all your lovin' and your tur-HUR-tledovin'"—suggested he'd been up to a certain kind of no good at least a few times. Another rock 'n' roll degenerate, then, this time disguised in respectable attire.

Furthering this sense of confusion was a strange instrument hanging from his shoulders, which was appearing on national TV for the very first time with a rock 'n' roll band. If Buddy's look and bearing presented him as something familiar, his guitar rejected that assessment. Its body seemed to have two horns sticking out of its side, like jet wings or tongues of flame. A white patch was splattered across its body like the side panel of a Chevy Bel Air. The thing was so thin it barely jutted outward at all; it seemed to hug Buddy's torso with its curves. Compared to the hollow-body guitar held by sideman Niki Sullivan, Buddy's axe looked downright space-age, a sci-fi, comic-book sort of thing. Even with the awful microphones and mixing of the Sullivan show, the tone of it cut right through: a clear, jangling ring that seemed to let the strike of each string linger in your ears. It stuck out above the din of a rock 'n' roll band the way it stuck to Ed Sullivan's viewers' eyeballs. It was Leo Fender's latest creation, and perhaps his greatest.

But even as the rock 'n' roll storm reached hurricane strength in 1957, this radical instrument appeared only rarely on stages and screens.

Just a few of the first-generation rock 'n' roll singers played electric guitar themselves, and even fewer played solid-bodied instruments. Elvis Presley sometimes wore a Martin acoustic onstage but let sideman Scotty Moore grind out the hot licks. Bill Haley led a band whose debt to swing honchos like Bob Wills and Benny Goodman was obvious. Meanwhile, Chuck Berry created the archetype of the singing, soloing rock 'n' roll superstar. Shuffling and duck-walking out at the front of the stage, a Gibson hollow-body hanging off his muscled shoulders, Berry imported the role of the R & B bandleader into the realm of rock 'n' roll, and in the process became its original guitar-playing genius. Chess Records had issued his first single, "Maybellene," in 1955, and watched it rumble to more national success than his labelmate and hero Muddy Waters had ever managed, peaking at no. 1 on the R & B charts and no. 5 on the pop Top 40 chart.

Berry's music was not like Muddy's, but a sped-up, teen-targeted hybrid of various styles: the jazzy jump-blues of Louis Jordan, the grinding shuffle of electric Chicago, and even the thumping western swing of Bob Wills. "Maybellene" itself was based on "Ida Red," one of the more raucous numbers in Wills's repertoire, showing just how closely rock 'n' roll modeled itself on the sounds of the prior era. Berry borrowed the earlier song's tempo, souped up the rolling, battering, *boom-chk* rhythm, and updated the lyrics into a teen drama complete with a two-timing love interest and a battle between a villainous Cadillac and a heroic Ford. So a tune that thrilled white high schoolers was built from what Bob Wills had used to get their parents dancing the jitterbug. Many grown-up western swing and country fans even recognized "Ida Red" inside "Maybellene"—and liked it.

Of course, the songs told of different worlds, from Wills's "Chicken in a bread tray, peckin' out dough" to Berry's "Cadillac doin' about ninety-five," with Berry compacting a full narrative into just over two minutes and summoning a wry attitude that was entirely of its moment. And as a black man singing songs aimed at white teens, Berry embodied, as perhaps no other artist had, the profound cultural and racial convulsion that accompanied the rise of rock 'n' roll.

Like Americans themselves, American music had long been segregated into white and black charts, styles, record labels, and radio stations, all in an effort to disguise the fact that members of each race regularly found things to like in the other's music. DJ Alan Freed first adopted the "rock 'n' roll" label to make it more acceptable for young whites to buy and appreciate the vital black sound of rhythm and blues. But the music's evident blackness made many white listeners uncomfortable, and canny producers and artists deemed further accommodations necessary. "There was something in many of those youngsters that resisted buying this music," Sam Phillips once explained. "The Southern ones especially felt a resistance they probably didn't quite understand. They liked the music, but they weren't sure whether they ought to like it or not."

To find commercial success in this divided landscape, artists blurred racial lines. Phillips found a white singer—Elvis Presley—who could sound black. Chuck Berry disarmed white listeners by training his black voice to sound white. Honing his act in St. Louis clubs, he'd taught himself to sing with a harder, whiter diction, as he explained in his autobiography. In those days, fans rarely saw pictures of recording stars, leaving skin color open to imagination—and anyway, "photos of black faces only required less exposure to appear as bright as white faces," Berry noted. Berry sounded hillbilly enough that he found himself accidentally booked into white clubs in segregated states, clubs it was illegal for him as a black man to enter, much less headline. He later recounted the confused mutterings of one such white promoter: "It's a country dance and we had no idea that 'Maybellene' was recorded by a niggra man."

But if Berry could summon white attributes to broaden his appeal, he arranged his bands in the style of black R & B, making its structure the standard for a rock 'n' roll group. After the war, as jazz had grown more abstract and less danceable, black bandleaders like Louis Jordan and Lionel Hampton had built small, rhythm-focused combos around a powerful lead instrument like a saxophone. Half a decade later, Berry borrowed their format—but replaced the sax with his electric guitar.

Rising to fame a couple of years after Chuck Berry's arrival, Buddy Holly became Berry's style of bandleader, filling a role that would later be called a front man. Like Berry, Holly wrote most of his songs, sang them onstage, and played rhythm and lead guitar. Though Berry was the greater innovator, Holly was in some ways more modern—in his choice of instrument, for one thing. A few other rock 'n' rollers used solid-body guitars, even Stratocasters. Gene Vincent and His Blue Caps could be seen wielding double-cutaway Fenders as they scratched out "Be-Bop-A-Lula." But no early rock 'n' roller would shape the future through a solid-body guitar the way Buddy Holly would. Because no audience felt the allure of Holly and his Strat more than the teenagers of Britain.

21.

"TWO DONKEYS ON EACH END OF A ROPE, PULLING IN OPPOSITE DIRECTIONS"

FULLERTON, 1955–1957

On a warm Thursday morning in June 1955, salesman Charlie Hayes drove out to Fullerton to visit the Fender factory. Hayes had been recently married—to the surprise of his friend Don Randall, who wondered whether Hayes's pretty new wife, Dorothy, knew what she was in for. How could the prankster Charlie Hayes keep a wife, especially one who seemed so mild? But marriage seemed to calm Hayes down a bit. He still loved to pour too much lighter fluid on the barbecue, but he seemed to have realized that, along with all the opportunities for practical jokes, there was serious money to be made in the Fender operation. And as its vice president of sales—a corporate officer along with Don Randall, Leo Fender, and F. C. Hall—the lanky Texan was in a position to earn plenty.

Leo, eternally occupied in his lab, kept Hayes waiting all morning, and Hayes used the time to gab with the still-new plant manager, Forrest White, about the increasingly tense relationship between Don and Leo. In his easy-going drawl, addressing White as "kid," Hayes said that the two men were behaving like sparring generals on the same side of a war, communicating only cryptically through their secretaries, each refusing to bend to what the other wanted. Sales were erupting, but frustration was mounting on both sides of the company. Leo wanted to create radical new products, to make improvements anywhere possible. Don wanted to produce what customers would buy. As White soon learned, the two men were like "two donkeys on each end of a rope, pulling in opposite directions trying to get some food."

Around noon, Leo emerged from his lab and went to lunch with Charlie, Forrest White, and George Fullerton. They lingered over their hamburgers, finding a lot to talk about. Hayes's personal life had just undergone a radical change: he now had a wife, a new house in Tustin with a lawn he'd just planted, and a dealer-fresh Cadillac Coupe De Ville—baby blue with a white roof—to ferry him around on sales trips. Leo asked about the car and gave tips about cultivating the lawn, both subjects on which he considered himself an expert.

There were urgent developments at work to be discussed, too. F. C. Hall, who owned part of the company that sold Fender instruments, had recently purchased the Electro String factory in Los Angeles, maker of the venerable, competing line of Rickenbacker electric guitars and amps. Leo and Charlie were furious that Hall had bought a local rival: it seemed Hall was hedging his bet on the electric instrument industry across two separate manufacturers, rather than putting all his faith in Fender. Leo especially hated the idea that, through Hall, Rickenbacker would know how many guitars and amplifiers Fender was selling.

It was the longest lunch Leo had taken in a while. Afterward, Hayes stuck around the factory to continue talking business and spent all afternoon there, walking out with Leo, Forrest, and George as they were locking up the plant just after seven p.m. "So long, kid," Hayes told Forrest White. Then he got into his new Cadillac and headed south toward the Fender Sales office in Santa Ana.

The area between Fullerton and Anaheim was then largely empty. The roads were country two-laners, nothing like the ribbons of freeways that would later crisscross the region. Golden hills rose to the north and east, and long rows of fruit trees undulated in neat lines, filling the foreground in every direction. The only blip of civilization was the lone Fullerton drive-in, dusty and vacant in the fading summer light.

Hayes's Coupe De Ville rolled south down Placentia Avenue, just coming into Anaheim. Racing in the opposite direction, unbeknownst to Hayes, was a drunk twenty-one-year-old named Raul Rivera. Roaring north out of town, Rivera suddenly nudged his car into the other lane to pass a local doctor, who was driving that evening with his three children in the car. But in the haze of his intoxication, Rivera miscalculated the distance. His car struck Hayes's Cadillac head-on, and both vehicles all but exploded in the crash. Hayes's massive new Caddy absorbed the brunt of the impact and was mangled into ribbons, virtually unrecognizable. Rivera, the passing driver, was killed instantly. The doctor Rivera had been trying to pass got out to give aid to Hayes, and found the lanky Texan critically injured, lying unconscious in the Caddy's glass-strewn interior.

Later that evening, Don Randall's eldest son was getting ready for bed when he heard the phone ring. At thirteen, he was old enough to know immediately that something was wrong. From his bedroom at the back of the Randall home, Don Jr. heard his parents talking in brittle tones, heard a quaver in his father's usually firm voice. No one told him any news that night. The elder Don Randall was too upset to explain, and left to try to comfort Hayes's wife. Don Jr. sat up with his grandmother late into the night, finally falling asleep on the sofa.

The next morning, Jean Randall went into her son's room and sat down next to him on the bed. "Uncle Charlie isn't here anymore," she said. By the time emergency workers had gotten the vice president of Fender Sales to Orange County Hospital, all life had fled from his body.

Hayes's death leveled Don Randall. He and Charlie were best friends, travel partners, golf buddies, and close confidants. Hayes was a regular around the Randall family dinner table and a beloved uncle to Don's kids. For all that Don and Charlie's relationship had been about selling instruments, for all the barbs they traded in letters back and forth, their friendship was about much more than sales goals and product announcements—it was personal. The two men had loved and understood each other, and had had big, if untold, dreams for the future. But Randall, so used to running things along with this wisecracking, supremely capable older companion, would now have to helm Fender Sales on his own.

Hayes's absence ripped through the entire organization. Fender had lost not just its most talented and best-known salesman, a figure well-known in music industry publications, and a corporate officer. It had lost a crucial communications link between Don in Santa Ana and Leo in Fullerton, between the inward-facing inventor and the outgoing president of sales. Hayes had been the one person who spoke both Leo's and Don's languages, who could make one man see problems from the other's perspective, and who commanded unquestionable respect from both sides. He'd been hugely important in building this motley assemblage of peddlers and craftsmen into a profitable enterprise—and even *with* Charlie Hayes around, the relationship between Don and Leo had been fraught. Now he was gone, and no one knew quite how to continue.

In the painful weeks after Hayes's death, however, one certainty declared itself to both Don and Leo: Fender couldn't maintain its relationship with F. C. Hall. The businessman had been a crucial support from the earliest days of the operation, wagering money from his wholesale radio parts store on Leo Fender's novel ideas for electric instruments. He'd let Don Randall, a onetime stock boy, run an entire arm of his company. He'd given Leo at least two loans to keep his factory running. But Hall had become a skeptical, glowering parent for a Fender enterprise then entering an awkward adolescence. He wasn't willing to take the same risks in the new guitar business that Randall was, and he had little patience for Leo's perfectionism and chronic unreliability. Leo had grown so distressed by Hall that, according to Fender historian Richard Smith, he often had to pull his car off the road and vomit after meetings with the investor.

The final count against Hall was his purchase of the Rickenbacker factory, which Don and Leo saw as an intolerable betrayal. They wanted him out, and Charlie Hayes's death provided a way to do it. Don and Leo decided they'd buy not only the shares of the company now owned by Hayes's widow but Hall's shares, too, consolidating ownership of Fender Sales between the two of them.

Hall of course didn't want to sell. But Don and Leo had the leverage:

Hall only owned shares of Fender Sales, the company that sold the instruments (it had been separated from Hall's wholesale radio parts business two years earlier). The Fender factory, which actually made all the valuable products, was owned entirely by Leo. "We told Francis either you sell to us or we sell to you," Don Randall told Richard Smith. If Hall had refused to give up his shares, Leo could've simply sold his instruments under another name through another distributor. But rather than fight, Hall gave in. "The parties have encountered differences of opinion as to the management, control, and operation of the corporation," read the separation agreement drawn up that fall. For the paltry sum of $45,000—less than half of what his lawyer claimed it was worth—plus the repayment of a $10,000 loan, F. C. Hall grudgingly agreed to sell his fifty shares of Fender Sales to Leo and Don Randall. A few years later, such a move would have been unthinkable. But no one could see, at that moment in 1955, just how profitable the electric guitar business would one day become.

If Hall was embittered by his ejection from Fender, he was too dignified to complain loudly about it. It seems he did feel betrayed by Randall, his longtime employee, whom he'd groomed from a provincial, radio-obsessed teenager into a sophisticated salesman and manager. But Hall wasn't one to linger over his feelings. Business was business; he didn't hold Fender or musical equipment in any special regard. If he no longer had a piece of Fender, he at least owned Rickenbacker, one of the electric guitar industry's most venerated names, and he could now turn his attention to building that firm into a stronger competitor.

Leo and Don had agreed that they needed to run Fender themselves, but this did nothing to improve their dysfunctional relationship. Increasingly, each occupied a separate world. With White now largely managing the factory, Leo retreated into his lab, working with a close circle of employees and musicians to develop new products and features. He began to feel that his group was the only one truly focused on the fortunes of the company, that Randall was too distracted by his golf game or his newest hobby, flying airplanes.

Randall, meanwhile, put on sharp suits and spent twelve-hour days talking to outside people, either on the phone or in person, nose-deep in the reality of trying to sell Leo's instruments. He sometimes came home from work so infuriated, usually by something Leo had done—or not done—that he'd leap up from his chair at the dinner table and disappear for an hour or two until he could calmly interact with his family. Just ten miles separated the Fullerton factory from the Santa Ana sales office, but the divide between Don and Leo felt far larger. It was growing almost as fast as the company's sales.

In 1954–55, the first year the Stratocaster was offered, Fender had shipped 720 of them. Leo believed in linear technological progress, in a new thing coming along to replace the old. He thought the updated model would wipe out demand for the original Telecaster. He was wrong. Even with the Stratocaster circulating that year, Fender had sold 1,027 Telecasters and single-pickup Esquires, showing that plenty of players thought the original Fender solid-body was newfangled enough.

The combined success of the solid-body guitars, plus the increased demand for Fender amplifiers caused by the changing currents in music, pushed Fender's net sales above $1 million for the first time in 1955. From May 1956 to May 1957, that number increased to $1.7 million, bringing Don and Leo a net profit of $100,884—the equivalent of nearly seven figures today. Business was booming. Large western swing outfits were in decline along with the old ballrooms, but replacing them was a whole eco-system of smaller groups—in rock 'n' roll, country, blues, and pop—who played halls and clubs and depended on electric amplification.

Photographs of the most successful musicians in the second half of the 1950s captured Fender's growth. Leo's guitars and amplifiers—either or both—appeared with Elvis and Chuck Berry, with B. B. King and Muddy Waters, with Wes Montgomery and Oscar Moore, with Hank Williams and Johnny Cash, with Frankie Avalon and Ricky Nelson. And why not? The equipment sounded exquisite. The chief character of the Fender tone was its lushness, the way notes came out full and rich and somehow *refreshing*. The amplifiers produced more clean, undistorted volume than anything else on the market. But the spectrum of sound available from both Leo's electric guitars and amplifiers felt tremendously wide, and any note—lows and highs especially—seemed to punch right out of the speaker, demanding attention. This sonic character would animate innumerable concerts and recordings, and would be copied (or at least imitated) by countless competitors.

Just a year after the release of the Stratocaster, Fender was succeeding beyond what Leo could have imagined. He and Esther finally ended their long tenure as renters and purchased their own home—actually, they had one built by Grady Neal, the contractor who'd erected the Fender factory. It was a modest little two-bedroom on the east side of Fullerton, at 221 North Lincoln Avenue, less than five minutes' drive from the plant. The house had one story, a tiny porch, and Cape Cod shutters on the front windows. Leo took advantage of the spacious lot by having a large shed built off the alley, which he used as storage for the company.

Leo was literally bringing home his work, and his inability to escape from the goings-on at the factory created new problems. He was always sensitive about his health, but in 1955, he got a streptococcus infection, and no matter what he did, it wouldn't seem to go away. His doctor injected him with penicillin and other antibiotics, but every time Leo got a chill, the infection flared back up. Soon, the doctor declared that Leo simply couldn't work seven (or six and a half) days a week anymore, that he needed to take his mind off the plant. They didn't call it "stress" then, but rather, "worry." Leo had to stop worrying so much. He needed a distraction.

Leo despised golf, which he associated with Don Randall. But when the doctor suggested fishing, a light must've gone off in Leo's mind. Fishing meant a boat, and boats were interesting. Leo had been in the kayaking club at Fullerton College, but the first real vessel he purchased, around 1955, was no kayak. The Chris-Craft had sweeping, modern lines rendered in fiberglass and fine teak, and, at forty-two feet in length, ample deck space on both the bow and stern. In a fit of literalism, Leo named the boat *Aquafen*: water plus Fender. He outfitted it with every electronic gizmo available: fish finders, depth sounders, radar. "It was kind of like being in a rocket ship on water," one family friend remembered. The way Leo looked at it, just because his new boat was meant as a distraction from work didn't mean it shouldn't perform as effectively as possible.

22.

"IF WE'RE GOING OVER WELL, OUR GUITARS WEIGH LESS THAN A FEATHER"

The Gibson Les Paul Model's finest moment in 1950s rock 'n' roll came in the hands of rockabilly hero Carl Perkins, who used his gold-top to play "Blue Suede Shoes"—a slab of stop-time genius and a huge hit in 1956. Recording for Sun Records under the guidance of Sam Phillips, Perkins bent notes and slid around the fretboard in a casually smoldering style, careful not to break the spell of studied indifference coursing through the song. There was the merest hint of the snarl this guitar would one day be associated with, a clue that if handled a certain way, this thing might peel the paint right off the walls. But even as recorded by Sam Phillips, a lover of distortion, Perkins's Les Paul didn't howl or scream or growl. Rather, it chimed and purred, supplying cool dignity rather than unhinged rebellion. Black bluesmen were achieving wickedly raunchy tones on Les Pauls at this time in near-total obscurity, but popular rock 'n' roll hadn't yet caught up to what the guitar could do best. By the late 1950s, even Gibson's constant improvements to the Les Paul Model couldn't mask a bleak reality: the instrument simply wasn't selling well.

Nearly every hot guitarist had at least given the Les Paul Model a shot. But in an age when even the brashest rock 'n' roll tunes used mild distortion, and when electric guitars still competed with pianos and saxophones for the lead in songs, no one had managed to discover (or value) what would later be hailed as the guitar's greatest strength. The more obvious aesthetic niceties of the Les Paul didn't seem to make up for its excessive heft. A newspaper writer in Florida reported that Les and Mary's guitars weighed eighteen pounds each—a mistake (they were more like nine to eleven pounds), but a revealing one. "If we're going over well, our guitars weigh less than a feather," Mary had said, hinting at her discomfort. The difference between the weight of a Gibson Les Paul and a Telecaster's or Stratocaster's roughly seven pounds might seem slight, but over several sets in a long night, it meant a persistent ache in the shoulders. Even Mary, when at home, preferred to pick up Les's old hollow clunkers.

The popularity of the Gibson solid-body had peaked in 1953, with 2,245 shipped. Four years later, the company was selling less than half that number, even when including the more upscale, black-finished Les Paul Custom model. With the guitar failing fast, Gibson made major changes to its sound and look.

In the mid-fifties, at the direction of president Ted McCarty, an engineer at Gibson named Seth Lover had developed a pickup that produced no hum when plugged into an amplifier. Most other electric guitars, including all of Leo Fender's designs, used pickups consisting of a single magnetic coil, which sent an audible sixty-cycles-per-second buzz through the amplifier. This sound wasn't loud enough to drown out any music, and many took it as a matter of course, but the hum was noticeable, especially with an amp set to high volume. Seth Lover's new design consisted of two magnetic coils joined together, their reverse polarities canceling out the hum. Quietness wasn't their only benefit: Lover's pickups issued a thick, punchy sound, a pleasing alternative to the often piercing character of single-coils. Placed in the Les Paul's dense body for the 1957 model year, Lover's new pickups, identified by their "Patent Applied For" stamp, made for an instrument with tremendous sonic muscle.

The following year, Gibson gave up on that gold paint Les Paul had liked so much and instead offered the guitar with a beautiful cherry sunburst finish, similar to the more traditional look of Gibson's other models. On these "bursts," as they'd become known, the center of the guitar was stained a transparent yellow, which faded to a deep translucent red toward the edges of the body.

But while Gibson's designers certainly improved the guitar, the new humbucking pickups and cherry finish did little to change the Les Paul's declining sales. Even in 1959, a year seen in retrospect as the model's best, Gibson sold only 643 standard Les Pauls, along with 246 black Customs. Such paltry figures didn't threaten the company; Gibson still retained the largest market share of any electric guitar maker. But solid-bodies were only growing more important, and the Les Paul Model had become a weak spot for America's premier firm.

Though Fender enjoyed rising sales of its radical solid-bodies, the Fullerton crew remained mostly clueless as to where the action was in guitar music. Buddy Holly, the Stratocaster-wielding front man, had turned kids in America on to the company's Jet Age shapes, but hardly anyone in Fullerton seems to have noticed or cared. When Buddy's Strat was stolen on a tour stop in 1958, a bandmate with connections called Fullerton and got the company to send out two new guitars and amplifiers free of charge. It was the typical Fender arrangement: Don Randall would never pay artists to use Fender products, but if an established performer wanted them, he or she could often get them at no cost. Holly was apparently deemed just important enough to get gear for free.

In the eyes of Don Randall, a more crucial Fender player was someone like Buddy Merrill, a clean-cut young man in the country-jazz mold of Les Paul, who performed on *The Lawrence Welk Show*. Welk himself was a big-band leader—the high-priest of so-called champagne music, staunchly old guard—but he gave a nod to the kids by featuring Merrill, who lit up his short spots with acrobatic runs, a gleaming Fender tone, and the confident grin of a prodigy. Merrill's Stratocaster heroics were beamed into living rooms once or twice a week, at prime time, and doubtless incited plenty of demand for a two-horned guitar with an asymmetrical headstock. He certainly earned his portraits in Fender ephemera, as did James Burton, the gifted Louisianan and Fender guinea pig who chopped out wily licks behind Elvis manqué Ricky Nelson on *The Adventures of Ozzie and Harriet*.

Meanwhile, Fender never even mentioned Buddy Holly in a magazine ad. Like most adults, the company leaders in Fullerton and Santa Ana were oblivious—convinced, as it seemed safe to be, that this rock 'n' roll music would be no more than a passing fad.

23.

"I REALIZED IT WAS ALL OVER FOR MUSICIANS LIKE ME"

At home, Buddy Holly's reign on the charts was brief. "That'll Be the Day" and "Peggy Sue" yanked him out of Lubbock and onto the package tours that trundled around the US through the boom years of rock 'n' roll, but he'd only had those two major hits. In England, however, Holly's singles were outright blockbusters—not just the initial pair, but follow-ups like "Maybe Baby" and "Rave On," which failed to do much in the US. When Buddy arrived in London in early 1958, he was regarded as a giant: only the second real rock 'n' roller (after Bill Haley) to make it over the pond.

The signal moment of Holly's trip came on Sunday, March 2, when the Crickets appeared on *Val Parnell's Sunday Night at the London Palladium*: the British equivalent of *Ed Sullivan*, but with even worse sound. Onstage, Buddy radiated confidence, tilting his shoulders suggestively, holding his long frame taut, as if ready to pounce at any moment. Under the Palladium's lights, his face no longer seemed gawky or nerdy but casually handsome. On "Oh Boy," the Crickets' second number, Buddy let out a wolfish yelp and laid into his Stratocaster, pounding its strings with the abandon he'd learned from watching rhythm and blues artists at home.

Live, especially, Buddy's songs were feasts of guitar—and just *his* guitar, since the Crickets were now a trio. This forced Buddy to conjure all the magic that in other groups might come from two or three performers. They had only modest equipment: an upright acoustic bass, a standard drum kit, and that Stratocaster run through a four-speaker Fender amplifier. Yet with this they attained heights of volume their listeners wouldn't soon forget. Ronnie Keen, the leader of a large British jazz orchestra, had stood watching Holly and the Crickets perform the night before they appeared on *Palladium*. "At that moment," Keen remembered, "I realized it was all over for musicians like me. This was the future. They hardly had any power—only the house mics and that one little amp . . . The bass player, I remember, wasn't even amplified. But they still managed to make as much noise as the whole of my thirteen-piece orchestra."

The Stratocaster was so rare in England that it qualified as a star next to Buddy himself. Its space-age outline floated before the bare backdrop of the Palladium stage, its pickups chirping through the tinny speakers of a million British televisions, its body a shock of curvaceous brilliance from the country where fun seemed to be a major export. The England of 1958 was still bound by Victorian propriety, still in such a state of recovery from World War II that food rationing was a recent memory. The impressions left by this skinny, charming lad and his sleek guitar had an incalculable effect on the younger generation of Britons. "It showed that to play rock 'n' roll you did not have to be a bespangled Technicolor freak," the English Holly biographer Philip Norman wrote. "You did not have to be a pouting Adonis like Elvis . . . You could be thin, hollow-faced, a little goofy; you could even be a foureyes!"

All over that rainy island, the first generation born since the horrors of the war watched in delight as Holly played on the telly. A twelve-year-old boy in the village of Ripley, southwest of London, stared at Buddy's guitar, listened to the music, and thought he'd gone to heaven. To Eric Clapton, Fenders seemed like instruments from outer space, promising glints from

To their millions of fans, Les Paul and Mary
Ford were "Mr. and Mrs. Guitar"—accessible
innovators who brought flashy electric licks and
multiple sonic layers to the pop charts.
Copyright © Gilles Petard/Getty Images

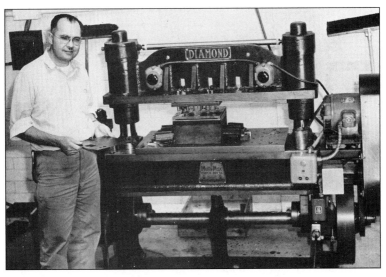

Leo Fender adored tools like his Diamond punch press the way players adored
their guitars. It was an extravagant piece of machinery for his tiny firm in 1950.
Courtesy of Richard R. Smith

Esther Fender covered the salaries of Leo's early employees with her earnings as a telephone operator. Pudgy the dog lived at Fender's first factory.
Courtesy of Richard R. Smith

Anything that went fast or got loud, Paul Bigsby was into—first as a motorcycle racer, later as a gifted craftsman and designer.
Copyright © Centerstream Archives

When he wasn't selling Fender equipment out of the trunk of his Cadillac, Charlie Hayes loved to pull pranks like setting Don Randall's golf bag on fire.
Courtesy of Richard R. Smith

Don Randall "was definitely the high moral type," as one colleague put it—a well-adjusted, hardworking manager whose efforts were essential to Fender's success. Yet Leo almost never saw eye-to-eye with him.
Courtesy of Richard R. Smith

The Fender workforce celebrates Christmas 1952 in a photo likely taken by Leo. George Fullerton stands at far left. *Courtesy of Richard R. Smith*

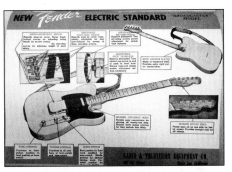

Fender announced its radical new instrument to the world in the February 1951 issue of *Musical Merchandise*, only to discover weeks later that Gretsch held the trademark on the name "Broadcaster." Musical Merchandise *magazine*

The thin electric guitar Paul Bigsby built for Merle Travis in 1948 drew lots of attention. Travis didn't complain. *Photo by Scotty Broyles, copyright © Deke Dickerson Photo Archive. Licensed through Deke Dickerson Photo Archive*

Forrest White started managing the Fender plant in 1954. He worshipped Leo Fender so much that he later bought a house across the street from his boss. *Courtesy of Richard R. Smith*

Armed with the brand-new Fender Telecaster, Jimmy Bryant became one of the hottest guitar slingers on the LA country scene. *Courtesy of Richard R. Smith*

A cheeky, mischievous domesticity defined Les and Mary's public image. The phallic suggestion here is perhaps the first in a long line of electric guitar double entendres.

Copyright © Michael Ochs Archives/Getty Images

In the mid-fifties, George Fullerton tested a freshly built Stratocaster in the expanded Fender factory in Fullerton.
Courtesy of Richard R. Smith

Muddy Waters got a white Fender Telecaster before his trip to England in 1958. The tones he conjured with it scandalized British purists who'd never heard the electric style Muddy developed in Chicago.
Copyright © John Cohen/Getty Images

Elvis never brought American rock 'n' roll to London. But Buddy Holly and his Stratocaster did.
Copyright © John Rodgers/Getty Images

Armed with his Fender Stratocaster and Dual Showman amp, Dick Dale may have been the first rocker you could reliably hear from out in the parking lot.

Copyright © Michael Ochs Archives/Getty Images

Carol Kaye endured leering drunks and long hours to become the top electric bassist in the LA recording studios. Her imaginative bass lines animated some of the greatest hits of the mid-sixties.

Copyright © GAB Archive/Getty Images

The T.A.M.I. Show, featuring the Beach Boys, the Rolling Stones, and Chuck Berry, was the first real rock 'n' roll concert film. When it appeared in 1964, Leo and Les were eyeing retirement, but their electric instruments were just taking off.

Copyright © Michael Ochs Archives/Getty Images

George Harrison and John Lennon play the Rickenbacker models F. C. Hall gave them on the Beatles' first trip to the United States in 1964. Their guitars sparked a global frenzy for the instruments of Fender's crosstown rival.
Copyright © Michael Ochs Archives/Getty Images

James Jamerson reached new heights of funky artistry in the Motown studios, using his 1962 Fender Precision Bass on nearly all of the label's indelible 1960s hits.
Copyright © Michael Ochs Archives/Getty Images

Jimi Hendrix arrived in London in 1966 with virtually nothing but a white Stratocaster. Within a few months, he'd dethroned the country's best guitarists and recorded "Hey Joe" and "Purple Haze."
Copyright © Val Wilmer/Getty Images

By cranking his Gibson Les Paul to obliterating volume so his blues licks positively sang through a room, Eric Clapton revealed the guitar's potential for hard rock.
Copyright © Michael Putland/
Getty Images

Playing "The Star-Spangled Banner" at Woodstock was a defining moment of the 1960s and of Hendrix's career. It gave the electric guitar a new status in the popular imagination.
Copyright © Barry Z. Levine/
Getty Images

the future. Here, he realized, was what he wanted and needed—that instrument, that sound, the exhilaration they brought. Even at twelve, Clapton felt deeply alone in the world, and for good reason: His mother had given birth to him when she was sixteen, in the bedroom of her parents' Ripley flat, and then had largely disappeared. When Clapton later learned that the people raising him weren't his real parents, but his grandparents, it sent him spiraling into a fever that would last for decades. He hungered after something, perhaps the love he'd been denied, perhaps a way to numb the pain of its absence, and he'd use the guitar as a means to find it.

That same night, in the Liverpool suburb of Woolton, a nearsighted seventeen-year-old named John Lennon slouched toward his grainy screen and studied the chordal riffs Buddy Holly played instead of single-note solos. A few streets over, in a working-class neighborhood of modest town houses, Lennon's friend Paul McCartney also sat mesmerized by the curves of Buddy's guitar.

Three weeks later, when Holly and the Crickets came to Liverpool, neither Lennon, a struggling art school student, nor McCartney, a high schooler, could afford tickets. Instead they pried details out of friends about his set list, his appearance, his guitar. Afterward, Lennon pushed to change the name of their band from the Quarrymen to something like the Crickets, the name of Holly's band. They settled on the Beetles, which Lennon, a lover of puns, soon changed to reflect the so-called beat music they played. They'd practice in Paul's living room on soggy afternoons, learning Buddy's vocal harmonies, which they adopted as their own. Lennon, legally blind, took a new attitude toward his spectacles. Both dreamed of a Fender guitar.

The curvy shape of the Stratocaster illuminated something else beneath Buddy Holly's surface, hinted at an aspect of his appeal not obvious from that gawky, white exterior: sex. Outwardly, Holly was no Adonis like Elvis; nor did he radiate lust like Little Richard. But Holly never lacked sensuality—he and Little Richard reportedly shared some wild dressing-room encounters, none strictly heterosexual. "Peggy Sue" may have conveyed a simple, sweet devotion, but those feelings belonged to drummer Jerry Allison (who'd make the real Peggy Sue his bride). Other entries in the Holly catalog, like "Ting-a-Ling" and "Oh

Boy," revealed a libido raging for satisfaction, a young man utterly familiar with the yearning of the flesh.

Holly's Stratocaster revealed it, too. For all the practicality that Leo
Fender had carefully instilled in his handiwork, his new instrument had
arrived hot—not some workman's modest tool, but a gorgeous object of
desire. The Telecaster hadn't had such an effect, and neither quite had
the Les Paul. The Stratocaster was the lone hot rod—a pinup model
among musical instruments. For the teenagers watching Buddy Holly at
home, its lascivious shape was a tell that this singer, for all his nice neckties, for all the adult tolerance he might receive next to the likes of Elvis
Presley, wanted to get it on just as much as they did.

TO ERIC CLAPTON, John Lennon, and Paul McCartney, Buddy Holly
linked the sound and look of the solid-body electric guitar to rock 'n'
roll, the music they'd spend their lives pursuing. But even if few of its
original purveyors had so far performed in England, rock 'n' roll was
a familiar style by then on both sides of the Atlantic. Later that year,
English observers got a taste of a ferocious American music that even
most Americans had never heard of.

By the time the invitation arrived from the other side of the world,
asking him to tour concert halls in England, Muddy Waters's career had
fallen far from its onetime peak. In 1954, Chess Records had released
what would become Waters's biggest hit: a thick, strutting testament to
his own mythical stature called "Hoochie Coochie Man," whose lyrics
left audiences as much laughing in disbelief as howling in appreciation.
(It began: "The gypsy woman told my mother / Before I was born / 'I got
a boy child's coming, / Gon' be a son of a gun.'") In the wake of its success, Muddy bought himself a house and a car and a Hoochie Coochie
Man's guitar: a Gibson Les Paul gold-top. When he brought it to a gig,
everyone in the band marveled, but Muddy had a turbulent relationship
with those nine pounds of mahogany and maple. "He didn't like it, 'cause
it was thin and real heavy," Jimmy Rogers told the writer Sandra B. Tooze.

The summer after "Hoochie Coochie Man," Chuck Berry had

announced himself to the world with "Maybellene," and Elvis and Bill Haley became major national stars. Sales of Muddy's records fell off and never recovered. Younger black listeners increasingly thought of his music as slow, down-home stuff, old-fashioned and even a little shameful. By 1958, he was taking almost any gig around Chicago that would fill the schedule, even playing bargain nights when he had to.

News of Muddy Waters's decline hadn't reached England, though. The country was in the midst of a full-scale folk and jazz explosion, led in part by Chris Barber, a bandleader who invited Muddy over. Barber's 1920s-style New Orleans jazz had become popular among white college students and liberal intellectuals in England, and this same crowd appreciated folk blues records of the kind Muddy had made before moving to Chicago. To these Brits, appreciating blues and jazz was a stance against the crassness of modern pop music, a way to differentiate themselves from the younger (and often poorer) teens who salivated over singers like Buddy Holly and Little Richard.

Two months before Muddy Waters left for England, he realized that he'd need to relearn the guitar. He'd stopped playing onstage around 1955, due to a bad cut on his left hand, and had never picked it up again. It was partly laziness, but he'd also grown a little embarrassed by his playing, a little less confident in his music after the rise of rock 'n' roll. In England, since he'd only have a pianist to accompany him, he'd need to play guitar. Yet for reasons that are unclear, he didn't pick up his old Gibson. Perhaps the Les Paul had been stolen, or perhaps he'd just grown tired of its heft. Instead, he brought with him a white Fender Telecaster.

The first England gig was at the Leeds Festival, after which Muddy and his accompanist were written up under the headline "Screaming Guitar and Howling Piano"—a hint of what was to come. In London, a decent press contingent came to see him along with the local blues intelligentsia. The *Sunday Times* had warned that "this is not the voice of the 'old-time' American Negro but of the American Negro as contemporary conditions have made him." Yet many arrived at St. Pancras Town Hall apparently expecting a poor sharecropper with overalls and a drawl and a shabby acoustic guitar.

What they saw instead was an urban hustler in a crisp suit, wringing overwhelming volume from a thin, white Fender. As Muddy strummed the first chords on the Telecaster and adjusted the sound of his amp, one well-known critic and his entire retinue got up and walked out. "[Muddy] fiddled with the knobs [of his guitar]," the critic wrote. "The next time he struck a fierce chord, it was louder, and I realized that this was the established order of things. As he reached for the volume knobs again, I fled from the hall."

American blues players had toured England before, and some had used amplified hollow-body guitars, but Muddy's electric blues played through a Fender solid-body made for a dramatically different experience. In the years since his earliest hits, Muddy's style had grown only heavier and more aggressive—and that sound had never crossed the Atlantic. "Electric guitar had not really been heard, not loud," one witness recalled. "The chords, yes, but not that kind of wild playing." Even those who appreciated Muddy's performance felt stunned by the volume and tone of his guitar:

By the time the spellbinding "Blues Before Sunrise" came up, Muddy had the audiences hooked on the end of those curling blue notes that shot, shimmering, from the big amplifier box. Mr. Fender would be amazed at the sounds that Muddy Waters, out of Stovall, Mississippi, can wrench from his usually fiendish invention. And when Muddy slipped a short piece of brass pipe onto the little finger of his left hand, the sounds were eerie and yowling, a distorted electronic voice singing back at the intensely human one—answering, commenting, affirming.

As Muddy scraped that little slide up the neck, over and over, making one of his climax-inducing moves, the Telecaster screamed, shrill and piercing, all but overwhelming. Muddy loved that sound.

Many English listeners didn't. Some were jazz and folk purists who saw the electric guitar as a symbol of commercial rhythm and blues. Some were simply rattled by the forcefulness on display. "It was tough, unpolite, strongly rhythmic music, often very loud but with some light and shade in each number," Max Jones wrote in *Melody Maker*. "I liked his singing very much. I also liked some of the violent, explosive guitar accompaniment—though there were times when my thoughts turned with affection to the tones of the acoustic guitar heard on his first record."

Muddy was surprised by the reaction his Telecaster playing got in England. Aside from perhaps a few curious white faces in a South Side club, he'd never performed for an audience outside of his core black following. In 1958, his music was virtually unknown to white listeners in America. He was wounded by the harsh criticisms these foreigners initially made, and as the England tour progressed, he gradually turned his amplifier down.

Yet despite the controversy, or perhaps because of it, nearly all of the shows in England sold out. Over those two weeks, Muddy saw that his music had found an appreciative audience all the way on the other side of the Atlantic, an unimaginable distance from the South Side, and this realization rejuvenated him. "I didn't play guitar until about two months ago, but I'm gonna keep on playing now," he told Tony Standish. "I won't rest no more—when I rest next time, I'll be through." All the electric guitars he'd played before had not stuck with him, but Muddy would play the Telecaster he used in England for the rest of his life, later repainting the guitar red and adding a thicker neck.

By the end of the tour, receptions had grown so warm that Muddy talked about making plans to come back. "Now I know," Muddy told *Melody Maker*, "that the people in England like soft guitar and the old blues." But he'd already begun to change that. Among those who saw Muddy Waters in England were a few art-school students who'd soon start a couple of bands. One of those bands would be called the Animals. The other would become the Rolling Stones, after one of his own hits. Older English fans, those who wrote for the magazines, who swooned over Chris Barber's 1920s jazz, might have preferred the acoustic Muddy Waters. Those younger listeners would never forget the way he made that Telecaster howl.

So by the end of 1958, two Americans with Fender guitars—a white Texan and a black Chicagoan—had demonstrated raw, electric-guitar-driven music as it had never been heard in England. Surely neither Buddy Holly nor Muddy Waters realized how fully, and how soon, a few English players would come to master it themselves.

24.

"WHY DO YOU HAVE TO PLAY SO LOUD?"

"Like many adults, I've been in the habit of switching the radio off rather quickly the last couple of years," Les Paul's old friend Bing Crosby wrote in the *New York Herald-Tribune* in 1960. "Two bars of rock 'n' roll and I reach for that dial. But despite those jangling guitars, I've stayed optimistic about the future of popular music . . . Now, I guess I was right. Rock 'n' roll seems to have run its course." Crosby wrote that teenagers had lost their taste for "thumping electric guitars" and a big beat, and that something else would soon take their place as the musical fad of the day—perhaps even the slow, gentle ballads he loved.

Surveying the music of the time, it would have been easy to agree. After a ruthless rise in the mid-1950s, rock 'n' roll seemed to crater by the end of the decade. Elvis Presley entered the army in October 1958 and returned to civilian life in 1960 more a crooner than a greaser. Little Richard announced his plans to retire and enter the ministry. Jerry Lee

Lewis, on a tour of England, revealed to the press that he was married to his thirteen-year-old cousin—and that she was his *third* wife—thus banishing himself from polite society.

The following February, in the greatest tragedy to befall the first generation of rock 'n' rollers, the plane carrying Buddy Holly and the rising stars Ritchie Valens and the Big Bopper crashed, killing everyone aboard and cutting short the career of that lanky, bespectacled, Strat-wielding genius from Texas. In November, Alan Freed, the DJ who'd helped start the rock 'n' roll craze, was implicated in a payola scandal. The following month, Chuck Berry was arrested for transporting an underage girl over state lines; he'd spend the next three years fighting a Mann Act charge and serving time for his conviction.

So Crosby's claim that the "thumping electric guitars" had met their end perhaps had some backbone. A folk music revival led by groups like the Kingston Trio was capturing the attention of older youth, while novelty song-dances like Chubby Checker's "Twist" stormed the pop charts. Whatever those were, they weren't rock 'n' roll.

In Southern California, however, a particular strain of original rock 'n' roll endured among middle-class teenagers. It was largely instrumental music: tough, lean, easy to play, led by the electric guitar and the saxophone. The first signs of it had surfaced in 1956, when Bill Doggett's "Honky Tonk" replaced vocals with jaunty electric guitar and shot to no. 2 on the *Billboard* Hot 100, becoming a rock 'n' roll standard. Two years later, Duane Eddy's "Rebel Rouser" offered up little besides the echoing, metallic sound of a Gretsch hollow-body guitar as its centerpiece, inventing "twang" and exuding unimpeachable cool. Link Wray's "Rumble" of 1958 was even rawer, foregrounding a crackling, distressed tone that Wray achieved by cutting holes in his amplifier speaker.

Ritchie Valens, the Latino rocker from Los Angeles who died in the plane crash with Buddy Holly, had contributed to this movement with "Fast Freight," an instrumental that featured him tooling around the neck of his Stratocaster, flicking out licks over a steady beat. Like "Rebel Rouser" and "Rumble," "Fast Freight" was two minutes of utterly basic music: three chords, a chugging rhythm, and Valens's Fender issuing attitude. It showed obvious debts to Chuck Berry, but Valens had also borrowed from a friend and brief label-mate in LA. That friend was a handsome young man who'd moved out to California in high school, a lefty developing a strikingly powerful style on the guitar, which he played upside down, its strings reversed from the usual order. Born to Lebanese parents as Richard Monsour, this friend of Valens's had started out playing local talent shows, and showed enough ambition that one night a four-hundred-pound country-western DJ named T. Texas Tiny bestowed on him a stage name: Dick Dale.

Los Angeles had facilitated Dick Dale's evolution from a would-be Hank Williams to a would-be Elvis Presley, even giving him a bit part impersonating the King in a Marilyn Monroe flick called *Let's Make Love*. But Dale's initial rockabilly recording went nowhere, and working in metallurgy at Hughes Aircraft was a drag. So in the late fifties, he moved south to Orange County and joined a little folk scene on the Balboa Peninsula, a spit of land jutting out from Newport Beach into the Pacific. Balboa was a kind of Hamptons of Los Angeles, and a favorite spring break destination for local high schoolers, whose annual "Bal Week" festivities shattered the usual seaside calm. There was one beatnik coffeehouse in town, and an ice-cream parlor with a stage where Dick Dale and his cousin started playing folk and country music on electric guitars, building a little following. In the summer of 1960, their audiences overflowed the ice-cream parlor and clogged the street outside. So Dale moved one block away, to a cavernous venue called the Rendezvous Ballroom.

Built in 1928 to present traveling jazz orchestras, the Rendezvous had once hosted Tommy Dorsey and Benny Goodman, though lately, its staid offerings barely drew a few hundred people to a parquet floor that could hold three thousand. Its hulking, Spanish-tiled exterior and vast parking lot sat right on the sand, their concrete pad occupying more than 160 feet of beachfront, so close to the breakers that ribbons of sea foam spilled into the parking lot at high tide. It made a perfect birthplace for what would become known as surf music.

Starting in July 1960, Dick Dale and the Del-Tones performed at the Rendezvous every Thursday, Friday, and Saturday, from eight p.m. to midnight. After spreading the word around local high schools, their audiences swelled from dozens to hundreds within weeks. To satisfy authorities nervous about rock 'n' roll's corrupting local youth, Dale imposed strict rules. There'd be no alcohol, of course, and no letting attendees in after they'd left the show, to limit any parking lot mischief. A strict dress code was enforced: no "short pants"—not even capris for the girls—and for the boys, collared shirts and neckties. A box of ties was even kept at the door, to be handed out to the rebellious or forgetful.

With Dale now using guitars, bass, drums, and as many as three saxophones, his folk tunes were replaced by more forceful numbers, especially rock instrumentals. Much of the Del-Tones' set was soon wordless, with Dale's guitar simply buzzing out lead melodies over a tumbling rhythm. His guitar style grew out of his fascination with the drums, particularly the haywire soloing of big-band leader Gene Krupa. Trying to re-create Krupa's percussive force and blinding speed on a guitar, Dale started chopping at his strings with a pick so fast that every note came out serrated, his wrist a blur, the amplifier spitting a steady tremble of barbed wire. Sawing at the strings required formidable strength and precision from Dale, and as his playing grew more intense and powerful at the Rendezvous, he began to have problems with his amplifiers. He kept setting them on fire.

That, anyway, is what Dale *said* was happening, though any conflagrations were likely small and short-lived. He'd paired his white, left-handed Stratocaster with speaker boxes from Gibson, Fender, and the smaller Southern California company Standel, but no matter which amp he played, he'd destroy it. He sought the fattest, thickest sound from his Stratocaster, the heaviest bass possible, a gut-punch. To get such a sound in such a large room, he turned up his amps so loud that he either fried the capacitors inside—sending up small puffs of smoke—or shook the speaker into incoherent flatulence.

It was a problem Leo Fender just couldn't understand. By then, Leo had taken a liking to the young Richard Monsour, bonding with him after the young player apparently came around Fullerton begging for a guitar. The two would call each other with new technical ideas late at night, and spent time sitting in Leo and Esther's living room, listening to Marty Robbins country records. Leo found Dick Dale's amplifier conundrum intriguing. He and his lab assistant, Freddie Tavares, spent weeks developing improvements for Dale, building stouter versions of the new amplifier line they were developing. Dale would drop by on Thursday afternoons in 1960 and play through the new circuits and the wall of speakers Leo used for testing. Inside the concrete bunker of Leo's lab, his guitar sounded like a machine gun. It was deafening how Dale played the instrument, his tanned left arm bulging as he knifed the strings with his pick.

Yet at the end of every weekend, Dale trudged back to Fullerton with whatever supposedly powerful amp Leo had given him, and it ended up with its capacitors smoked or the speaker cone torn or both, and Dale still claimed that it hadn't given him the sound he wanted. "Leo kept asking me, 'Why do you have to play so loud?'" Dale remembered. After what he claims were some forty or fifty amps destroyed, Freddie Tavares finally told Leo that to truly understand the problem, they'd have to go see Dale perform in person.

Mr. Fender and Mr. Tavares, middle-aged professionals heading out to get a taste of the local teen mania, must have been quite a sight: Freddie in his round metal glasses and Hawaiian shirt, grinning, the ever-curious musician; Leo in plain khakis and a blue button-up, slightly frowning, battling an ulcer after nearly fourteen years of running his own instrument company. On that weekend evening, they joined a line of cars three miles long down Balboa Boulevard and found the Rendezvous parking lot crammed full. The two grown-ups must have moved awkwardly through the crowds of teens hanging around, the kids surreptitiously drinking or necking or getting into precisely the mischief the town fathers had feared. Out on the darkened beach, the crashing waves left trails of white foam that glowed in the streetlights.

After the cool damp of the outside, the humid air inside the Rendezvous hit like a wall. In the ballroom darkness they could just make out the bulk of the crowd: three thousand teens knotted together, twirling, spinning, stomping. Boys in neat gray jackets and ties; girls in flannel skirts and closed-toed shoes, leaning on one another. A few more rebellious types in Pendleton flannels and huaraches, their collars torn open, dancing alone. The boys would put one foot down, slide it a little, then the next foot, slide, and so on: the surfer's stomp. A forest of young faces, sweating, smiling, their white skin turning pink with exertion, everyone absorbed in the music and each other.

Leo and Freddie clumsily made their way to the center of the room and focused on the stage, where their friend was leading his band. Dale was a marble statue, animated: a shovel-chinned superman wearing a madras blazer and a tie. A curl of greasy hair fell over his face while his dark eyes stared down at the veiny hands pummeling his Stratocaster. There were perhaps five more musicians up there, all dressed as immaculately, all swaying in unthinking unison to the beat, which was relentless. There was a drum kit alongside a Fender Precision Bass cranked up, and a trio of horns, but the star was Dale's left-handed Stratocaster. It wasn't playing just rhythm or lead, but somehow both. As the loose shuffle of the band swayed beneath him, Dale jackhammered electric notes out into the ballroom, as if trying to stab the sound of his guitar through the chests of his fans. His picks disintegrated on his thick guitar strings, and flurries of white plastic rained down on the checkerboard stage at his feet. Dale was punishing his guitar, pounding it, sawing it, threatening to tear it in half, and the resulting blare was like nothing Leo Fender or Freddie Tavares had heard. It wasn't a sweet, clear melody. It was a jagged rhythm, a howl of steel, a squall of electric nails to which every single one of the three-thousand-something young people inside the Rendezvous Ballroom appeared desperately and completely in thrall.

Amid the din and the sweat, Leo turned to Freddie. "Now I know what Dick is trying to tell me," he yelled.

Some weeks later, Leo called Dale down to the factory. He'd ordered a new fifteen-inch speaker from the James B. Lansing company and installed it in its own cabinet. An amplifier he'd built for Dale was housed separately, to make the rig easier to move. During use, the amp box stacked on top of the speaker cabinet. Both pieces were wrapped in cream-colored vinyl.

"This is you," Leo said to Dale. "You are the Showman. This is your amp."

It was the first amp Fender had made specifically to meet the needs of one player. The Fender Showman was also one of the first so-called stacks, the towering amplifier arrays that would become common as rock 'n' roll evolved into rock. Based on other Fender circuits, but heftier—and, at eighty-five watts, more than twice as powerful as a common Fender Bassman—the Showman pointed the way to an even louder future, an age in which electric guitarists would require speaker boxes the size of refrigerators—or, at least, would really, really *want* them.

It still wasn't loud enough for Dick Dale. Just as with the earlier trials, the Showman roared in Leo's lab, but inside the Rendezvous, a room filled with thousands of sound-absorbing bodies, the thick bass Dale wanted wasn't there. Even the new JBL speaker couldn't stand up to his playing. Dale remembered Freddie Tavares holding the JBL cone in his hands and marveling at the strange contortions his *rat-at-at* guitar style forced out of it, eventually tearing the edges of the paper. Dale told Leo he wanted even more power, and two fifteen-inch speakers in the cabinet, not one.

One afternoon, Leo and Dale worked inside the beige walls of Leo's lab, tweaking the Showman. As Dale's guitar shot out of the speaker, Leo thought he heard a malfunction in the electronics and told Dale to stop playing. He reached over to the amplifier chassis and turned up the volume to maximum. Then he put an ear to the speaker grille and listened carefully for any unwelcome hum or hiss. This was a common procedure for troubleshooting amps, the best way to hear a faulty circuit—just turn it up and listen to what should be silence. But perhaps Dale bumped the guitar, or tripped over it, or smacked it; maybe he didn't see where Leo's ear was. Something struck the guitar, which was still plugged into the amp, which was turned all the way up and had Leo Fender's head against its speaker. The full force of the machine bulldozed into Leo's skull—the chomp of a Stratocaster at eighty-five watts, producing a violent metallic blast. Leo felt his eardrum crumble. He leapt away from the speaker, howling in agony, his hand covering his ear. But the damage was done;

Leo's ear collected only silence and pain. For days afterward, he could hear nothing out of it, and only a meager sensitivity ever returned. It was a cruel stroke of irony. Leo had already learned to live with one eye; now, he'd have to develop musical instruments using little more than one ear.

And yet he did. For Dick Dale, Leo created an even more powerful amp stack, with a huge output transformer and two revamped JBL fifteen-inch speakers in its cabinet. The regular Showman model was now in the Fender catalog. This "Dick Dale Showman," as Leo called it, was not.

But it worked. Within a year of taking over the Rendezvous, and with his custom Fender amplifier punching out the heavy, tight bass he'd so long imagined, Dale's performances became legendary around Southern California. As word spread about the band's new sound, curious listeners came down from Los Angeles, the Inland Empire, and beach cities from San Diego to Malibu. Seeing Dale perform became almost a rite of passage. Among the visitors to Balboa that year was a high-school-age singer and songwriter named Brian Wilson, who brought the group of boys he was singing with. They left stunned by the vigor of Dale's shows, the heaviness of his guitar. "On entering the building, you could hear the shock waves of energy even before you heard the music," one fan remembered. It was a scene neither they nor many others would forget.

There's a story, possibly apocryphal, that Dale was recording a performance at the Rendezvous in August 1961. When he tried to explain that the next song wasn't quite finished, the crowd of boisterous young fans, many practitioners of a new sport called surfing, interrupted him with one of their favorite calls to action: "Let's go trippin'!" A title was born, and so was a style of music. For the youth of coastal Southern California in the early 1960s—who either surfed themselves, wished they surfed, or at least thought surfing was cool—Dale's instrumental music seemed to capture the bracing experience of riding a wave.

Dale himself had learned to surf shortly after moving to Orange County. His long, strong limbs had no trouble handling a nine-foot Hobie, and his dark complexion and chiseled figure meant that he looked positively godlike out there, riding the ocean, gleaming in the sun. Some Dale fans surfed at Huntington Beach or the Wedge in Newport all day before showing up to Del-Tones gigs at night, and the link they heard between the sport and the music wasn't just in their saltwater-clogged ears.

Dale *intended* his overwhelming volume and the hypnotic rhythm of his instrumental music to evoke the awesome power of the sea. You could all but hear a surf rider in the movement of his lead guitar, the way it ventured from lower pitches to higher, crisscrossing the wave of the rhythm section as far up the fretboard as it could go. In this new sound—*surf music*, as it was beginning to be known—electric guitar was no longer an accompaniment, no longer a sideline. There wasn't even a singer to compete with. The instrument had taken over the music, had become the very protagonist of the songs. And after another collaboration between Leo Fender and Dick Dale, the electric guitars themselves began to sound *wet*.

25.

"YOU WON'T PART WITH YOURS EITHER"

SOUTHERN CALIFORNIA, 1961–1963

The acoustic guitar produces a natural richness. The steel guitar sustains almost forever. The saxophone blows raspy and aggrieved. But an electric guitar run straight through an amplifier often comes out sounding plain. Since the earliest days of the instrument, players have felt that it needs some additional element to give it character and make it a compelling lead voice—some sort of distortion, or, perhaps, echo. With echo, each note builds on the last, and the sound becomes layered, complex, three-dimensional. Les Paul used echo to add sparkle to his clean tones. Sam Phillips's Memphis studio was famous for its tape echo system, which gave a surreal tint to Elvis Presley's voice and guitar. Such dimensionality is integral to the character of many instruments: a pipe organ, for example, derives plenty of majesty from the way its sound bounces around a cathedral.

That church-organ echo was exactly what Dick Dale wanted. Dale, told Leo Fender that his Hammond organ had a button to induce artificial reverberation, adding a little warble and a lot of sustain to the notes. The Hammond reverb was created by a metal chamber with springs inside, built into the organ. Dale wanted this effect for his singing voice, and Leo was presumably happy to give it a try.

At Dale's request, Leo took a Hammond reverb tank and placed it in a standalone box. Dale ran his voice through it. Suddenly, he "was able to sing and sound like Elvis," he remembered. Next, almost on a lark, Dale tried running his Stratocaster through the reverb. Dale and Leo knew in an instant that they'd found something even more amazing. The crisp edges of the Stratocaster, always so present and cutting, seemed now to waft around a damp, metallic cavern. The plucks of his strings, always so prickly and pointy, now seemed to float, their edges rounded off, their chords buoyant. Dale's crisp electric guitar was transformed into a smear of tonal color. The sharpness of the Fender Stratocaster blurred by the wet atmosphere of the reverb made for a thrilling juxtaposition, like a knife gleaming underwater.

Dale wanted this sound for his stage show, and Leo gave the first Fender Reverb units to Dick Dale and the Del-Tones in 1961: cream-colored rectangles, each a little larger than a shoebox, containing a spring tank (licensed from Hammond) and displaying a few knobs. You plugged the guitar into the Reverb, then the Reverb unit into the amp, and then basked in the humid glow. Many of Dale's acolytes were starting surf bands of their own, and as soon as they heard his Stratocaster transformed by this new Fender gadget, they had to have one, too.

The Chantays were one such group. For a show at the Tustin Youth Center in January 1962, guitarist Bob Spickard somehow obtained Dick Dale's very own Fender Reverb without his knowing it. (The device had been in Leo's shop for repair.) He and his bandmates were so impressed that they bought their own—a wise investment, as it would turn out. The Chantays were just a group of friends from Santa Ana High School, playing casually, but that year they recorded a moody, mellow single, titled "Pipeline," with their new Fender Reverbs. A small LA label released the song, and somehow, by the following spring, "Pipeline" had reached no. 4 on the *Billboard* Hot 100 chart, and had sold more than a million copies in the United States, becoming the most successful surf music recording yet made. Spickard and his friends were stunned; their young lives would be transformed forever. Importantly, "Pipeline" featured none of the saxophones or horns that often appeared on early surf records. There was an electric piano, but the Showman-amplified, reverb-soaked Fender electric guitar stood alone, front and center.

Dick Dale's crowd-favorite songs like "Misirlou"—later to become iconic in the opening credits of *Pulp Fiction*—and "Shake n' Stomp" had made Fender equipment much desired among the surf bands forming around Southern California. But after the Chantays' "Pipeline," Fender gear was all but *required*. Surf music was now defined, first, by the sharpness and clarity of a Fender guitar through a Fender amp, and second, by the watery echo of the Fender Reverb and the hisses and pops it made when heated up. Only Leo's creations had that knife-in-the-water character.

Yet Fender's near-ubiquity in the early 1960s also came through marketing efforts shrewdly attuned to the teenage sense of cool. The company had been largely oblivious to 1950s rock 'n' roll, but in part because this latest movement was happening in its backyard, Fender quickly grasped the appeal of surfing and surf music, hot rods and hot-rod music. Around 1957, the company started offering guitars in a bright "Fiesta" red. The idea of a musical instrument painted the color of an Italian sports car was so novel that at first Don Randall's sales team laughed it off. Then Fiesta red, first mixed at a hardware store by George Fullerton, massively caught on with young players. Fender soon offered guitars in the same hues as Detroit dream machines: Lake Placid Blue, Firemist Silver, Foam Green, Candy Apple Red Metallic, Burgundy Mist.

These instruments' chrome components mirrored those of flashy cars, and Leo's new solid-body electric models seemed to fit with the vehicles' sleek silhouettes. The Jazzmaster offered a rounded, amoeba-like body shape to go with the tail-fin mania of 1958. It never succeeded as a jazz guitar, but surf rockers loved it. The Jaguar of 1962 added more knobs, switches, and chrome to the same body shape. Leo thought both models made improvements to the Stratocaster and Telecaster, though many players disagreed. Meanwhile, cheaper models like the Music-master and Duo-Sonic put Fender sound and quality within the reach of players just starting out.

Firms like Gibson and Gretsch marketed their products to serious musicians: adults. At Fender Sales, Don Randall and his number two, Stan Compton, targeted young people. After all, young players were the ones who'd take lessons at music stores, see the instruments hanging on the wall, and ask their parents to buy one. Randall hired an artist-turned-adman, Robert Perine, whose images showed Fender guitars in places one would never expect a professional-quality instrument. He took a picture of a man riding a motorcycle with a Jaguar model on his back, or a kid riding a skateboard down a suburban sidewalk while strumming a Stratocaster, or a surfer fingering a chord as he rode a longboard down a wave, and turned these into magazine ads with a pithy caption: "You won't part with yours either." The message was clear: You didn't have to be an expert to play a Fender. A Fender guitar wasn't a professional tool, it was a leisure accessory. For the readers of the national music magazine *DownBeat*, on whose back cover many of Perine's ads ran, Fender became a part of the Golden State dream, a sexy, cheeky contrast to the self-serious professionalism of Eastern-made instruments. Jazz elites might still never play Fender instruments (its amps were an exception), but young people everywhere would want them.

Band photos and record covers from these years can themselves seem like Fender advertisements, with every member proudly cradling their favorite company product, often in matching colors. Groups gave themselves names like the Fender IV and Eddie and the Showmen, testifying to their adoration. And if uninitiated high schoolers needed a lesson in the charms of a Fullerton export, the company erected booths at teen fairs, like one at the Hollywood Palladium in March 1964, to give it to them. Amid displays of hubcaps and beauty supplies, Fender set out Jaguars and Strats and Showmen and let the kids rock out. Further guidance was offered by Dick Dale and the Del-Tones, who pounded the LA teens into sonic ecstasy at the fair one evening while the image of bandleader Lawrence Welk gazed down from a billboard, hopelessly obsolete in a world where three-chord rock blasted out of refrigerator-size amplifiers.

In 1955, Don Randall had been thrilled to sell a million dollars' worth of merchandise. In 1963, at the height of the surf craze, Fender's net sales in just three months totaled more than $2.2 million. A study found that Fender claimed 26 percent of the national electric guitar market that year, crushing Gibson's 11 percent. And yet the surf obsession couldn't last forever. Even in Southern California, not everyone could surf, not everyone looked good at the beach, and not everyone appreciated a wordless style of music that often expressed little more than smug naïveté. Surf rock was distinctly upper-middle-class, too, dominated by teens who had both a car to get to the beach and the cash to buy equipment like a Fender Showman. (The amplifier's initial price in 1960 was an astronomical $550, more than $4,000 today.) The scene was dominated by white, middle-class males, who created a sound that spoke to their rarefied and rather circumscribed existence.

Dale himself didn't care much about making his music a national phenomenon, even after signing to the heavyweight Capitol Records. Rather than touring, he preferred to stay home and play with his surfboard, his exotic cats, his sports car, and his girlfriends. Perhaps he could have helped define surf music for the outside world as tough, instrumental, guitar-driven rock 'n' roll, but instead, another group sold the California dream in a strikingly different form.

One night in December 1961, a few brothers and friends from the LA suburb of Hawthorne went onstage before Dale's set at the Rendezvous and sang two songs. It was just during the intermission, for barely ten minutes, and no one thought much of it, especially not the group's leader, Brian Wilson. They'd arrived in Balboa looking rather like carpetbagging fops, wearing navy blue dress shirts and tight white pants, hoping to back the unexpected success of a novelty record they'd made called "Surfin'" with a live performance—their first. But their singing was shaky, and the reception from Dale's loyalists was vicious. To hard-core surf fans, this group's intricate, high-pitched vocal harmonies amounted to heresy, especially since only one of the soon-to-be Beach Boys had ever ridden a fiberglass board down a curling swell of the Pacific. Never mind that the group would soon outfit itself with full surf-rock equipment—Fender Showman amps and matching white Fender guitars (with a Precision Bass for Brian Wilson)—and issue the attendant volume. They were seen in Orange County as impostors.

For the rest of the country, whose listeners couldn't know that the motifs of Dick Dale's guitar embodied "the boom of the barrel and the hiss of the lace"—that is, the very experience of riding a wave—the clarion voices of the Beach Boys proved a far more compelling advertisement for the Southern California lifestyle. Here were not just the sounds of the ocean but words about it, and words about the romances and souped-up cars that supposedly went with it. California boys might have loved a pounding, reverb-soaked electric guitar, but young people everywhere loved the lush harmonies that Brian Wilson wrote and the Beach Boys performed.

Underneath their college-boy exterior, though, the Beach Boys essentially paired doo-wop vocals with electric-guitar-driven rock 'n' roll. "Surfin' USA," which in 1963 outperformed any instrumental surf song on the pop charts, was essentially a rewrite of Chuck Berry's "Sweet Little Sixteen" from 1958, complete with a furious, Berry-style guitar solo played by Brian's younger brother, Carl, in a tone that would've suited Dick Dale. The Beach Boys hadn't thrown out loud guitars, despite the criticisms of Dale loyalists; they'd simply added to them. This basic combination would fuel the next great wave of rock 'n' roll—one rolling in from the far side of the Atlantic.

It was 1960 when Bing Crosby argued that rock 'n' roll had "run its course." Just three years later, his claim would've looked absurd. "Thumping electric guitars" had returned to the pop charts and the repertoires of high school dance bands around the country—and powered largely by Leo Fender's creations, they were now louder and more dynamic than ever. The big beat was back.

26.

"I JUST DON'T UNDERSTAND HIM AT ALL"

MAHWAH AND LOS ANGELES, 1958–1963

While teenage rockers bumbled their way onto the charts with a few sunglass riffs and an aquarium of Fender reverb, Les Paul and Mary Ford bumped along the nostalgia circuit, playing state fairs, army bases, policemen's balls, and second-rate nightclubs. The Houston Auto Show and Birmingham Fashion Week were a long way from Friday night at the Chicago Theatre, but they were gigs. The couple's fans in the press, many sporting a hardened distaste for rock 'n' roll, still penned the occasional glowing review. Capitol Records let Les and Mary go in 1958, but Columbia picked them up, with rock-loathing producer Mitch Mitchell helping the duo turn out a spate of releases aimed at proper adults.

For Mary, though, playing and pretending the good old days might somehow return wasn't worth the effort. She'd been ready to give up the stage for years, wanting to settle down in New Jersey and live an actual domestic life, instead of the slave-driving simulacrum of one presented on their TV show. Scarred by the sudden loss of her infant daughter, she'd pushed Les to take custody of a newborn baby girl in April 1958. They named her Mary Colleen. The following October, Mary gave birth to a boy named Robert. With Les's two sons from his previous marriage, Mr. and Mrs. Guitar now had the family Mary had always wanted. They spent the children's infancy on a reduced schedule, calling it a "retirement" in the press, but by early 1961, needing to support their output on Columbia, they'd resumed traveling regularly. The mother of two hated being away from her kids. For Mary, performing live always had required a battle with stage fright, but now, knowing there was so much else she *could* be doing made it far worse.

Les, of course, wouldn't allow himself to think of *not* performing. For him, no crowd was too small or sad, too old or young. Jack Paar would still have him and Mary on *The Tonight Show*—Paar always loved to laugh at Les's stories—and Les was almost impossible to embarrass. Indeed, he treated signs of the couple's reduced status as comedy material, happily telling a newspaperman about the time their electric Gibsons blew out the speakers of one state fair stage in upstate New York. Lacking any kind of amplification, there was no way they could perform. So Les just told the audience to sing "The Star-Spangled Banner," and as the crowd rose and began belting, he and Mary fled.

The warmth Les showed in public would often disappear in private. By the end of the decade, he was pushing Mary to perform and travel, threatening, if she didn't, to find other women out on the road. "You bet your ass I was tough to work for, but who wouldn't be?" Les wrote in his autobiography. "You may have five things going at once, and they're all important, and the only way you can keep it all going is to constantly be going a hundred miles an hour." For so many years the couple had both wanted the same thing. But now, Mary wanted to stop performing altogether, and Les didn't. There was no way to break the impasse. "I understood how she felt," he later claimed, "but to cut it off completely was something I couldn't do."

In the midst of this argument, in 1961, Les's contract with Gibson came up for renewal. Gibson still wanted him, though the company had come to view the Les Paul Model itself as a failure. Fender guitars now wore chrome accents, candy-flake paint jobs, and modernist-blob body styles; other makers had followed suit. In comparison, Kalamazoo's output—those elegant, wood-grain-sporting instruments—looked old-fashioned. Ted McCarty and his luthiers had tried a few more-radical designs: the Flying V was, as its name suggested, a giant arrow of a solid-body electric guitar, while the Explorer took the outline of a stylized lightning bolt. Both were introduced in 1958, when the Cadillac Eldorado was growing two-foot metal sails on its trunk. Yet both guitars failed in the marketplace.

A more traditional model that launched that year would prove an instant classic. Gibson's ES-335 was semihollow, with a solid block in its thin acoustic body to counter feedback and provide some of the rich sustain of the Les Paul Model, but at a far lower weight. It found success with jazz, country, blues, and a few rock 'n' roll players (Chuck Berry adopted a variation), and in the process pinched the already lackluster sales of the flagship Gibson solid-body, that heavy and unbalanced Les Paul.

So in 1960, Gibson finally gave up, creating an entirely new guitar and sticking the name Les Paul on it. This instrument would become better known as the SG, for "solid guitar," and it was one of Kalamazoo's clearest admissions yet of the prescience of Leo Fender. Like a Stratocaster, the SG had two cutaways, contoured edges to fit comfortably against a player's body, and a whammy bar. Once confident in their superiority over the California company that bolted boards together into guitars, Gibson luthiers now bent to the Fender belief that comfort (in terms of body shape and lighter weight) was paramount. Still, the new guitar was definitely a Gibson. The SG had the same muscular pickups as the rest of the line, a glued-in neck, and the company's iconic headstock with three tuners per side.

Les claimed to have first encountered this guitar—branded as the new "Les Paul Model"—in a music store one day. "I didn't like the shape," he told guitar historian Tom Wheeler. "A guy could kill himself on those sharp horns. It was too thin . . . The neck was too skinny, and I didn't like the way it joined the body; there wasn't enough wood." But the lack of wood was part of the point: the SG weighed only about seven pounds. And per Les's contract with Gibson, he was still obligated to play the guitar that bore his name. So in his early-sixties publicity shots with Mary, the two of them held new, red and white Gibson SGs. Their skinny, pointy guitars looked as misplaced and strange as the forced smiles on their faces.

One night, after a fight with Les in a Chicago hotel room, Mary snuck out and boarded a flight to Los Angeles, seeking the warm embrace of her family. It took three weeks for Les to coax her back to New Jersey, where she found only the same misery she'd tried to leave behind. "I just don't understand him at all," Mary wrote in a letter to her parents. According to Les's biographer Mary Shaughnessy, he told Mary that if she tried to divorce him, he'd seize custody of the children and leave her without a cent.

But eventually Mary felt she had no other choice. On June 19, 1963, she escaped Mahwah and flew to California, where her oldest sister greeted her in the airport, aghast at her sibling's look of despondency. The next month, Mary filed for legal separation from her husband of nearly fourteen years, accusing Les Paul of cruelty and a failure to support her.

Les was deeply wounded at this rejection and responded by having Mary trailed by private detectives, according to Shaughnessy. That fall, he countersued her, alleging in a widely reported-on complaint that Mary had "openly, publicly, and notoriously consorted with . . . other men," even committed adultery with two she'd known before him. Les further accused her of abandoning their professional engagements, humiliating him in public, and boasting of her affections for other men.

Reporters penned their breakup as a tale of juicy, illusion-puncturing gossip. Many adults could fondly recall the flush days of Les Paul and Mary Ford after the war but before rock 'n' roll, the sweet couple and their Gibson solid-bodies appearing on tiny TV screens all over America. The two performers had embodied domestic bliss, inspiring optimism and a faith in technology. It seemed that a couple could work in showbiz, hit the highest echelons of stardom, and still live a wholesome life. But if the easygoing, creative domesticity of *The Les Paul and Mary Ford Show* had ever really existed, it was now gone for good.

Two weeks after Les filed his countersuit, President John F. Kennedy was shot and killed while riding next to his wife in a Dallas motorcade, shocking the country out of any lingering postwar innocence. By the end of the next year, Mr. and Mrs. Guitar were also no more, the details of their divorce painfully public. Les won custody of their son, Robert, and planned to adopt Mary Colleen. Mary Ford got a settlement worth more than half a million dollars over a period of years, a sum that likely represented only a fraction of the couple's wealth, though she'd been the voice and the face of their act. Though, undeniably, Les contributed numerous technical achievements and a knack for knowing what would sell, few would contest that much of what the couple actually sold was Mary's warmth and charm, and the interplay that resulted from it. Les had talked and tinkered, but Mary had sung and smiled and swooped around her guitar with skill and grace. Without her, Les Paul would have been a brilliant sideman and a revolutionary guitarist with a host of creations to his name. But he never would have been a pop star.

The only thing Mary Ford had wanted in her divorce from Les—custody of the children—she failed to get. The mischievous pastor's daughter from Pasadena had long been sliding into alcoholism and depression as she fought with her husband over the future of their career. Legally separating from Les would end the stalemate that had caused her so much pain, but it would do nothing to halt her bouts of self-destruction.

Les was now losing his longtime guitar maker as well as his wife and costar. He decided not to renew his Gibson endorsement, in part out of fear that Mary might try to claim some of his future income from the deal, but also because he just didn't like the new model on which the company had slapped his name. After his contract expired, Gibson renamed that skinny guitar the SG. The thick, single-cutaway shape of the original Kalamazoo solid-body soon disappeared from the display windows of music stores and retreated to the racks of pawnshops. Everything about Les Paul—his music, his instrument, his stage act—at that moment seemed to be headed for obscurity. Les himself would shortly withdraw to his mountainside house in New Jersey, unaware that on the other side of the ocean, further unimaginable changes in music were taking shape.

27.

"WHERE YOU GOING, LEO?"

ORANGE COUNTY, 1960–1962

The village of Avalon sits on the southern end of Santa Catalina Island, some twenty-six nautical miles from Newport Beach. It's a resort, a little hamlet of tourist shops and a casino encircling a gorgeous azure bay. A good place to get away from life on the mainland. Leo's boat could make the trip in about two hours.

It didn't even feel like it took much effort that day. The summer sun peered down with seemingly infinite warmth, a glow that made the coastal waters of California look downright tropical—as crystal clear and blue-green as the waves on Hawaii, which Leo was coming to know well. He stood up on the bridge of his yacht, scanning the waters ahead for any sign of disturbance, watching the two-humped outline of Santa Catalina grow larger in front of him. Esther gazed out behind him, smiling in a dress, her hands gloved, her hair bundled under a neat scarf, as usual.

On the bow, old friend and steel guitarist Noel Boggs, his wife, and their three teenage children were lying out on the deck, bodies soaking up the sun. Besides the sons of Leo's sister, Wilda, Noel's kids were the closest Leo and Esther had to their own. They gave Leo new screwdrivers and pliers for Christmas, swung by "the plant," as everyone called it, with their father, and came out on the boat almost every long weekend. Though a first-rate country sideman, Noel Boggs was almost like a Fender employee, one of Leo's closest advisers. Leo gave him a company car, a Ford station wagon, to help him transport the fifty-pound amplifier and forty-pound steel guitar that were his professional burden. And because Boggs was stricken with chronic road rage—and enjoyed a good gag—Leo wired up an ultra-loud "ahooga" horn so that Boggs could vent his frustration at other drivers.

There was no frustration now. The Boggs family was lying on the bow of the boat, listening to the churn of the waves and the hum of the engine. From far back, they heard Esther's voice, a chime in the breeze: "Where you going, Leo?"

They looked and saw that he'd left the bridge and was scurrying forward through the cabin. A moment later, his skinny arm shot up through the deck and reached to close the hatch nearest them. But as Leo tried to pull the hatch closed, his little mustache crinkled in frustration. His tool pouch had gotten stuck, trapping him in the open space in the deck. The Boggs family watched amusedly as Leo fiddled and cursed to himself. Suddenly, they all felt the boat plunge downward. Then—splash: a wall of chilly salt water crashed over the bow, washing all the warmth off the sunbathers' skin, smacking Leo in the face, and pouring into the stateroom where he was standing.

Boggs and his kids rubbed their eyes and tried to figure out what had happened. Then they saw Leo, sopping wet, still in the hatch, and heard the high-pitched whine of his laughter. It was like a storm had come over him; he was laughing so hard that he'd started to cry. What the hell was so funny, Boggs asked. His wife was furious: They could have been washed away! Drowned!

Between howls, Leo tried to explain. He'd seen the wave coming long ago from up on the bridge. He'd concocted a little plan to sneak up and close the hatch without warning Boggs and the kids, so they'd get a good smack from the swell. But the plan had hit a snag. As he reached for the handle to pull the hatch closed, his tool pouch had hooked him in place right as the boat hit the wave.

Boggs was now guffawing just as hard as Leo. The two friends thought it was the funniest thing: Silly Leo had tried to pull a fast one on the family, tried to give them a good splash without getting his boat all wet inside. But he'd gotten caught right in the middle of his own plot.

Leo had bought his first yacht in 1955. Over the next thirteen years, he'd purchase eight more, each time trading in his current model—usually just a year or two out of the boatyard—for a new one, and each time changing the Roman numeral after *Aquafen* on the stern. Just as with radios and then guitars and amplifiers, Leo became obsessed by the mechanical details of these vessels. Later years would find him writing letters to the elite Stephens Brothers boatyard in Stockton, California, in which he discussed the minutiae of propeller shapes and battery alignment. Leo once wrote the boatyard saying that on plans it had sent, one bulkhead was shown three-eighths of an inch too high, and another was off by a half inch. A builder soon wrote back, "You were correct, they were a bit off."

His other hobby was photography. Leo had loved taking pictures since he was a boy, but he was now acquiring photographic equipment at a furious pace—first Leica cameras, later Nikons. He learned to process the thousands of rolls of film he shot both at work and on the increasingly lavish vacations he and Esther were able to take, to places like Hawaii and Alaska. In one sense, photography was a visual analogue to what Leo did in music: like the amplification of music, photography extended the aesthetic experience, made it accessible in a way the original never could be. It was a way to participate in a moment while remaining removed from it. There was also a deep appeal for him in simply capturing the physical world: many of Leo's photographs weren't of idyllic vacation scenes or his family, but of construction sites or technical objects like the gadgets on his boats.

Even amid their newfound wealth, Leo and Esther lived in well-matched harmony, each spouse's idiosyncrasies helping those of the other seem less unusual. In their quiet way, husband and wife adored each other. To most eyes, they would have seemed hopelessly stodgy, the total opposite of rock 'n' roll: Leo with his perpetual tool pouch and pocket protector, and plain, dusty work clothes; Esther with her matching gloves, a leather handbag that sat upright on her lap, and her habit of pulling her hair under a scarf during the windy crossings to Catalina. The couple didn't drink, or smoke, or get out of control; nothing seemed to penetrate their veneer of privacy and reserve. Still, they radiated a kindness and an odd sense of humor that inspired loyalty from their inner circle.

Fender researcher Geoff Fullerton, George's son, remembers being at Leo and Esther's house—the second house they owned, a spacious ranch built in 1960—for a dinner party. After the meal, Esther rolled out a new tea cart, which she was obviously proud of. It was elegant and practical, enabling her to serve her guests efficiently. Leo had never seen the cart, so he immediately leaned over and started inspecting its mechanical parts. After a moment, he bolted upright. This tea cart was absolutely terrible, he announced to his wife and their guests. The wheels on it were shoddy, the whole contraption poorly built, and why would they bother owning something so inferior?

Esther turned to her husband. "Well, hell, Leo," she retorted. "I'm not going to *ride* it."

Everyone—everyone but him—erupted in laughter.

Esther had been promoted from an operator to a manager at the phone company but found that her new position didn't allow much time off. The Fender factory shut down for two weeks every year around the Fourth of July, and she and Leo could finally afford to travel. "Leo said there's not much point in being married if you can't ever find your wife to go anywhere," his nephew Gary Gray recalled. So Esther went back to being an operator and left when she wanted for their cruises and trips.

Having Esther present helped Leo feel more comfortable in social gatherings. The company's growing success, and his and Esther's tight circle of friends, had only somewhat eased his social awkwardness. "He didn't know how to have polite conversation," remembered Noel Boggs's daughter, Sandy. "You would ask him a question and then he'd respond and then he would think about it, and twenty minutes later he would make a comment that would drop you dead it was so funny. Because he had thought about it, had processed it."

His quietness seemed to reflect confidence, and his talents attracted total loyalty from factory hands like George Fullerton, Forrest White, and Freddie Tavares. Sandy Boggs remembers watching him at the plant, working on a technical problem with a few employees. "He would be listening to the conversation the whole time, everyone would be yabbering about, 'Well, this is the problem, this is this, and this is that.' And it would be like he'd just lift up something and fix it. All of a sudden it would be perfect, and people would stand there with their mouths open. He didn't do it to show off or show them. It [was] like, 'Oh I just figured it out, thank you. You were saying all these words, and I heard them all, and here it is.' "

To most employees, though, Leo Fender was the solitary genius whose research-and-development lab occupied all of the Fender factory's Building Six. He was a legend, a specter. One day, a new arrival named Babe Simoni was asked to take some boxes over to Building One on a handcart. A sturdy seventeen-year-old with a quick temper, Simoni stacked up the cart and started pushing the swaying load at high speed toward its destination. On the way he nearly crashed into an older employee, who jumped back about three steps to avoid getting run over.

"Don't you think you could probably handle that a little bit better if you didn't take quite as much?" the older man asked.

"If you think you can do better than me, why don't *you* just take it down to Building One," Simoni shot back.

The man just scratched his head and walked away. When Simoni got to Building One, the stock clerk there glared at him. "What the heck did you do?"

"What?" Simoni said.

"Don't you know that guy you're talking nasty to out there, that's *Leo Fender*!"

Simoni had no idea. Many Fender employees would have similar experiences, realizing with a start that the quiet figure who hovered behind them was born with the name they emblazoned on every product. Abigail Ybarra, a young lady of Mexican heritage, had been hired by George Fullerton at first to grind frets for guitars. Later she moved to winding pickups, a skill for which she'd eventually acquire an international reputation. Working at Fender wasn't really like a job, she thought. There were hardly any rules as long as you got your work done. You could talk to your coworkers, walk around barefoot on hot days, adjust your hours if you needed to. At first, she figured the older guy in khakis with all the keys must be a maintenance man. But at Christmas, he rolled around a wheelbarrow filled with candy bars and gum and cigarettes, letting everyone take anything they wanted. A few Christmases later, Leo Fender was handing out whole hams and three-pound boxes of See's Candies to every employee.

Success had arrived; by the early sixties, that was unquestionable. But people like Noel Boggs and George Fullerton worried that Leo had never given much thought to what success would mean—for him. With Forrest White managing the factory, Leo had won the freedom to largely disappear into his lab and design new products. Yet he still bore ultimate responsibility for the organization, and the burden wore on him in ways that a new boat or a trip to Hawaii couldn't ease. Even with his hobbies and his huge Chrysler and his comfortable house, Leo struggled to sleep at night, his mind consumed by problems at the factory. His ulcers worsened. His strep infection, the one he'd picked up back in 1955, still hadn't gone away. At fifty-three years old, Leo Fender could have anything he wanted—anything, it seemed, except peace of mind.

28.

"PRONE TO LOOSE TALK"

In 1963, none of Fender's handful of salesmen earned less than $35,000, the equivalent of more than $270,000 today. One had earned $100,000 for more than three years straight, nearly all of it on commission. The company hadn't hired a new salesman since 1957, and in that time sales had grown by about 600 percent. If the sales reps were doing a good job, Don Randall was happy to let them keep their territory. Mike Cole, who handled the East Coast, owned a sportfishing yacht that he kept down in Florida.

Nine rectangular buildings stretched across the Fender factory's three-and-a-half-acre plot, but all of that space—some seventy thousand square feet inside—still wasn't enough. With no room indoors, finished amplifiers in their cardboard shipping crates were stacked outside the factory buildings in the dry Fullerton sunlight to wait for a truck to take them away. The perpetual struggle between the Fender factory and sales office was approaching a crisis, as the plant struggled to keep up with orders. By the following year, the company backlog was pegged at fourteen to sixteen weeks for many products, estimated at $1.5 million. Randall had to tell the salesmen not to take orders for more amps and guitars than they thought the factory could produce.

Leo rented other buildings around Fullerton to get more space, but things just kept growing. Fender started an acoustic division, with instruments designed by a German luthier named Roger Rossmeisl, who'd built hollow-body electric guitars for Rickenbacker. That needed a plant. For some years, Leo had been intrigued by the experiments of a fellow tinkerer named Harold Rhodes, who was trying to build an electric piano. The technology was enormously complex, and most everyone but Leo and Harold thought it would go nowhere, but Leo invested anyway. That project needed space.

George Fullerton would now wake up in the middle of the night, terrified he'd forgotten to lock one of the factory doors. There was a chain-link fence around the parking lot these days for security, but that didn't help him sleep. He'd replay Leo's admonition in his mind. "Are you sure everything's locked? You're really sure?" It took an hour every morning and every night to unlock and lock up, with *two* men doing it: George Fullerton and Forrest White, who had other projects aplenty, and hated each other besides.

And there was still more to the operation: A distribution center in Tulsa, Oklahoma. A service center in Flushing, New York. Randall's sales office was planning its own expansion, a larger Santa Ana home for Randall's forty-seven employees and the goods they shipped. The Fullerton factory's 270 workers were now churning out a thousand amplifiers and a thousand electric guitars every week—as much as the company had sold over an entire year in the 1950s.

No matter how much more they made, though, it was never enough. Leo Fender's company had become a behemoth, its daily operation an almost unimaginable contrast to the rickety operation he'd started in downtown Fullerton. He'd become a rich man, a homeowner, with a new yacht every two years. Don Randall now owned a nimble two-seater

plane that the air force had used to train combat pilots. There was absolutely no one to answer to, other than the two of them, since Leo owned
all of the factory and half of the Fender Sales company. With no one else
to share profits with, he and Randall paid themselves enormous salaries
of $242,000 each, the equivalent of nearly $2 million today.

Their idea, that a durable, reliable, good-sounding electric guitar and
amplifier would find an eager reception among musicians, had succeeded
beyond their wildest dreams. From virtually nothing in 1946, Fender
had grown into the largest maker of electric guitars and amplifiers, second
in total size only to Gibson, which sold many acoustic models. Fender had
changed the sound and look—and the very course—of popular music,
and was still doing so. Yet Leo was the furthest thing from happy.

The combination of his strep infection and a slight breeze could leave
him with an energy-sapping cold. The infection showed no sign of abating, no matter how many treatments his doctor gave him. Carrot juice
didn't help; neither did his constant trips to the chiropractor. The very
size of his namesake firm intimidated him—it felt beyond his control,
perhaps even beyond his understanding. The western swing and country
players he loved were far out of the spotlight now, even if a few of his old
favorites, like Speedy West and Bill Carson, had become Fender employees. When Leo looked at the musical landscape, at all those Dick Dale
acolytes with their loud guitars, he felt that he didn't belong. He'd helped
create this world, but he didn't see any place for himself in it.

Overwhelmed occasionally by bouts of deep insecurity, Leo Fender
assessed his position in 1962 and 1963 and reached two conclusions:
First, he decided that his self-taught electrical skills would become irrelevant soon, as vacuum tubes were replaced by the smaller but far more
complex transistor.

Second, given his strep infection and what he felt were numerous
other health problems, he didn't figure he'd live very long.

Meanwhile, the company had to expand. Demand was unyielding;
the backlogs were growing untenable. But expanding meant borrowing
money, and Leo, sick with strep, felt queasy at that idea. "Prone to loose
talk," as the historian Richard Smith described him, Leo Fender caught

Don Randall off-guard one day in a private meeting and said something deeply unexpected.

Leo told Don Randall that he'd sell him his half of the Fender companies—for $1 million.

Don Randall was stunned, too aghast to respond. The company was thriving beyond anything he or Leo had dared to dream of. Fender dominated the industry it had had a singular hand in creating. There were problems, logistical issues, sure, but money was rolling in, more of it than they knew what to do with.

Yet Leo wanted out. On top of his illness, and his fear of the transistorized future, Leo may have also believed that Fender simply couldn't sell that many more electric guitars. According to Geoff Fullerton, Leo thought that surely, everyone who wanted a Fender instrument by now had one—and since the guitars and amps were made to last, those customers wouldn't be buying another any time soon. The company had already experienced more than a decade of straight upward growth. How much bigger, how much broader, could the electric guitar really get?

But all around the country, all around the world, a new generation of musicians was preparing to answer that question in a way that Leo Fender, seeking to retreat from his company, and Les Paul, slowly resigning himself to the idea of retirement, would never have believed. Only through the sounds and stories of these musicians would the ultimate legacy of Leo Fender and Les Paul become clear.

29.

"THAT MAN JUST DONE WIPED YOU UP"

Jimi Hendrix played guitar on the way to the gig, onstage during it, back-stage afterward, in the car on the way back, and once he'd returned to the hotel. He dozed off with the instrument in his arms. "He played all the time," one collaborator remembered. "It wasn't like a thing you were lis-tening to, though, it was a simple observation—like, the sun is shining; Jimi's playing his guitar." Jimi Hendrix was a sideman, a guitar player for hire, shuttling around a network of black-run theaters and clubs called the Chitlin Circuit, taking any gig he could get, and trying to master his instrument along the way.

At eighteen, he'd left his home of Seattle for the army, which shipped him off to Fort Campbell, Kentucky, near the Tennessee border. He'd been thrilled to join the 101st Airborne but soon found his electric guitar far more interesting than parachute jumps and military discipline. After ten months and a ruthless campaign to convince army doctors that he'd been seized by homosexual tendencies, Jimi found himself discharged from the army with a few hundred dollars in his pocket and a Danelectro six-string at his side. He quickly lost his virginity to a local woman, and with it, any intention of returning to Seattle. Instead, Jimi Hendrix—raised by a struggling, indifferent father, long accustomed to feeling holes in the soles of his shoes—set off to become a famous guitar player.

He moved to Nashville with some musician friends and soon decided to show off his growing abilities. Jimi often went to watch a talented guitarist named Johnny Jones, a Mississippi native who'd learned from bluesmen like Muddy Waters and Freddy King, and who played in a band called the Imperial Seven. Hendrix would often ask to hold Jones's guitar when his band took a break, trying to parse the older man's sound. One night, encouraged by a friend, Hendrix challenged Jones to a cutting contest—a classic encounter in jazz and blues wherein one band or musician contests another's superiority onstage, tries to "cut their head," as the phrase went. Hendrix and his friend wheeled an amplifier into the club where Jones played and announced that they were coming after him, that he'd better get ready. They set up their gear, and the head-hunting contest began: young Jimi Hendrix and his occasional tutor, sparring on electric guitars over what was likely a spare blues song.

Immediately, it was clear that Hendrix's amp couldn't match Jones's for power or clarity. Then, when Hendrix pulled out some of his favorite licks, the crowd in the room snickered. Through Jones's tutelage, Hendrix had recently met B. B. King and Albert King, titans of electric blues guitar. He'd had an intimate conversation with B. B., in which the older man explained his preference for slow, singing notes, notes that radiated out from his large hands and his Gibson guitar like a good vocalist's vibrato.

The influence had gone to Jimi's head, and as he tried to replicate B. B.'s sound onstage, hoping to beat Jones with it, the crowd had started laughing. *Laughing*—that was how transparent Jimi's imitation of B. B. King was, how obvious, how facile. Meanwhile, Jones, schooled by the greats and having lived the tumultuous life of a Southern bluesman, had conjured his own deep, yearning voice through the guitar and brought the house down, exposing his challenger as naive, inexperienced, perhaps even a phony.

"Jimi left the stage dejected," according to biographer Charles Cross, "and Jones remained the headman." Afterward, Jimi explained to friends that he'd been trying to sound like B. B. King but had simply failed. "That man just done wiped you up," Jimi's friend told him. The failure wasn't merely in the execution, though—it was in Jimi's attempt to imitate rather than express. An electric guitarist couldn't truly move an audience (at least not a savvy one) merely by copying someone else. The only route to the chilling power Jimi sought was to live and play and evolve into the truest, most fluent version of himself. And he still had some evolving to do.

These dues he'd chosen to pay as a sideman, joining the tours of stars like Little Richard, Ike Turner, the Isley Brothers, Curtis Mayfield, and Solomon Burke—witnessing a golden era in American soul and R & B music that looked decidedly less glamorous up close. In these years, Hendrix could barely keep himself clothed and fed, since he refused to take any job outside of music. He'd pawn or lose numerous guitars—Epiphones, Fenders, some bought for him or rescued from hock by his employers. And he'd learn the power of pure showmanship. To audiences on the Chitlin Circuit, playing music well meant nothing without a good stage act, and Hendrix soon began to incorporate flashy moves into his sideman's routine. He learned to play guitar behind his back and with his teeth, to act like he was fucking the guitar onstage, to fall to his knees while soloing, to flick his tongue at the ladies in front when he shredded the high notes. It drove the audiences wild. His bosses were less enthusiastic.

"Five dates would go by beautifully," recalled soul singer Solomon Burke, "and then at the next show, he'd go into this wild stuff that wasn't part of the song." Burke ended up leaving Jimi Hendrix by the side of some Southern road.

While touring with Little Richard, Jimi once wore a ruffled shirt onstage, eliciting howls of outrage from the star. "I am Little Richard!" the bandleader screamed at him. "I am the only one allowed to be pretty!"

Hendrix played briefly with R & B singer Bobby Womack, who would never forget the experience: "He'd turn his git-tar down but he would still overshadow a person . . . Everybody he would play with, people wouldn't be payin' no attention to the artist, they'd be sayin', hey, look at *him*. When he would play with his teeth, they'd give him an ovation because they thought he was crazy, but the artist at the front would think he was tryin' to take the show."

The singers who hired Jimi weren't looking for a rival star. They wanted a clean, obedient employee, someone to stand on the side of the stage and play rhythm guitar, maybe add a solo when one was called for. The problem with Jimi Hendrix, even then, was that he couldn't stay off to the side of the stage. Wherever he stood was the center.

30.

"I CAN'T BELIEVE I HAVE TO PLAY THIS SHIT"

Carol Kaye would nudge her Chevy Impala into the recording studio parking lot barely ten minutes before a session, park, and wearily open the trunk. In it were the half-dozen instruments a studio guitarist like her was expected to carry: an Epiphone hollow-body, a Fender Jazzmaster, a twelve-string acoustic, a six-string Danelectro electric bass guitar, and more, plus an amplifier. She would trudge inside the studio with just two guitars and an amplifier, and there would be five minutes left to grab a cup of vending machine coffee and look over the charts for the current session: another three-chord rock tune, most likely. And Carol Kaye would think to herself, maybe even mutter to one of the other studio musicians—all of them male—whom she worked with: *I can't believe I have to play this shit.*

But she did have to play it. After taking her first studio gig in 1957— backing Sam Cooke on "Summertime," at the request of storied R & B producer Bumps Blackwell—Carol Kaye had joined a corps of musicians who performed anonymously on nearly every disc the LA recording studios put out, regardless of who the named performer was. Employing such uncredited pros was standard practice around the country. Producers looking to hustle out product weren't about to let rock 'n' rollers, many still in high school, waste time and money with sloppy musicianship. They wanted experts who could either read charts or invent clever parts on the fly, getting a song perfectly on tape in just a few takes.

Yet bringing in jazz-trained musicians of Carol's caliber to record the music of the day—surf rock or pop, usually—was like using a nuclear warhead to destroy an anthill. The style of jazz Carol Kaye loved most, bebop, took brains and fingers like nothing else: it was to swing jazz what cubist painting was to classical portraiture, but improvised at a hundred miles an hour. The electric guitar was so much about accents and flowery little touches, but bebop rose and fell on hard, swift, positive notes. You got a moment to cut away into a solo, and Carol could take it and go, each tonal color flying off her Epiphone hollow-body like raindrops splattering the windshield of a car racing down the highway.

By 1963, though, the hundreds of jazz clubs that had once dotted LA County, the places where Carol had earned her reputation, had shuttered or transformed into rock clubs, following the money in the industry. One by one, the jazz players she knew had moved to New York, or accepted starvation as a way of life, or started working in the studios.

Sixty-three dollars was union scale that year for a three-hour recording session, during which a good group might lay down as many as four or five songs. So by playing music she hated, Carol was earning good money. She could give her children all the food they wanted and plenty of Christmas presents, could keep them safe in a quiet neighborhood in North Hollywood. Compared to her childhood, theirs was a miracle. She was determined that they wouldn't know the want she'd suffered, not live with the fear that there might not be enough to eat. She knew she should be grateful for the good life she'd built by playing guitar—but she still couldn't stand the music she spent her days recording. She was grieving for a jazz world that had mostly disappeared. Musically, Carol Kaye had died.

One day that fall of 1963, Carol arrived for a session at the circular Capitol Records tower on Sunset Boulevard. She had no reason to expect anything besides the usual three hours of playing "idiot music," as she thought of it. And she had a lot of other things on her mind. All her life, Carol had had bad luck with men. She was then thinking about leaving her third husband, who loathed the fact that Carol spent many long hours and late nights working with musicians and producers who were often black men. The husband had recently smacked her son so hard with a rake that he'd had to skip school and see a doctor, which sent Carol tumbling into a nervous breakdown. It's a testament to her troubles that she would later remember nothing about the details of the session that fall day—who the producer was, what the songs were. All she would remember is that the bass player didn't show up.

Producers knew Carol could handle the modified Danelectro six-string bass guitar she kept in her trunk. But on this day in 1963, it was a Fender Precision Bass player who didn't come to Capitol. Recording sessions often used both a Danelectro and a "Fender bass," as the Precision was commonly known, and the producer that day chose Carol to take the Fender player's place. Someone put a borrowed Precision in her lap and told her to play any line she thought would work. The instrument had four thick strings instead of six thin ones, with a neck significantly longer than that of an electric guitar or a Danelectro bass. Carol had never really played it before. She was an expert guitarist, but she had no idea what might come of her trying out this thing.

As it turned out, something big came. After the session, Carol drove to the Fife and Nichols Music store in Hollywood and bought two Fender Precisions for herself. Then she went straight home to practice on them.

Playing guitar in the studios, Carol was usually not a soloist but a rhythm player—thus a middle layer in the thick cake of a final recording. She was barely audible on songs like the Righteous Brothers' "You've Lost That Lovin' Feelin'," a Phil Spector–produced masterpiece from 1964, strumming chords on an acoustic guitar somewhere within Spector's titanic production. Her job was to support, not stand out, and she did it well.

Support was also considered the bass's role. Most studio players did little more than plunk out single notes in reference to the changing chords of the song. But starting at that Capitol session on which she played the Fender bass, Carol saw that the electric four-string sat at a crucial juncture in the studio ensemble, one that offered her a unique opportunity. The Fender bass linked the pure percussion of the drums to every other melodic element in the group. Sitting at the bottom of the mix, playing Leo Fender's radical electric bass guitar, she became the "bus driver," as she thought of it—the one player besides the drummer that everyone else had to follow. Few songs came into the studio with a written bass line; instead, session players were expected to invent one. So by playing electric bass, not only did Carol get to drive, but she often got to choose the route she took, calling on the melodic fluency she'd developed in jazz.

The benefits of her helmsmanship were evident from the first moments of "Lipstick Traces (on a Cigarette)," by Ohio funk-soul group the O'Jays, recorded a few months after Carol's first encounter with the Fender four-string. Her Precision Bass pumped and throbbed, pressing an elastic energy into the lower registers that drove the song forward. She locked into Earl Palmer's drumming, and the two of them seemed to meld together into a single fat beat. Played with a heavy pick, the electric instrument let her highlight every subtlety in the rhythm. Palmer's kick and snare drums punctuated the stride of her bass, she underscored his fills, and together, they carved out a thrusting groove.

Playing with such intricacy at such a high volume would have been impossible on a traditional upright bass—it required an electric bass guitar. But the even greater revelation of Carol's playing was the way she found to weave her bass line through a song's melody. In "Lipstick Traces," she painted variations in pitch with her Fender Precision that guided the singers, effectively unifying groove and melody, rhythm and vocals, into a single movement. When she responded with her bass to what the singers were doing, the entire recording became more intense and athletic. Leo's Precision Bass, in Carol Kaye's hands, was helping to make music funkier, to make every layer of it more alive.

It made Carol Kaye feel more alive, too. In "Lipstick Traces" and other recordings, like Irma Thomas's "Wish Someone Would Care," it's almost possible to hear how much the Fender changed her attitude toward playing in the studio—indeed, how much it changed her life. She loved the punchy sound of the Fender Precision, which she played with a heavy pick through a four-speaker Fender guitar amp. Working down in the lower registers, driving the bus, inventing complex routes through the simple pop songs of the time, brought Carol a joy that playing guitar in the studios never had.

The job of a session musician is to make songs into hits, and producers soon found that having Carol play bass increased a record's chances of reaching the charts. She, in turn, recognized that the instrument she'd stumbled into playing would occupy an ever more important role in the music coming through the LA studios. She changed her listing in the local musicians' union directory, putting her name under "Fender bass" as well as guitar, but word spread organically through the recording community that she was available for dates on the instrument and had a powerful new style. Brian Wilson, who'd chosen Carol to play guitar on a few early Beach Boys recordings, took note. A bass player himself, and an acolyte of Phil Spector's, he wanted to work with someone who could execute his very specific vision of the instrument's role.

Soon Carol was the first bass player many Los Angeles producers would call for a recording session. After a fellow bass pro left to direct music on a TV show, Carol got even more work. In 1964, she started earning $104 per three-hour session, an astronomical sum at a time when gas was 30 cents a gallon, her mortgage $233 a month. The money she was earning made it possible to hire a live-in nanny to care for her kids and the house she now owned on a quiet corner in Toluca Lake. With no more prejudice to accommodate from a husband—she'd left that abusive spouse late the previous year—Carol Kaye was free to lay down all the Fender bass grooves the Hollywood studios wanted. She enjoyed playing music again, and she was changing the sound and structure of it with each new session. Her main problem now was getting enough sleep.

31.

"IT'S A RICKENBACKER"

The photograph reached Francis Carey Hall in the fall of 1963—a letter from across the world that would change his life, and the story of the electric guitar, forever. In the eight years since Leo Fender and Don Randall had severed their relationship with him, furious over his purchase of the factory that produced Rickenbacker guitars, Hall had utterly modernized the brand, shifting the Rickenbacker line from electric steel guitars to electric standard models. He'd set technical specifications on new instruments himself, had hired designers and luthiers who saw to it that Rickenbacker offered some of the most striking body shapes in the industry.

It was those unmistakable outlines—quirky, asymmetrical, half art deco and half atomic age—that Hall saw in the photograph he received in November 1963. The black-and-white image, cut out of an English newspaper, showed three male musicians in identical collarless jackets

193

and shirts. Their band was just a specter in the States then, an oddity creeping into news stories from across the Atlantic. Adults at NBC News and the *New York Times* were quizzically reporting a new obsession among British teenagers, something about musical bugs—handsome insects who caused screaming fits, near-riots, ridiculous holdups at airports. Who had "pudding-bowl haircuts." In America, Capitol Records had done its best to ignore them, refusing to issue music its British parent company, EMI, found so successful at home.

But there they were: the Beatles—three of them, anyway—in the picture on F. C. Hall's desk. The only visible head belonged to the drummer, and was turned to show just a shaggy brown scalp. The other two figures consisted of merely shoulders and chests—but those were all that mattered, because in front of them hung Hall's own Rickenbacker electric guitars.

The cover letter from the company's London distributor ran just two sentences: "This shows both the Rickenbacker's [*sic*] used by the group I mentioned to you," Roy Morris wrote. "We'll need samples of both these models, please." His clear urgency was cloaked in British understatement. But how, knowing nothing about this group or the tsunami it was causing in England, could Hall have grasped that?

By late December, Morris showed even more excitement. "We think it would be an excellent idea if you, as the manufacturer of Rickenbacker guitars, were to contact The Beatles' manager and offer them a certain amount of American publicity on their forthcoming visit to the States," he wrote to Hall. Three days later, Capitol Records at last issued the single "I Want to Hold Your Hand," accompanied by a massive promotional campaign, and Beatlemania began in the United States. It reached even a middle-aged businessman in Orange County who'd seemed, to Leo Fender and Don Randall, about as dynamic as a church pew.

By January, Hall was practically chirping to his best salesman: "Buck, this is the hottest group in the world today as they have the two top records by popular poll in Europe; and, in addition, they have the two top LP albums for the same territory . . . If the boys are as popular in the United States as they are now in Britain, it would be impossible for us to begin to make enough guitars to supply the demands."

The salesman, Harold Buckner, wrote back in agreement. "To keep them on Rickenbacker would prove a promotion so big that it could not be measured in dollars and cents," he wrote. "But watch out for those Fender promoters, or they will have them all using Jaguars and Piggybacks (and don't say I didn't warn you)."

Hall followed his distributor's advice and arranged a meeting with the Beatles' manager, Brian Epstein, during the band's upcoming visit to New York. Rickenbacker's owner was deeply worried, however, that he might not be the only guitar maker seeking to win their favor. "Please do not mention [the meeting] to a soul," Hall wrote to Buckner, "as I do not want our competition to know I will be in New York while they are there."

A few weeks later, five thousand young people howled into an iron February wind while the bugs scampered off a Pan-American flight and onto the tarmac of the newly named John F. Kennedy International Airport. These greeters were the fiercest of the new fans, a mere drop in what would become, two nights later, an ocean of seventy-three million—setting a record for American television, and carving the name of *The Ed Sullivan Show* into history's eternal slate.

Everything began to change the instant a TV camera panned across the screamers in the *Ed Sullivan* audience and revealed the four bugs onstage. The first thing heard (besides the screams themselves) was those guitars: not one but three, if you counted that odd-looking electric bass. All held by mop-headed boys in suits. What was this? *How* was this? There were only four of them, smiling as they stirred up a racket that seemed at once familiar and exotic, cheerful and brusque, friendly but also vaguely threatening. They wanted to hold your hand. You could take that as bubblegum, but underneath, the songs carried a toughness largely absent from the pop landscape. There was nothing in the music to soften the rasp in those voices, the grit of those electric guitars, no tinkling piano or jazzy saxophone or easygoing strings.

The closest thing America had to this were the Beach Boys, who offered lush four-part harmonies atop their undercarriage of rock 'n' roll. Even counting their own simpler harmonies, these Brits made no similar accommodation. The Beach Boys were a vocal group; the Beatles—that ridiculous name—were a guitar band. In the two minutes and twenty-five seconds it took to deliver "I Want to Hold Your Hand" to television screens nationwide, pop in America became rhythm and blues, and rhythm and blues—or at least the closest thing to it that a quartet of Liverpudlians could muster—once again became pop.

Theirs was actually the sound *of* America, disguised just enough to seem foreign. English wit expressing Presleyan rebellion. English accents singing Buddy Holly's vocal harmonies. English-cut suits on a group formatted like Holly's Crickets. Only the haircuts and the accents—and some of the songs—wholly belonged to the Beatles. The rest of the tunes came from America. Delivering those familiar Chuck Berry riffs, however, were instruments largely unfamiliar to the American public.

Stateside teens had seen Stratocasters and Precision Basses on *Ed Sullivan*; they'd thumbed past Gibsons on the covers of their parents' jazz records. But what were these things in the arms of the Beatles? Paul McCartney plunked an electric bass the shape of a viola, made by a German company called Hofner. George Harrison that night chose not his Rickenbacker, but a guitar from the Gretsch company out of New York called the Country Gentleman. (Three years earlier, in Hamburg, he'd meant to buy a Stratocaster, but another expat Brit beat him to the only one for sale.) Ringo's drums were made by Ludwig (from Chicago, not Frankfurt); the amplifiers were English prototypes bearing the name Vox. Much of this was new kit to American eyes.

Leo Fender and Don Randall hadn't seen many of the Beatles' instruments, either—save for one. Noticing it as the Beatles in three minutes conquered America, Randall must have shuddered. Leo would have, too, if he'd bothered to watch. On *Ed Sullivan*, and soon everywhere else, John Lennon held a bright-sounding electric guitar with a graceful silhouette and three pickups, a striking instrument that had originated all the way back in Southern California. The guitar Lennon brought across the Atlantic to change the music of the United States was a Model 325 from Rickenbacker. Randall could only watch as an instrument produced by his and Leo's former partner rocked on the shoulders of the lead Beatle. It would become, almost overnight, the most desired electric guitar in the world. In those three minutes of black-and-white television, the near-hegemony Fender had enjoyed in early 1960s rock 'n' roll came crashing to an end. What the kids wanted now—perhaps would want evermore—was what the Beatles had. February 9, 1964, the day of the Beatles' first appearance on *Ed Sullivan*, would prove a great day for F. C. Hall and Rickenbacker. For Hall's crosstown rivals, the British rockers' television appearance was the first portent in years that Fender's lofty position in the world of electric guitars might not always be so assured.

Meanwhile, Hall himself was there behind the scenes, fussily preparing for his meeting with the Beatles by arranging a miniature trade show inside his suite at the Savoy Hotel. He was willing to give the group almost anything they wanted. Amid the torrent of the band's first days in the States, after their first rehearsal for *The Ed Sullivan Show*, Epstein kept the appointment. On February 8, the manager shuttled the Beatles out of the Plaza Hotel—it was thronged by fans even before their arrival— and guided them across a corner of Central Park to Hall's nearby hotel. George Harrison, ill with the flu, stayed behind.

The Beatles arrived at the Savoy to find a spread of Rickenbacker models, along with a pro musician, Toots Thielemans, whom Hall had brought to demonstrate the instruments. Two electric guitars and an electric bass, representing the company's finest creations, stood on stands in the room. Paul McCartney tried out the electric bass. He may have found it too heavy compared to his viola-shaped Hofner, or Hall may have brought a right-handed model, not realizing McCartney played left-handed. In any case, at the meeting, McCartney refused the Rickenbacker four-string.

One of the guitars Hall showed off was an experimental new model. Folk players had long used twelve-string acoustic guitars, whose additional six strings were tuned an octave higher than the originals to give the instrument a chiming, airy quality. Meanwhile, among Rickenbacker's specialties were so-called semihollow guitars, hybrid models that provided a woody warmth while resisting feedback better than a full acoustic. (With their minuscule chambers, they were still dependent on amplification, but had a lighter sound than a solid-body.) Semihollow six-string guitars were common, as were fully acoustic twelve-strings. But at the Savoy, there stood a *semihollow, electrified twelve-string*, finished in an incandescent red fade—a Rickenbacker prototype that had yet to reach the market.

Knowing his bandmate's interest in twelve-string guitars, John said he wanted George to try it. But of course, flu-stricken George wasn't present. Hall, eager to accommodate, packed up the guitar, and the whole entourage—Hall, the Beatles, Epstein, and perhaps even Thielemans—put on their coats and snuck across Central Park back to the Plaza and George's room.

The Beatles and their retinue had taken over the entire twelfth floor of the hotel, and its pillowy carpets and gilded chandeliers had become the backdrop for a 24/7 chaos machine. The band members were staying in a series of interconnected suites, with Epstein off by himself on the far side of the building, shielded from sneaking fans and pushy DJs. The group found George, laid low by the flu, lying in bed under the covers, listening to the radio. He'd just started strumming chords on the new Rickenbacker twelve-string when a radio station, besieged by teenage listeners, called his room. Harrison answered. When the DJ asked what he was doing, he explained on air that he was trying out a new guitar. The voice on the other end asked if he liked it.

"Yes," George said dryly. "It's a Rickenbacker." The radio station offered to buy it for him, but Hall insisted on giving it to Harrison free of charge.

Lennon was then relying on the 1958 Rickenbacker Model 325 he'd been scuffing and strumming since the Beatles' hardscrabble Hamburg days. Its original natural wood color had been refinished black. At the Plaza, Hall arranged to get John a replacement for the instrument, a new, black Model 325, with three pickups and a white pickguard. It would be shipped to him later in the month, while the Beatles were in Miami.

So later that afternoon, as Hall strolled back through the winter-barren corner of Central Park that separated his hotel from the Plaza, he must have felt satisfied. He'd given the Beatles two new Rickenbacker guitars, including a prototype of a new model. But even he probably couldn't have understood the magnitude of what he'd accomplished. Lennon's new Model 325 would remain with the Beatle through the group's long career, becoming the guitar with which he was most closely associated. Harrison would begin using his red twelve-string immediately. Recording at Abbey Road studios in London later that year, he'd reach for it to play the iconic opening chord (and every other subsequent one) of a new song called "A Hard Day's Night."

Thus, in only an hour or two with the Beatles, F. C. Hall had outfitted George and John with what would become their most iconic set of guitars, had ensured that the Beatles-Rickenbacker link would endure for decades. Before long, Rickenbacker's London distributor would be advertising some of the company's models as "Beatle backers." As Hall's firm rode the wave of Beatlemania sweeping the world, he would be forced to radically expand his little Rickenbacker factory in Santa Ana. It stood just a few miles from the wholesale radio parts store Hall still owned, the store from which onetime stock boy Don Randall had sold the very first Fender instruments.

32.

"I'D BROKEN MY CARDINAL RULE"

NEW YORK AND FULLERTON, 1964

The arrival of the Beatles transformed the American music industry. The band tore open the market for electric guitars, and launched formerly secondary players like Rickenbacker and Gretsch to new prominence. For Don Randall, who watched as his local rival experienced a sudden onslaught of new business, the situation looked like an emergency. Beatlemania threatened to consume anything and everything having to do with music in America. Beatles gear was the fashion of the day, and legions of copycat bands began appearing overnight. As ever, kids wanted to play what their heroes played. Fender could not be left out. Randall knew he must try to get his equipment into the hands of these new arrivals, whatever it took.

In the early months of 1964, though, Don Randall had another major challenge before him. Leo Fender, the partner with whom he hadn't seen eye to eye in years, had declared that he was finished with their companies. Leo wanted to sell Fender off, to get out of it entirely.

Leo firmly believed that his strep infection, from which he'd been suffering for nearly a decade, was going to kill him. He saw a doctor several times a year for shots of penicillin or streptomycin, but the medications only helped in the short term. The infection, centered in his sinuses, leaked fluid all down the back of his throat, especially in cold weather. His insides burned with a soreness that no remedy could ease. Having tried seemingly endless fixes—new diets, juices, doctors, stress relief via boating—Leo gloomily assumed that strep would soon end him completely. In his own mind, he was a worn-out tool, a machine that would soon have no more utility to offer.

Looking at his company, now spread across twenty-seven buildings in Fullerton and Anaheim, Leo could hardly recognize it. Hundreds of cars clogged the parking lot each day. Daily operations proved so massive, so absorbing, that Leo couldn't, as he wanted, completely dedicate himself to the task of research and development. And when he did, his efforts didn't have the world-rearranging effects they'd once had. After introducing the Jazz Bass, an updated and modified Precision Bass, in 1960, Fender's instrumental innovations often faltered. The six-string bass Leo invented to rival Danelectro's Longhorn missed the point of its cheaper and simpler competitor. The design of his latest, supposedly high-end guitar, the Jaguar, also got bogged down in needless frills. Of late, the only truly great new Fender design was the black-panel amplifier series, including the Twin Reverb and the Deluxe Reverb, which would rank among the most iconic and popular guitar amplifiers ever made.

Fullerton employees had formed a union to represent themselves back in the 1950s, and relations between the hundreds of union members and the ten or so managers had long been amicable. The employees were paid on an incentive system that allowed them ample freedom and comfortable pay. By the early 1960s, however, new employees rekindled talks of an outside union. Forrest White strongly discouraged the effort, posting an antiunion screed on a company bulletin board. Like Leo, he was a fiscal conservative who loathed taxes and any other perceived interference in business. Leo left the union issue to White to deal with, but he seems to have regarded it as yet another sign that the company he'd built had grown far too large.

Doubt now filled Leo like his pens and tools filled his breast pocket. Everywhere he looked, the world—even the little corner of which he was ostensibly in charge—seemed unrecognizable. In music, mop-headed youngsters in stovepipe suits had replaced cowboy jazzmen in Stetsons. Their songs were loud and simple, their guitars often deliberately distorted. Leo didn't see the appeal. Music fans now carried around tiny radios powered by a transistor. Leo, along with many observers, believed the device would render vacuum-tube amplifiers obsolete. And lacking any formal education in engineering or electronics, he couldn't venture into the new, transistorized world.

He was a product of the age of home inventors and backyard tinkerers, untrained men who could build or fix almost anything because, back then, anythings were simple: cars had carburetors, not fuel injection; radios and amplifiers were a few wires soldered to a handful of vacuum tubes and a speaker. Now cars and electronics were built, it seemed, by scientists. The world had utterly changed, and if some part of that was Leo's doing, it was of little comfort when the new currents threatened to sweep him into irrelevance.

Introverted to the core, Leo Fender was happiest when experimenting alone or working closely with people he knew well. By 1964, the Fender factory had exploded into a hydra that seemed to need a voluble, outgoing leader of its own, someone who could take its reins and drive its small army into an even more prosperous future. Leo Fender had no desire to fill that role.

The idea of selling Fender first surfaced in a 1957 letter written by a hired accountant who suggested that Don and Leo sell the company to him. That idea went nowhere, as did a February 1962 proposal that the accountant made on behalf of outside buyers.

Leo had made another suggestion to Randall: buy him out for $1 million. Randall, however, probably assumed that his partner was in the depths of another strep infection. Six months after initially floating the idea, Leo told Randall his price was now $1.5 million. By August 1963, the number had risen to $2 million, according to a document written by Randall and unearthed by historian Richard Smith.

It would have been a great deal for the buyer: Fender was soon selling $2 million in merchandise every quarter, and earning more than a million dollars in pretax profit every year. Randall, however, was deeply wary of the idea of buying out Leo like this. He'd seen plenty of others take advantage of Leo's myopia and generosity, musicians who came in with sad stories seeking new guitars, only to pawn them to settle gambling debts or divorces. The relationship between Don and Leo was deeply troubled, but Randall didn't want to cheat his partner. "If I bought it now, a year from now, you would say I robbed you," he told Leo. "You'd hate me."

Randall also suspected that Fender was worth far more than Leo realized. He decided to pursue acquisition by an outside firm—one big enough to handle Fender's thriving business and intractable backlogs, and with pockets deep enough to pay what it was worth. Early in 1964, delicately and without drawing much attention, Randall spread the word that the Fender companies, stupendously profitable but chronically hobbled, were for sale.

That summer, Randall saw an opportunity to court the Beatles, as the band embarked on its first proper tour of the United States. After beginning in California, the trip brought the Beatles via chartered plane to Forest Hills Stadium, outside of New York City, on August 28 and 29. According to Andy Babiuk's authoritative history of the Beatles' equipment, Randall sent a deputy to New York to try to meet with Brian Epstein and encourage the Beatles to use Fender gear. This encouragement, however, was to include something unusual for Fender: cash.

"It was a huge amount, I can tell you that much," Randall told Babiuk. "Not by today's standards, of course, but it was a lot of money for us at the time." Other sources have pegged Fender's offer at $10,000—enough, in 1964, to buy a pair of brand-new Chevrolet Corvettes. Of course, along with the money, the Beatles would be able to get all the Fender equipment they wanted, free of charge. Meanwhile back in Fullerton, an oblivious Leo Fender continued to tell even close family that his firm never paid artists to use its instruments.

It's unclear why Randall sent Jim Williams, his advertising director, to meet the Beatles, rather than go himself. Since the company's earliest days, whenever a salesman struggled to close an important sale, or when there were major deals near consummation, Randall would bring to bear his own forthrightness and charm, usually with success.

Williams, however, seems to have been a mess. According to Babiuk, he was frayed by nerves ahead of the big meeting in New York. The stadium where the Beatles were playing was built as a venue for tennis competitions and sat adjacent to the quaint, village-like downtown of Forest Hills. To calm himself before going to see the Beatles, Williams apparently stopped at a local watering hole and put back a cocktail or two. By the time he made it over to the tennis stadium, Williams was likely past the point of business-friendly lubrication. He met with one of the Beatles' submanagers, clumsily presenting Fender's offer. It must have had all the charm of a naked bribe: $10,000 to play the company's instruments, plus all the free gear the Beatles could ask for.

Williams didn't get past that first meeting. As Randall told Babiuk, the Fender representative never even got to speak with Brian Epstein, the Beatles' all-powerful manager. Rather, he was fended off by one of Epstein's deputies. The Beatles' response to Fender was simply, as Randall put it, that "the boys had been successful with what they were playing, and they were going to continue to use that." Neither Williams nor Randall could find a good counterargument.

Rather quickly, it seems, Randall realized the blunder of this gamble. Fender was a giant by the standards of the electric instrument industry of 1964, and the Beatles looked upon its products favorably, even if they weren't then using them. The offer, clumsily delivered, made the company look domineering and desperate.

The botched maneuver also proved the paranoia of F. C. Hall and his Rickenbacker salesman quite justified. "I felt I'd broken my cardinal rule, but it was imperative to do it," Randall said of the episode. He must have also realized his mistake in sending Williams to close a major deal, rather than going himself. It was one he wouldn't make again.

33.

"HE IS CLEARLY NOT GROWTH-MINDED"

FULLERTON AND NEW YORK,
SUMMER 1964–WINTER 1965

The first real interest in purchasing Fender came from the D. H. Baldwin Company, a large Ohio maker of pianos and organs. Owning Fender would mean instant entry into the booming market for electric guitars, and Baldwin executives quickly began negotiating with Randall. Leo stayed behind in Fullerton, leaving it entirely to his partner to sell the companies. By July of 1964, Baldwin was throwing out numbers that made Leo's earlier request, for $1.5 or $2 million, look hugely shortsighted. In the guitar-crazy, post-Beatles landscape, Fender, it seemed, could go for something closer to $10 million.

There was one hang-up. By 1964, Leo had invested in two somewhat risky enterprises that lurked uneasily on Fender's fringe: the acoustic guitar division, overseen by German luthier Roger Rossmeisl, and the electric piano project run by Harold Rhodes. Neither of these had yet earned a dollar in profit, and neither looked to have a much brighter future. By July, Baldwin had agreed to pay a hefty price for Fender, but it didn't want the acoustic or electric piano businesses. Randall, however, insisted that the company give Leo at least the cost of his investment in the two operations, some $470,000. By mid-August, he had the Cincinnati contingent convinced, with Baldwin offering the following terms: It would pay market value for all of Fender's assets, about $4 million. Then it would pay Don and Leo 50 percent of after-tax profits up to $5 million, or for fifteen years, whichever came first. The deal even included $470,000 for the acoustic and Fender-Rhodes companies.

All the boxes were checked. The amounts were tremendous. Baldwin was an experienced musical instrument company that, through its organ projects, had a deep familiarity with electronics and amplification. It seemed like a great new parent for Fender.

But by then Baldwin was no longer the only suitor. That summer, while fighting to get Baldwin to pay Leo his $470,000, Randall had considered other options, including taking the company public. A financial adviser counseled against this and instead put Randall in touch with representatives from Columbia Broadcasting System in New York. Soon Randall was shuttling back and forth to Manhattan, meeting at hotels with representatives from CBS's Columbia Records division. One was a promising young executive named Clive Davis, who couldn't understand CBS's interest in a musical instrument manufacturer. Under CBS president William S. Paley and Columbia Records president Goddard Lieberson, however, "synergy became the byword," as Davis recalled in his memoir. The broadcast firm was growing at an enormous rate, acquiring interests far out of its core specialty—including, that year, the New York Yankees baseball team.

Through that summer, Davis worked to determine whether Fender would make a smart addition to the growing CBS empire, and whether it could get a fair price for the California company. To decide this, the New Yorkers called in outside help: a consultant that would evaluate every aspect of Fender and advise whether CBS should acquire it.

Remarkably, even as observers from the Arthur D. Little consulting firm visited Fender, interviewing managers and salesmen, reviewing catalogs, and asking pointed questions, no one at either the Fullerton factory or the Santa Ana sales office guessed that the company employing them might soon change hands. Everything seemed to be working as normal—except, perhaps, for Leo Fender himself. Starting that summer, Forrest White noticed that Leo seemed quieter than usual, more distant even than was his introverted habit. Leo was absent from the factory more than in the past, and there weren't as many new ideas coming out of his lab. Even Leo's right-hand research-and-development man, Freddie Tavares, had noticed a change in his boss. He figured that Leo was simply slowing down, his drive to best the competition fading. His apparent apathy seemed deeply out of character, though.

That fall of 1964, the Arthur D. Little consultants released a forty-page analysis of Fender's past, present, and future, along with an assessment of the electric guitar industry as a whole. It is a fascinating document, both for what it perceived and what it missed about the company and the times. "Unquestionably, Fender's name ranks very high in the industry," the report said. "It has established a reputation for producing a first-quality instrument. . . . Fender's major competitor is Gibson, [which] enjoys a position almost on a par with Fender in the top-quality guitar market." Asking whether any competitor enjoyed a natural advantage over Fender, the consultants concluded, simply, "No."

The report detailed the "excellent" design of the amplifiers and guitars, explaining to CBS executives that "Fender amplifiers can be kicked, dropped, vibrated, or allowed to overheat, and still continue to give excellent service." There was no improvement to be made there. Yet the observers were appalled by Fender's lack of college-trained technicians and surprised to find that "virtually all of the engineering talent is concentrated in Mr. Fender himself." They saw an absence of formal education all across the company. Of Fender's nine salesmen, spread around the country, they wrote: "The men we met were presentable, articulate, and possessed of considerable sales enthusiasm and drive. They are a little rough in terms of social polish. Few, if any, have college degrees. They are probably very well suited for the type of trade they call on and are obviously doing a good job."

Also shocking to the consultants was the "rather substantial compensation" earned by the salesmen, as well as by Leo, Don, and senior managers like George Fullerton and Forrest White. Remarkably, in their interviews with the Arthur D. Little consultants, Forrest White and Don Randall apparently kept the dysfunctional relationship between the sales office and the factory completely concealed. The outsiders had no idea that White was basically guessing which products and how many of each Fullerton should build each day.

Randall, having enchanted the consultants, was deemed to be worth his pay. In fact, the report recommended that CBS should purchase Fender on two conditions: first, that it got a reasonable price; second, that "Randall's enthusiastic services are secured." The president of Fender Sales was found to be integral to its marketing activities and in command of "strong loyalty" from its staff—only natural, since they viewed "his leadership as the factor which has primarily contributed to their economic success."

Of Leo Fender, that self-taught, half-blind, now half-deaf factory denizen, the consultants took a drastically different view.

They couldn't help but note some of Leo's talents. "He has the successful, practical inventor's genius for detecting early those relatively small design features in a new product which will be the 'right way to do it.'" But they framed Leo's achievements in a way that, however accurate, served to diminish their importance. "Most of these developments do not involve either highly theoretical or complex concepts. They involve rather simple practical elements; for example, the offsetting of the side depressions in the body of a guitar so that it will fit the contours of the body more comfortably." True as this was, the consultants, as nonmusicians, didn't seem to appreciate how much difference those simple practical elements had made.

Apart from Leo's designs, the consultants quite accurately found Leo an odd fit for the Fender of 1964. "Mr. Fender finds it hard to believe that the little business which he started in the late Forties has grown to such proportions. He finds that the size of the business is such that he has virtually no time left for doing what he enjoys, namely, engineering. He is clearly not growth-minded. Mr. Randall, on the other hand, immensely enjoys his ever-widening sphere of activity."

Along these lines came their verdict. Randall, the report said, was essential if CBS was to succeed in running Fender. But if the purchase went through, the consultants viewed "a sharp diminution in [Leo's] contribution . . . as a relatively minor risk." His responsibilities in overseeing production could be handled by any competent engineer. As for developing new products, "it would be highly desirable, at least for a period of four or five years, to maintain the active interest and creativity of Mr. Fender." After that, the consultants suggested, CBS engineers could surely design and introduce successful new electric instruments on their own.

The consultants' report changed the tenor of Don Randall's discussions with CBS. He finally informed Baldwin that he was in talks with other buyers and took every measure to strengthen his bargaining position. He had the wind at his back that year, with the arrival of the Beatles and the subsequent realignment of America's tastes in pop music. Gone were the saccharine solo singers, the cutesy novelty dances, the songs written by Brill Building pros. Back was the age of the pop-rock group, with the Beach Boys suddenly upping their game to compete with the British Invasion bands. Even the American folk music revival, which long saw itself as the antidote to a mainstream of inconsequential pop, would soon meet its end (as such) in the aftermath of the British Invasion, done in by a Fender Stratocaster and a former folkie from Minnesota.

The Beatles may not have used Fenders, but they exploded American teens' interest in electric guitars, and Randall played the new landscape to maximum advantage. Previously, he'd forced his salesmen to hold down new orders to what they thought the factory could reasonably produce. While negotiating with Baldwin and CBS, Randall, according to historian Richard Smith, told them to instead take all the orders they could possibly get. Fender's sizable factory backlog grew even longer, and conjured visions of huge profits in the minds of the New York and Ohio negotiators. Randall watched the offers from CBS,

in particular, grow higher and higher. He'd later say that these negotiations, which he likened to forging a Middle East peace accord, were the
most exciting period of his professional life: "Everything afterward was
anticlimactic."

Early in the fall, CBS executives floated a number that Randall
received with terrific excitement. Fender's financial adviser wanted to
push for more, but Randall was satisfied. The total amount of the deal
would be $13 million—an immense sum for a relatively obscure com-
mercial enterprise, and a historic price for an electric guitar company.
The offer included the Fender factory in Fullerton, its sales office in
Santa Ana, and its service center in Tulsa; the V. C. Squier Company,
maker of Fender strings, in Michigan; and—crucially—the acoustic
guitar and Fender-Rhodes divisions. It would also include a plot of land
next to the existing factory, owned by Leo, on which a new manufacturing plant was envisioned. Randall was to be kept on as vice president and
general manager of CBS's new Fender Musical Instruments division, and
given a $50,000 salary (with bonuses) and a corner office in New York.
Leo would be hired as a design consultant for five years and couldn't
do any competing work for ten. This, it seemed to Don and Leo, was it.
Fender had grown from two tiny tin sheds and a radio wholesaler to a
potential new division of the Columbia Broadcasting System. The offer
had all the prestige, and money, that the company's two leaders could
have hoped for.

So on October 16, 1964, an agreement was signed outlining the terms
of CBS's purchase of Fender. The deal was to be kept secret until the following January, and it mostly was. No one in Fullerton or Santa Ana had
any idea of the major changes about to occur until that December. It was
late that month when, on a cool winter evening, Forrest White went over
to see Leo in his lab.

The founder and inventor presented a humble sight: seated at his
messy workbench, he huddled near a small heater, pulling his jacket up
over his neck to stay warm. White could hear Leo sniffling, still suffering
from his strep infection. It was obvious he should have been at home, in
bed, instead of working late into another evening.

"Sit down, I have something to tell you," Leo said, as White recalled. The plant manager had sensed that something unusual was occupying his boss, but he had no idea of the news he was about to hear.

"You know, I haven't been able to shake this sinus condition, and I think it's time for me to get out," Leo continued. "Don and I have been talking to CBS Records about them buying the company."

White grasped for a response. He finally muttered something sympathetic about Leo's health. White had long noticed a strange change of character in his boss, but hearing this news, he was so surprised he could hardly speak.

34.

"WHICH IS WORTH MORE?"

FULLERTON, WINTER 1965

CBS's purchase was formally announced in a press release on January 5, 1965, and hit papers across the country the next day. Fender Musical Instruments was to become a division of the Columbia Records Distribution Corporation. The electric guitar industry had graduated from a niche business to a visible and expensive corporate player. Electric guitars were now officially a part of mainstream American life, suitable for suburban homes and sprawling corporations and sensible adults.

Check number 8339, for $5,735,000, was made out to Leo and Esther Fender from Columbia Record Distributors. Leo couldn't be bothered to go to New York to pick it up. Instead, Don Randall went alone, and deposited both Leo's check and his own, for $5,265,000, into their bank accounts. An additional $2 million was placed in escrow to be distributed in two years.

January 6 was a dark winter day, as cold and dim as Southern California gets. At the Fender Sales office in Santa Ana, Bill Carson, the former western swing sideman whose ideas had shaped the Stratocaster, answered the phone to hear someone asking about a strange story they'd seen in the *Wall Street Journal*. Carson had heard nothing about a sale of the company, but in the afternoon, he went out and bought his own copy of the paper. There, sure enough, was a piece announcing the news. Carson took it to his boss, sales vice president Stan Compton. "You know as much as I do," Compton said. Despite whirlwind negotiations on both coasts, Randall had kept this dramatic change of guard a total secret.

Phone calls deluged the sales office and the factory—from friends, competitors, and family members—all asking if the news was true and what it meant for Fender and its employees and products. No one had any answers. Abigail Ybarra was working on the factory floor, winding coils for guitar pickups, when the rumor spread that Fender had new owners and that Leo would be handing over control of the plant. After eight years of work at Fender, Ybarra was frightened. She had no idea what to expect.

Eventually, Leo's nasal voice crackled through the factory's public address system. "We have an important announcement for everybody; the rumors you've heard are true," he began. In less than three minutes, Mr. Fender himself explained what had happened and tried to calm the fears crossing his employees' faces. Everyone will still have a job, he said, and not to worry—"I will still be here."

Despite these assurances, the employees were in shock. The entire Fender production system—as well as every other piece of the company—was soon to be at the mercy of a New York firm that knew nothing about making musical instruments, let alone electric guitars. Regardless of what Leo had said, everything about the future seemed in doubt. These January days would eventually come to be seen as some of the darkest in Fender history.

The outside world received news of CBS's acquisition with a mix of bewilderment and hilarity. "Which is worth more," asked the Associated Press story: "A guitar factory or controlling interest in the New

York Yankees?" The fact that CBS had recently paid $11.2 million for an 80 percent stake in the Yankees would sneak into many reports on the Fender purchase, the contrast showing the arrival of a new age in which youth-led music could compete—not just for attention but for *cash*—with the oldest and greatest American pastime. The combination of baseball and guitar making under one corporate umbrella would also give sportswriters material for a few laughs. "It wouldn't surprise us if CBS split the Yankees into rock 'n' roll groups and sent them to England during the off season," quipped one hack in Chicago. *Music Trades* would call the deal "the largest cash transaction in music industry history," noting that the CBS corporation's sales volume exceeded that of the entire musical instrument industry.

Leo's little guitar-making project had shaken the world. That day, at age fifty-five, he became a multimillionaire many times over, a name known and respected far outside of music circles, his historic development of the solid-body electric guitar to be recorded in newspapers and magazines everywhere. As historian Richard Smith points out, Leo Fender was one of the first people to get rich off rock 'n' roll.

Yet he was turning over his life's work, his surrogate brood, his very *name*, to an army of East Coast corporate types with no inherent interest in the product or the musician it served, and no real appreciation for just how difficult and unlikely the path to this point had been. Could Leo trust CBS with his company? He preferred not to think about it that way. He just needed to get out.

At least he would get to stay in California. Don Randall would soon be flying back and forth to New York, holding endless meetings inside wood-paneled Manhattan boardrooms, a onetime stock boy with no degree negotiating among Ivy League egos and witnessing a conglomerate's total indifference to any detail not found on a balance sheet. Could Randall—a doer, a public face, a self-directed leader—really endure such a transition, even at $50,000 a year plus bonuses?

On January 4, two nights before the sale hit the papers, Forrest White walked down to Leo's lab. Leo was packing up his personal items, his favorite tools, in preparation for others to take over. Per his agreement with CBS, he'd do his consulting from another building he owned in Fullerton. A few close friends, including Noel Boggs, were there to help. There was an awl—a small, handheld punch with a walnut knob for a handle—that had been a favorite tool of Leo's father. Leo placed it inside his small box, along with his tool belt, a voltage meter, and a few other things. While White and Boggs helped Leo carry the items out to the trunk of his Chrysler Imperial, White pretended not to notice the tears welling in Leo's eyes, and tried to suppress his own.

After loading his trunk, Leo pulled up to the parking lot gate in his massive sedan. White waited by the fence to let him out before locking up, as usual. It was to be the last evening of this life they'd known, the last night in which White would see his brilliant boss, the owner of this entire Fullerton spread, drive out the front gate.

"I don't know what I would have done without you," Leo Fender said. It was, for him, a gusher of sentimentality.

Then, without waiting for a response, Leo hit the gas pedal and zoomed out of the parking lot, off for good, away toward some future as a CBS consultant—or, perhaps, as an invalid.

White, still sobbing, watched until Leo's car disappeared.

35.

"I THOUGHT DYLAN WAS ABANDONING US"

NEWPORT, RHODE ISLAND, JULY 1965

Leo Fender thought his story was over. The electric guitar he'd perfected for his country-western pals, the massive amps he'd developed for Dick Dale and the surf rockers—he looked at those tools and believed he was seeing the end of the line, the full maturity of the technology. Electric guitars were commonplace by 1965, Fenders especially. What could be next—ubiquity? Leo Fender and Don Randall, for all their ambitions, would never have dreamed of that. It must have seemed that they'd sold Fender at the best possible moment—that surely, in the wake of the Beatles, the electric guitar had reached peak popularity. Thirteen million dollars was an almost ludicrous sum for a guitar company in 1965, so large that even those who'd clawed the business into being could hardly believe they'd been there to catch the windfall.

Leo was now heading home to read a stack of Zane Grey western novels, develop pictures in his photographic darkroom, and plan vacations with Esther. Yet as he withdrew from the arena of innovation, the instruments bearing his name were still evolving in the hands of musicians—morphing themselves, and morphing the culture, into something Leo would struggle even more fruitlessly to understand. His retirement would be quickly followed by huge leaps in the sound and style of the instrument he'd helped perfect, by its transformation from a key accessory of youth pop music into an apparatus for more grown-up and dangerous modes of expression. The revolution continued—and the next phase of it began the very summer after Fender's sale became public, through a singer who released his music through a tentacle of the same CBS corporation that now sold Telecasters and Showman amps. This phase began on a stage in Newport, Rhode Island, on the night of Sunday, July 25, 1965, over the course of about seventeen minutes.

"Let's go!" Bob Dylan shouted, and the band jumped in behind the guitars—bass, drums, piano, organ, all radiating a wave of electric noise toward the audience. Out in the hot July darkness, the wave crashed into seventeen thousand attendees of the Newport Folk Festival, knocking them back on their bleachers and blankets. Dylan paused in his black leather jacket, black trousers, and blood-red shirt, and turned toward his wobbly accompaniment. He strummed furiously on a shiny new Stratocaster, its sunburst finish gleaming under a single stage light. The lamplight pushing through Dylan's unkempt hair cast a halo around his head, framing an expression somewhere between doubt and defiance.

Suddenly a note came ripping out of the darkness around him, a bent, distorted Telecaster yowl. Detonating camera flashes revealed Mike Bloomfield, a besuited figure on the left, huddled over his guitar, poised for attack. Dylan himself sauntered up to the mic, strumming, defiant. "I ain't gonna work on Maggie's farm no more," he snarled, and then leapt away. Bloomfield issued another electric blurt, his tone like a razor slashing at the night.

Dylan continued spewing out the lyrics to "Maggie's Farm" in a nasal monotone, and after every line, Bloomfield seemed to challenge him for the lead, slicing through the song in high, distorted notes. Perhaps Bloomfield knew what he was doing to the assembled throngs of folkies and college students. But it seems Dylan himself had no idea what was happening.

He found out as soon as "Maggie's Farm" crashed to its end. Up from the darkness of the crowd came a roar—a roar of negativity, of *booing*. Dylan had walked onstage that night as the young prince of Newport, the voice of the American folk movement, the main draw of this supposedly non hierarchical three-day festival. Now the devoted were howling in disapproval. He could hear their furor wafting up as he retuned his Stratocaster, the shouts that he, the supposed voice of the anticommercial movement, should go back to *The Ed Sullivan Show*.

There was a pause as the musicians prepared for the next song. The boos mingled with cheers as its first notes floated up from the unsteady band. Bloomfield outlined the chord changes with his crackling guitar, and in a moment Dylan was back at the mic: "Once upon a time you dressed so fine / You threw the bums a dime in your prime, didn't you?" Dylan's latest single had been released just five days earlier. "Like a Rolling Stone" was climbing the charts as he performed it live that night for the first time, his rendition mostly faithful to the hit recording.

As soon as it ended, though, the booing returned. There was applause, some cheering, but there were more angry shouts and bellowed insults, fans bewildered and disappointed. Rumors swirled of a festival organizer so infuriated by the noise that he was threatening to cut the sound cables with an axe. The crowd's rancor only worsened when Dylan and his band left the stage after just three songs. "We want Dylan," some shouted. "We want the *old* Dylan," others yelled.

It would be known as the night Dylan went electric. The night that American rock 'n' roll became folk rock or just *rock*. The night Dylan declared his allegiance to his own ideas rather than those of the folk community. "I thought Dylan was abandoning us," one witness said, and in a way, she was right. "Dylan was all of a sudden wearing a black leather jacket, and it was LOUD."

Folk was not loud. The folk movement favored old (or old-style) songs sung by anyone who cared to sing them, not for wide attention or profit but to express a feeling or tell a story. True folkies were people who lived in log cabins or roachy Greenwich Village apartments, who played "natural" instruments. At the Newport Folk Festival, most (though not all) performers used acoustic equipment. No one expected to hear a full-throated electric band pound through three-chord rock 'n' roll. And even for the fans who'd heard Dylan play electric on recordings, the sonic power of a full electric band playing through a large public address system made for a bewildering new experience. There were no rock concerts yet, with their jet-engine decibel levels. Even the Beatles, touring the world with custom-built hundred-watt Vox amplifiers, were regularly drowned out by screaming fans. As Elijah Wald writes in his history of Dylan's electric rupture, the levels of the night's set were assaultive, quite literally terrifying for those not used to them—which was just about everybody—and made even more grating by poor sound mixing.

But Dylan's greatest offense to the folk crowd was symbolic. His superamplified presentation inverted the festival's usual balance of power between performer and audience. Volume, after all, is power. When one person is heard loudly, another is silenced. Newport had always celebrated the communitarian ideal, the sense that everyone, onstage or not, famous or not, would have a voice. Fans would sing along in the crowd, and most stage performances were quiet enough that the audience's singing could be heard among itself and by the performers.

To those used to this arrangement, the overpowering volume of Dylan's electric set felt like a silencing—even an outright rejection. The sheer force of the music asserted what he'd been hinting at in his presence that year, with his black leather and his Ray-Bans. Dylan was now off on his own, following *his* ideas, no longer striving to be some voice of a generation. He'd become an artist, not an activist. "What he used to stand for, whether one agreed with it or not, was much clearer than what he stands for now," wrote one critic of the show. "Perhaps himself."

But if Dylan had chiseled himself free of the folk community with the electric guitar, this supposed tool of commercial pop music, he'd imbued the instrument with a new identity, too. The Beach Boys and even the Beatles wrote rock 'n' roll songs about girls and cars and having a good time—kid stuff, however charming. Now, electric guitars were a vehicle for Bob Dylan's surrealistic poetry. They were an accompaniment to his ambiguous verse about betrayal and cynicism and melancholy. Amid the crucible of Dylan's outrageous, overloud performance at Newport in 1965, electric guitars had suddenly become tools for serious art.

36.

"GIVE GOD WHAT HE WANTS"

LONDON, SPRING 1965–SPRING 1966

When the Yardbirds found a way to move out of small London clubs and onto the national tour circuit, their hotshot lead guitarist just quit the band. Eric Clapton was nineteen years old, had no other job, no place to live. But he also had no interest in the Yardbirds' catchy new single, "For Your Love," or in trading the smoky rhythm and blues on which the group had been founded for more widely appealing pop rock.

Clapton wanted to play the American blues, and only the American blues. He'd discovered the music as an angry young man in the London suburb of Ripley and felt then as if he'd already spent an eon with it—as if he were being reintroduced to something he already knew. With that self-seriousness particular to the lonely teen, he decided right then to dedicate his life to this faraway sound.

In America, the electric blues was by 1965 almost a decade out of fashion, with stars like Muddy Waters and B. B. King playing to the same aging, all-black audiences they had for years. The reality was utterly different in England, where an all-white intelligentsia—the elders of which had seen Muddy perform in 1958—regularly hired Americans to come over and tour. These visits had given Clapton, before his twentieth birthday, the chance to play with legends like Sonny Boy Williamson and Muddy Waters, to eye their technique and soak up the delicate feel of their music. Such experiences confirmed for Clapton that he—a white Englishman with fancy clothes, short hair, and a perpetual frown; a guitar prodigy on the run from a miserable childhood—was indeed on the right path.

John Mayall called as soon as he heard that Clapton had quit the Yardbirds. Mayall was a senior member of the British blues intelligentsia and a thirty-one-year-old husband and father. He was a blues purist and a showman who could play piano and guitar, sing, and write decent songs. But soon after Clapton joined John Mayall's Bluesbreakers, his guitar playing became the band's main attraction.

Clapton had long wielded a red Telecaster, as Muddy Waters did, while occasionally using hollow-body guitars made by Gretsch and Gibson. But he had a habit of moving restlessly through most things in life: bands, dwelling places, emotional states, girlfriends, guitars. After joining Mayall, Clapton decided to try out yet another type of guitar. It was a chance experiment—one that would have an incalculable effect on the future of the instrument.

Clapton had seen Keith Richards of the Rolling Stones playing an odd, out-of-production Gibson model: a heavy, single-cutaway, solid-body electric guitar. Richards had found the thing hanging, forgotten, in a London music shop, and immediately adopted it. Its finish was a cherry sunburst, and it had two dual-coil, humbucking pickups. Richards's guitar had been issued by its maker's Kalamazoo factory late the previous decade, in the vain hope of resuscitating the model's ailing fortunes. Only 643 were ever shipped. It was a 1959 Gibson Les Paul.

Furthering Clapton's interest in this Gibson model was a seminal blues album, *Let's Dance Away and Hide Away*, by the Texan Freddy King. The cover showed a besuited, blimplike King bent over, smiling, all alone in front of an orange backdrop except for the gold-top Les Paul hanging off his shoulder. Over twelve jaunty instrumentals, King coaxed a bright, spanking voice out of that guitar that obliterated the need for a singer, filling every rise and fall in the music with nimble runs and sharp, snarling licks. For an Englishman like Eric Clapton, raised in the bleak aftermath of the Second World War, even the name "Les Paul" on King's guitar would have seemed to belong to a different world. It would have symbolized the exotic realm of 1950s America, a place and time shrouded in the hopes of a thousand daydreams. And through Freddy King, this instrument held a link to the electric currents of the blues.

So in May 1965, as a newly furbished member of John Mayall's Blues-breakers, Clapton walked into a music shop on London's Charing Cross Road, looking for a Les Paul like the one King used. The little store was dedicated solely to guitars; it had become a haven for local players and the site of frequent jams among London session men. Clapton perused the hanging instruments, searching for the unmistakable gold paint that covered the early Les Pauls. He couldn't find it.

All he found was a later-model Les Paul, one from 1960, a guitar made when Gibson's cherry sunburst finishes had replaced the gold top. This wasn't Freddy King's instrument; it was basically the same model Keith Richards used with the Stones. But out-of-production Gibsons weren't easy to find in England, which was part of their charm. And this Les Paul was still a genuine piece of American artisanship—even its brown case had plush pink lining like the interior of some bluesman's Cadillac. So that spring day, Clapton walked out onto Charing Cross Road with the heavy case of the 1960 Les Paul in his hands, a boy carrying this enigma of an instrument into the future.

By then, Clapton hadn't just memorized the licks of American blues-men like Freddy King, B. B. King, Buddy Guy, and others, but had mastered them. With the freedom given to him by John Mayall, Clapton's playing had evolved beyond imitation, moving into the realm of deep personal expression. Fueled by a kind of madness that had dogged him since childhood—ever since he'd learned that his actual mother had left him to be raised by others and the whole story had been concealed from him—Clapton played the blues with an intensity and energy unmatched by anyone else on the London scene. It was a young and English energy, a white energy, but a thrilling one. "It was like the Eric Clapton show," Mayall's drummer remembered. "It wasn't John Mayall's Bluesbreakers."

Central to the Clapton show was a tone that had never before been achieved by an electric guitar. It issued from Eric's amplifier, a boutique device sold by a London drum shop owner named Jim Marshall. English guitarists like Pete Townshend of the Who had pestered Marshall for a high-powered, durable amp similar to those made in Fullerton, but available at a lower price than the imported Fenders. Marshall and his staff designed essentially a copy of the popular Fender Bassman, but made with parts that were easier to obtain in England. Due to their British tubes and speakers, the Marshalls issued a raspier, drier tone than the Fender amps. And because Jim Marshall didn't share Leo Fender's obsession with bell-like clarity—indeed, he'd only set out to satisfy young Turks like Townshend—the Marshall amps produced a thick, crunchy distortion, far more of it than any Fender did.

The most visible piece of Clapton's tone, however, was the guitar Freddy King inspired him to buy. Eric had meant to emulate the thin pricks of the Texas bluesman, but with his own sunburst Les Paul and Marshall amplifier, Clapton achieved a roaring, distorted blare that came out like war in the heavens. Or so his fans thought of it. Which is why the graffiti began to appear.

It first showed up in the spring of 1965, on a wall at the Islington Underground station in North London. Just a mess of spray-painted black letters that read, "Clapton is God." The line soon scattered over walls around the city and became a chant at shows: "Give God a solo!" "We want more God!" It became a catchword for the intellectuals, hippies, and art students who saw in Clapton's purism and intensity a model for their own.

In the eyes of English blues fans, Eric Clapton was a prodigy carving out a new role in the bands of the day. He wasn't some knock-around chap, not one of a group of Beatles or Stones or Yardbirds hanging with the boys. He was a solitary virtuoso, a hired gun. A king holding court, casting bolts of vengeful noise out from his electric scepter. He was a guitar hero. This template had existed before, but Clapton updated it to fit his tastes and biases. This portrayal of the mercenary guitar slinger—with fine clothes, a cold demeanor, and ruthless ability—looked omnipotent to much of Swinging London.

Being called God naturally boosted Eric Clapton's vanity. "In a way, I thought 'Yes, I am God, quite right,'" he told the writer David Mead. But the status also reinforced his overpowering loneliness. "I'm very conceited and I think I have a power," he told an interviewer at the time. "I haven't a girlfriend or any other relationship, so I tell myself of this power through the guitar. And I don't need people to say how good I am. I've worked it out by myself . . . My guitar is simply a medium through which I can make contact with myself. It's very, very lonely."

Neither God nor anyone else had high expectations for the album he and his mates were working on. John Mayall and his band planned to spend only a day or two on it: just go into the studio and play basically the same set they did onstage every night, live into the microphones.

Studio 2 at Decca Records' West Hampstead facility was a tiny room filled with near-obsolete equipment, able then to record only in monaural sound, not stereo. The four bandmates shuttled in on a March day in 1966: Mayall, the leader; Clapton, God; John McVie, the tipsy bass player who would later form Fleetwood Mac; and Hughie Flint, the thundering drummer. Producing them was a blues aficionado named Mike Vernon, who intended to run a session in which the band could record exactly as they pleased, with no pressure to appeal to the charts. Assisting Vernon was recording engineer Gus Dudgeon, a freelancer who had no idea what he was getting into.

The musicians set up while Dudgeon arranged the microphones. Eric Clapton hauled in his Marshall amplifier, a radiator-sized rectangle holding two twelve-inch speakers and producing forty-five watts of power. As was customary then, Dudgeon set up a microphone immediately in front of the amp. The prevailing practice in studios was to record with each instrument set to a low volume, screened off into its own microphone. That way, the instruments wouldn't bleed into each other, and the engineer would have utmost control over the levels of each element when setting the final mix. In this method, sheer volume wasn't necessary when recording. An electric guitar didn't even have to go through an amplifier—it could be plugged straight into the mixing board for a clear, dry tone.

But Eric Clapton wasn't going to plug his Les Paul into a mixing board. He reached down, picked up the microphone Dudgeon had left in front of his amplifier, and carried it over to the far side of the room, as far away from the amp as possible. Then he flipped the power switches on his Marshall and turned the volume knob to where he set it for a live show: Full. Ten. Maximum.

For even more power, Clapton ran his Les Paul through an effect called a Dallas Rangemaster, which amplified the trebly end of the signal before it got to the amp.

Then Eric Clapton played. And Gus Dudgeon, in the control room, began to freak out.

Hear it: a very large amplifier—not as loud as amps got, but still massively powerful—cranked to full volume, with a boost pedal also cranked, played in a tiny room. The sound careening around that cozy box, the mannered studio where Django Reinhardt once recorded, would have shaken the walls. It would have sent the hardware on Hughie Flint's drum kit chattering with resonant frequencies. It would have exploded into feedback the moment Clapton took his hands off the guitar strings, because with so much volume in a small space, there was no avoiding the ambient sound getting sent back through the amplifier. It would have *hurt* to be in there. For the uninitiated, it would have been terrifying.

Meanwhile, in the control room, Gus Dudgeon's VU meters would have been buried in the red on the far side of their primitive dials, far past "way too much" and into the territory where a recording engineer could lose his job. Dudgeon must have thought: *What kind of madman guitarist would think he could record like this?*

So the engineer raced back into the tracking room, went to Clapton, and asked him to turn it down. Begged him, according to some accounts.

Clapton refused. He said he planned to record with the guitar sound that he used onstage—a molten, billowing wail.

This wasn't the first time Clapton had infuriated a recording engineer unused to his technique. But as John Mayall biographer Dinu Logoz writes, the situation reached a stalemate. Dudgeon could do nothing until producer Mike Vernon returned. Only he had the authority to get this guitar player to turn down the volume.

"Is this absolutely essential?" Vernon finally asked the twenty-one-year-old Clapton. "Because Gus is having kittens, he doesn't know how to record it. He's never had to deal with anything like this volume in his life. Can't you turn it down?"

Vernon remembered Clapton responding with utmost politeness. "No, I can't, because if I turn it down, the sound changes. And I can't get the sustain I want. He's the engineer, you're the producer; tell him to engineer it and you produce it. But I'm not turning it down."

As the stalemate continued, Mayall decided to step in. He knew how important Clapton's sound was—he heard it onstage every night. He shouted at Vernon and Dudgeon the seemingly inevitable admonition: "Give God what he wants!" And that was that.

Much of Clapton's amplifier would end up bleeding into Hughie Flint's drum microphone, which was fine with him. As a guitarist, he didn't care which mic he went into as long as the right sound ended up on shellac. "I was on top of my craft, and I was completely confident, and I didn't give a shit about what anyone thought," Clapton said later. "If you didn't like what I was doing, then you weren't on the same planet as me."

But when the results of those three or four days in the studio were released, it became clear that no one was on the same planet as Eric Clapton.

No white person had ever played blues guitar so aggressively and with such emotional intensity—had ever played as if their life hung on every note. Here was the blues, unmistakable, laid out in all its soulfulness and splendor. Songs from greats like Freddy King, Little Walter, Otis Rush, and Robert Johnson, along with Mayall's own worthy compositions. The real thing. And since the wider world was then basically ignorant of these black American masters from whom Eric Clapton learned, his summoning of such immense feeling came across as a revelation. Many listeners would experience the terrifying power of the American blues for the first time through Clapton and Mayall.

But what was new, truly *new*—to England and the United States, to both white and black listeners everywhere—was the sound that Eric Clapton had discovered and that Mike Vernon and Gus Dudgeon had begrudgingly captured over those few days.

It hit in the first few seconds of the resulting album, *Blues Breakers with Eric Clapton*, on a minor-key tune called "All Your Love": a sonic arc that was half wail and half snarl, a few gleaming notes that just hung there, seemingly forever, as Clapton's fingers bent their pitch up and then down. He held a single note on the Les Paul for three full seconds, and he wasn't even soloing; this was Clapton playing *rhythm*. In the next minute he found a couple of simple phrases, outlining the chords, that set off a sublime cascade: solar highs that just floated, and as they decayed transformed into waves of abrasive distortion, then ghostly feedback. His guitar attained the fluidity of water, the notes pouring over one another, pooling together, then hitting some rocky shoal that revealed a coruscating darkness underneath. Each note sustained so long that the next one punched it out of existence. Electric guitar, as most humans played it, had been a pinprick, thin and sharp. Here it was a hydraulic press, every note three feet thick, yet somehow also singing and buoyant.

It was a sound you could not turn away from.

37.

"IT IS A GIANT STEP"

When it was released in July 1966, *Blues Breakers with Eric Clapton* stunned listeners and critics on both sides of the Atlantic. The recording put electric guitar at the forefront of a revamp of the electric blues, recasting it into something heavier and more percussive than any of the American records that inspired Clapton. The album spent ten weeks in the top ten of the British charts, peaking at no. 6 and far exceeding anyone's expectations. "No British musicians have ever sounded like this before on record," *Melody Maker* wrote at the time in one of the dozens of raving reviews. "It is a giant step."

Naturally, Eric Clapton's playing and his name in big letters on the cover had much to do with that success—though Clapton himself treated the effort, like so many others, as perfunctory. He was so indifferent during a photo shoot for the album cover that instead of looking into the camera, he glared into a copy of a *Beano* comic, hating to have his picture taken. To him, the album was simply a record of the shows he performed almost nightly, nothing more, nothing less. And by the time it was released—in fact, the month before—word hit *Melody Maker* that Eric Clapton had already left Mayall's band to found a new group, a trio called Cream.

But as the *Blues Breakers* album spread around England and the US, it began to acquire a near-mystical influence over guitar players. Clapton was pictured on the back of the album cover holding his 1960 Les Paul, and though the guitar was only shown from the back, careful observers would not have missed its outline. The sounds on the album were incredible, and the shape of that guitar on the back cover was a major clue about how to achieve them.

Clapton's playing had already made the old Gibson model into a precious commodity in England. His replacement in the Yardbirds, a young hotshot named Jeff Beck, had gotten a Les Paul. The Bluesbreakers had recorded some earlier tracks with a twentysomething studio guitarist and producer named Jimmy Page, and working with Clapton seems to have given him a few ideas. The *Blues Breakers* album's "Double Crossing Time" was a searing slow blues arrangement that foregrounded two major elements: a heaving, monolithic drumbeat, and the throaty wail of Clapton's Les Paul guitar. Both of these sounds would become key elements of a band Page would soon form, a vehicle for his own guitar-hero ambitions, called Led Zeppelin.

"Everybody started using the Les Paul Standard when Eric Clapton was using them with the Bluesbreakers," remembered guitarist Kim Simmonds, a London blues guitarist who'd find fame with the group Savoy Brown. "I would go and see all of Eric's shows . . . and I'd be standing in an audience filled with nothing but future guitar players. Robert Fripp would be on one side of you, and Jimmy Page would be on the other side."

In the States, Mike Bloomfield, the sideman who'd played with Bob Dylan at Newport, already wielded a 1956 gold-top Les Paul. After hearing the *Blues Breakers* album, he switched to a sunburst 1959 model, luring his American followers to do the same. With its sustain and tone, the Gibson Les Paul "was better than any other possible rock 'n' roll guitar at the time," Bloomfield insisted.

BY 1966, LES PAUL himself was languishing in New Jersey obscurity, his last bit of fame having withered away shortly after his divorce from Mary Ford became final. He'd tried to find a singer to replace her, but within a year had given up and all but retired from public performance. Beer and inactivity were adding girth to his waistline, and even at the relatively young age of fifty-one, arthritis was creeping into his fingers. Les Paul's recording innovations had come to rule the industry—multitracking, or, as he called it, sound-on-sound, was becoming a common technique—but the influence of his music had long since been forgotten. His signature guitar seemed to have met a similar fate.

Then something started to happen. Still playing and tinkering at his mountainside New Jersey home, conducting a few little experiments, Les would sometimes find his solitary work interrupted by a banging on the front door. He'd open it up to find some whippersnapper longhair asking if indeed this was the home of Les Paul—*wow, Les Paul really is a person!*—and asking if they could buy one of the Gibson models with his signature curling in gold across the headstock.

Gibson, of course, no longer made such a guitar. Starting in 1961, the original Les Paul Model had been replaced by the thinner, lighter SG. And while SGs and Les Pauls sounded similar, they didn't sound the same. Gibson had produced only 434 of the cherry sunburst Les Paul "Standards" in 1958, 643 in 1959, and 635 in 1960, according to researcher A. R. Duchossoir, plus a couple of hundred more of the black "Custom" models every year. Thus there were only about 2,400 examples of this guitar ever made, and with demand for them spiking virtually overnight starting in 1966, prices rocketed upward. One immediate effect of the Les Paul Model's resurgence was the adoption by electric guitar players of a belief long shared by collectors of cars, furniture, watches, and other fine goods: that items made in the past are superior to those produced in the present. It was in these years that the obsession over vintage guitars, which would eventually become a mania, took root.

Les witnessed the guitar's resurgence at gathering places for guitarists like Manny's Music in midtown Manhattan. "I'm going down 48th Street, seeing youngsters like Steve Miller, Jeff Beck, Jimmy Page, all these hot young guns looking for Les Paul guitars and paying huge prices when they can find one because they're out of production and getting harder and harder to find," Les recalled in his autobiography. It made him deeply proud to know that the model he'd helped create—the physical incarnation of his legacy as a guitar player—had so suddenly returned to favor. By 1966, the Les Paul Model guitar was becoming the must-have instrument among the heavy rock vanguard, who wanted to sound like Eric Clapton and Mike Bloomfield. Les didn't love hard rock music or the roar of a super-distorted electric guitar, but he did love the idea of being ahead of his time.

Meanwhile, Gibson's current line of solid-body electric guitars was struggling. Ted McCarty, the Gibson president who'd overseen the creation of the Les Paul Model and the company's golden era of electric instruments, had left the company to take over Paul Bigsby's business. Bigsby himself had spent his later years focused on producing the True Vibrato—the whammy bar that had prompted Leo Fender to design his own for the Stratocaster. The Bigsby version had become a classic; Gibson and Gretsch ordered them in large numbers, and Bigsby enjoyed his late-life success, spending time with friends and family, buying a new Cadillac every two years, finally even hiring others to help him produce vibratos. In 1965, he'd retired and sold the business to McCarty.

Without McCarty's strong vision, Gibson was a little lost. Les claimed the company was even considering ceasing production of fully electric instruments altogether, in order to concentrate on hollow-body and acoustic guitars. The older hands in charge had missed the news that among young rock players, their old, chunky, original solid-body was coming back into fashion. But Les Paul was happy to tell them.

38.

"I DON'T HAVE MY OWN GUITAR"

NEW YORK, SPRING–FALL 1966

The first thing she noticed was Jimi Hendrix's hands. They were enormous, spindly things—massive brown spiders on the ends of skinny little arms that crawled around his guitar fretboard seemingly without effort. They looked even bigger that night, shooting out of one of the cheetah-print tunics that were an odd choice of outfit for Curtis Knight and the Squires, especially for a show at a massive theater called the Cheetah Club, on Broadway and Fifty-Third Street in Manhattan. It was all just too much cheetah.

Linda Keith couldn't stop watching this nameless guitar player, following those hands as they coiled and slid around the little Fender Duo-Sonic guitar. Those hands outmatched both their instrument and their band, she thought. The sideman to whom they belonged seemed an obvious star, relegated to the supporting role of rhythm work, confined to a cheap, student-model Fender. Linda Keith, a twenty-one-year-old,

233

serenely beautiful English model then staying in New York, knew something about stars. She was the girlfriend of Rolling Stone Keith Richards.

Linda invited the intriguing guitarist to her table for a drink, and she and Jimi Hendrix and a few friends ended up back at her posh apartment on Sixty-Third Street. There they stayed up all night talking (and apparently only talking), listening to records and discussing music, art, their paths in life. Linda got Jimi Hendrix his first dose of LSD, and played him Bob Dylan's *Blonde on Blonde* for the first time, introducing him to a drug and an album that would become constant companions.

Linda wanted to know why such an obvious talent as Jimi Hendrix was languishing in a third-rate rhythm and blues band. She probably didn't find out then the full extent of Jimi's desperation—didn't learn until later that after years crisscrossing the country as a sideman in various groups, Jimi had landed in near-destitution in New York City. He was at that point essentially homeless, intermittently starving, bouncing from the arms and the cheap rooms of one paramour to the next, or relying on the kindness of friends for shelter and meals, always indentured to whatever band happened to be employing him.

Linda asked why Jimi didn't sing on his own. Jimi said he didn't think his voice was very good—although maybe, he mused, as Bob Dylan's vocals filled her apartment, properly good singing didn't matter much anymore.

Linda asked why Jimi was working for other bandleaders, debasing himself with cheetah print, instead of leading his own group.

"I don't have my own guitar," Jimi replied.

And it seems to have been true. Jimi was then using a sunburst Fender Duo-Sonic loaned to him by Curtis Knight, his bandleader, because Jimi didn't have his own instrument. He was an incendiary guitarist without a guitar.

Linda Keith decided right then to take on Jimi's career as a personal mission—to encourage him to sing and lead his own group, to spread the word about this unknown talent to her friends in the English music scene. She couldn't let Hendrix's obscurity stand. But before he could make any steps toward independence and perhaps recognition, Jimi needed his own guitar. When the Rolling Stones arrived in New York to begin a US tour a short while later, Linda made a bold move on Jimi's behalf: she apparently pilfered a white Fender Stratocaster from the hotel room of her boyfriend—snatched a brand-new guitar from the lair of Keith Richards himself—and gave it to this unknown guitarist. Rummaging around Richards's hotel room that day, Linda also grabbed a demo he had of a song called "Hey Joe," by the singer Tim Rose—a grim, moody tale of betrayal and murder—and gave it to Hendrix. These events would later seem almost impossibly auspicious, but Keith claims they happened. ("This is rock 'n' roll history," Richards confirmed in his autobiography.)

The white Stratocaster Linda Keith stole completely changed Hendrix's situation. He quit Curtis Knight's band and formed his own, based out of Greenwich Village, called Jimmy James and the Blue Flames: a trio focused on acid-soaked covers of blues and R & B hits—Howlin' Wolf, the Troggs, Bob Dylan, Wilson Pickett. It didn't matter that the Strat Keith had stolen was right-handed and Jimi was left-handed. He'd been playing righty guitars since he was a kid in Seattle, just by flipping them over and restringing them to maintain the usual string order.

It was likely that same Stratocaster, dangling upside down from his bony shoulders, restrung to work for Jimi's left-handed brain, that soon drew notice at a Village dive called Cafe Wha?. The club was basically a tourist trap, flypaper for underagers coming in to explore the big city, but it had a small stage and a regular crowd. Jimi now had a Stratocaster and a fuzz pedal, a card-deck-sized metal box that made his guitar sound like a buzzing bee or an electric razor. (Gibson had introduced the first commercial fuzz pedal in 1962, the one famously used on the Rolling Stones' 1965 hit "Satisfaction.") The bewildering things Jimi could do with these tools began to attract any New York denizen interested in the guitar or the state of rock music. "H-bombs were going off, guided missiles were flying—I can't tell you the sounds he was getting out of his instrument," said Mike Bloomfield. "He was getting every sound I was ever to hear him get, right there in that room with a Stratocaster . . . How he did this, I wish I understood."

Linda Keith came to Jimi's regular Wednesday afternoon shows and brought industry figures like Andrew Loog Oldham, the Rolling Stones' manager, to see him and hopefully sign him. But Oldham didn't see the appeal. Linda then brought the Rolling Stones themselves to a Blue Flames gig at a larger room in midtown, but Jimi could barely grab their attention with all the ladies strutting around. Her efforts to find a powerful believer in Hendrix seemed to have failed. Then, one evening, she ran into an acquaintance named Chas Chandler, bass player for a respected British R & B group called the Animals, outside a New York club. She told Chandler about Jimi, and they agreed to meet the next day at the Wha? for the Blue Flames' regular gig.

Chandler showed up in a suit—tall, proper, resolutely British, with a baby face that couldn't hide the fact that he was far older than the rest of the crowd. He sat down with Linda Keith and ordered a milkshake. Jimi had been tipped off to Chandler's presence, of course, and up on the tiny stage of the Wha? he set off even more fireworks than usual— including his own interpretation of "Hey Joe." Jimi juiced his version with fluid runs up and down his Stratocaster, inflecting it with the yearning, unstudied character of his voice, inhabiting the grim fatalism of the lyrics. Watching this happen, Chandler had such an epiphany that he spilled his milkshake all over himself. He already loved "Hey Joe," believing it could make a huge hit in England if performed the right way. And here was a tall, beautiful American black man, singing the song gruffly but with magnificent intensity, leaving pauses in the lyrics to pour out soulful lines on his Stratocaster. Here, Chandler thought, were the ingredients of a tremendous hit—and nobody but him seemed to have noticed.

Immediately after the gig, Chandler asked if Jimi was willing to go to England, where, Chandler said, he could make Jimi into a star. The Animals bassist had been looking for a way out of playing music for a living and into a career as an artist manager; in Jimi, he saw an ideal first client. Hendrix hesitated, not quite sure of the claims of this unknown British bloke—but sure, he said, he would go. Why not? It wouldn't be for another month or so anyway, since Chandler still had some US tour dates left to play with the Animals.

When Chandler returned to New York some five weeks later, though, he found that his would-be client had gotten cold feet. England was so, so far away, and Jimi would have to go all alone, without his Blue Flames. Jimi was only twenty-three; he hadn't been home to Seattle in six years, and England sounded like a strange place. Would he really be accepted over there? What kind of money did they use? Could you get LSD? What was the country even *like*?

Chandler persisted, and Jimi's hesitation finally came down to one question. He put it to Chandler that September of 1966: if he *did* move to England, would he get a chance to meet Eric Clapton, that great English guitar player?

Oh, yes, Chas Chandler assured him. Jimi and Eric Clapton would certainly get an introduction.

39.

"FROM COMPLETELY DIFFERENT ANGLES"

HOLLYWOOD AND DETROIT, 1966

Carol Kaye had played her Fender bass for the biggest names in music by 1966: for Nancy Sinatra and Tina Turner; for Ray Charles and Sam Cooke; soon, she'd play for the Doors and Simon and Garfunkel. She earned double the union scale—$208 per session—by never flinching at a late night or a merciless schedule. But for Carol and her fellow studio pros, a Beach Boys recording session was still an incomparable slog, an ordeal to be endured.

Brian Wilson preferred to record in Hollywood, at the Western or Gold Star studio, setting aside an entire three-hour block (or more) for a single song, instead of tracking several, as was typical. Like most studio tracking rooms, these were stark caverns with about as much charm as a middle-school cafeteria, their interiors so flooded with fluorescent light that Carol usually wore sunglasses inside. The linoleum floors were littered with discarded sunflower seeds, empty paper coffee cups, and gum wrappers. Blue-jeaned musicians sat on metal folding chairs, wearing headphones caked in the grease of a thousand previous sessions, telling jokes to ease their stress and boredom—usually with a punch line referencing someone else's race, gender, or body size.

As the sole female player in the room, Carol learned to curse and insult like the men did. She didn't smoke, but she chewed gum and swilled coffee to stay awake, and suppressed her hunger with sunflower seeds and cans of soup from the vending machine. If Brian Wilson, the artiste-in-chief, got so lost in sound that he forgot his players' comfort, she wasn't afraid to remind him. Racing to the restroom once after Wilson pushed the players for hours without even a five-minute break, Carol flipped the bird in the direction of the Beach Boys' resident genius. He was shocked—but afterward, breaks were more forthcoming.

Wilson worked tirelessly now, worried that new developments in rock music had made his band obsolete. Bob Dylan's "Like a Rolling Stone" had injected artful bitterness and wry observation into hard-driving rhythm and blues. The Beatles' *Rubber Soul* had introduced the concept of the rock album as a complete creative work, rather than just a set of singles interspersed with filler. The Beach Boys had been America's foremost producers of songs about cars and girls and surfboards and hot rods, despite the fact that Wilson, the band's chief creator, was always uncomfortable with such frivolousness. Now, challenged by the success of these high-minded rivals, Wilson pursued a mature sound for the Beach Boys. He made his old stage instrument—the electric Fender bass, now usually in the hands of Carol Kaye—a prominent part of it.

"Sloop John B" arrived March 21, 1966, the first single from a new album called *Pet Sounds*. The Beach Boys sang the opening lines a cappella, surrounded by flutes, then Carol Kaye's bass rumbled in with the drums, yanking the idyllic daydream into a torrent of sound. What began as a Bahamian folk tune about a ship and its sailors became, in Brian Wilson's composition, a refracted portrait of longing: "I feel so broke up / I wanna go home." High up in the mix, flutes and guitars fluttered, evoking the shimmering sea on a sunny day. Carol's bass followed the singers, seeming to identify with them, undergirding the rhythm but intertwining with their soaring melody. The song was impossible without her bass.

"Sloop John B" evinced obvious brilliance, but Carol and the other session players had doubts about the commercial potential of *Pet Sounds*. The album was moody and orchestral, complex and often slow. When it was released, the week after "Sloop John B" had peaked on the radio, *Pet Sounds* rose only to no. 10 on the *Billboard* 200, a poor showing for America's leading rock 'n' roll group. Even the critics were indifferent. Brian Wilson was deeply disappointed at the apparent failure of this full-length creative statement, but he resolved to try again.

HALFWAY ACROSS THE COUNTRY, another bassist had become essential to a project quite different from Brian Wilson's aesthetic jousting with the Beatles and Dylan. James Jamerson was a light-skinned black man with blue eyes and a mischievous smile. In 1964, he'd used his acoustic bass to conjure the warm, swinging throb of "My Guy" by Mary Wells, helping send it to no. 1 on the pop chart—the "white" chart, not the ostensibly "black" R & B chart. Afterward, the owner of the basement studio in Detroit where that hit was recorded decided that Jamerson was too important to be allowed to leave, and put him on a weekly retainer. Berry Gordy was building his Motown label into "the Sound of Young America," and he knew that hits would come easier with the energy of this man's grooves.

There was just something about Jamerson's style, as if he refused to accept the anonymity that had so long come with the bass player's role. Soon after joining Motown, Jamerson switched from the acoustic upright to the Fender Precision Bass, a sunburst 1962 model that would become known as "the funk machine." With the Fender, he could turn up the volume knob and be heard. Jamerson may have gone uncredited on every release, just like the rest of the Motown house band, but the way he played, there was no question he wanted to be out there, wanted to be known. Soon, he and the other artists at Motown were being heard more than ever before.

The Supremes had put Hitsville USA at the top of the charts three separate times in 1964, with Jamerson's bass more prominent on each song. "Baby Love" spent four weeks at no. 1 in the US and England, lifted up by the cooing of Diana Ross. In "Where Did Our Love Go,"

Jamerson locked in with the piano, building a rhythm so fine and airy it seemed self-propelled. Thanks to a new eight-track mixing console in the Motown studio, Jamerson bounced even more clearly through the chords of "Come See About Me," and things only picked up from there.

Jamerson was at Hitsville in 1965 when the Temptations recorded "My Girl"; he invented the pulsing, unforgettable bass part that is the very first thing heard in the song. He was there when the Supremes recorded "Stop! In the Name of Love," another eager, up-tempo no. 1, and was getting even more adventurous. He seemed to rummage through that Supremes hit, never remaining still, developing his signature, restless style. His approach worked that year when the Four Tops recorded "I Can't Help Myself (Sugar Pie, Honey Bunch)," another no. 1.

The Motown writers, producers, musicians, and stars were by then achieving the ambition Berry Gordy had laid out. Those impeccable rhythms, polished by the company's quality-control efforts, were increasingly unforgettable to any ears that heard them, white or black, British or American. By 1966, a stunning 75 percent of Motown singles were entering the *Billboard* charts, compared with an industry average of 10 percent. From 1960 to 1969, according to the critic and historian Jack Hamilton, the label landed a song on the charts at the astonishing rate of one every week and a half.

Detroit was even threatening to take over London. The Beatles adored the Motown sound so much that they tried their best to copy it, right down to the intricate bass lines issued by this unnamed funk master. Paul McCartney knew where the interesting bass playing was happening: "It was [Jamerson], me, and Brian Wilson who were doing melodic bass lines," he said later, "all from completely different angles: L.A., Detroit, and London, all picking up on what each other did."

So just like Carol Kaye, Jamerson was carving out a vital role for Leo Fender's electric bass in the popular sounds of the 1960s. Yet the success of the Detroit effort, the persistence of those Jamerson grooves, carried a particular historic significance in the United States.

The pattern in American music for decades had been that black musicians innovated new styles, while white players commercialized and profited from them. The choice of verbs varied with one's perspective (from "steal" and "copy" to "borrow" and "popularize"), and there were always exceptions (Louis Armstrong and Nat King Cole in jazz; Fats Domino and Chuck Berry in rock 'n' roll), but the American pop industry largely reflected the country's sharp racial division. Record labels, the press, and radio generally preserved a separation between radical, adventurous new black sounds and safe, salable white ones. Executives, parents, and concerned politicians believed that white youth had to be protected from black music. Others thought that black stars simply couldn't become as popular with whites as people of their own race. The music industry was like any other institution in America: if you wanted to make it to the very top, you pretty much had to be white.

Motown's success changed this. By 1966, the black artists of this black-owned company dominated the once-white charts in America—and not just one singer or style, but a rotating roster of Detroit stars, all pursuing their own funky excellence. Unlike in earlier eras, in which new sounds were quickly copied (and watered down) by white imitators, Motown's success couldn't truly be co-opted, because what produced it was not an individual or a small group. Rather it was as near as a label could be to a factory, a production apparatus that dictated everything from tempos and arrangements to its stars' diction and comportment. It was a system of being that had become an empire. Not every Motown release was a hit, and not every song was a classic, but in these years, African-American music, played entirely by African-Americans, was conquering the white mainstream to an extent never before seen. And Leo Fender's electric bass, in the hands of the brilliant James Jamerson, formed the rumbling core of it.

ALL THROUGH 1966, along with *Pet Sounds*, Brian Wilson had been working on something else: not an album, but a single song that would meld his ambitions as a classically trained composer with the strictures and possibilities of a pop single. Carol Kaye was called in for the second session on this work—the second of what would be twelve altogether, in her memory (others would report as many as seventeen), across five studios. By this point, Wilson was writing lines specifically for her: emphasizing a heavy beat, letting her bass meander through unusual melodies that tied the notes of every other instrument together. He had a specific sound he wanted out of the Fender Precision Bass: slightly metallic, but so loud and deep as to be oddly comforting.

After their twelve or so sessions, Carol got a pretty good sense of what the lead melody sounded like, which was unusual for a Beach Boys composition. Usually, the session players had no idea until they heard it on the radio. Carol generally hesitated to make judgments about the fragments of Wilson songs she heard while recording, but having agonized over this one, she thought it could be a masterpiece.

Her bass came in with a high-pitched figure: a crisp, throaty blurt from the Fender that repeated a minor-key plaint as it glided down the neck, drums clattering along with each retreating step. Over it floated Carl Wilson's voice, stratospherically high, achingly sweet: "I—I love the colorful clothes she wears /And the way the sunlight plays upon her hair." And in a moment the song zoomed into carnivalesque psychedelia, shaking, spinning, a sci-fi Electro-Theremin whirring up high as the collective harmonies sang about "good vibrations," circling around, seeming to rise a little farther up each time. Carol's sunset bass riff returned for the next verse, and Wilson chose to cut off two words completing a lyrical rhyme so that she could be heard more clearly as the bass launched into the following chorus. The Fender's huge low end supported everything in the song: it was the bus ferrying around this troupe of California freaks; it was helping to make Brian Wilson's marijuana circus heartfelt and elated but grounded, rather than untethered and nauseating.

The song moved at a ridiculous pace—two verses, two choruses, and a bridgelike section arrived in just over two minutes, all neatly colliding thanks to the splicing of magnetic tape. Then the whole thing fell down into a shocking near-silence. There came a breathy organ and a massive, soothing throb from Carol's Fender before the leap into one final chorus and a vocal-focused coda.

Three minutes and thirty-five seconds. Dozens of instruments, including Electro-Theremin, violin, harpsichord, and jaw harp. The tune had been produced at a staggering cost, estimated by Brian Wilson at $16,000, making it the most expensive pop song ever recorded at the time. But Wilson's "pocket symphony," as his publicist called it, went to no. 1. In fact, "Good Vibrations" was the Beach Boys' most successful song ever, hitting the top of the charts in both the US and the UK, becoming the group's third no. 1 at home and its first million-selling single. Future years would see the reevaluation of *Pet Sounds* and a near-universal consensus that it is, in fact, a masterpiece. But "Good Vibrations" was greeted immediately upon arrival as a magnificent work, almost certainly the pinnacle of the Beach Boys' recording career, and a perfect encapsulation of what the group did so well.

The artistic and commercial success of "Good Vibrations" illustrated the essential role that the Fender electric bass had come to play in popular music by the mid-1960s. Leo Fender had upgraded the low end from the awkward, underpowered, often-unheard doghouse to a light, portable instrument that stuck out over everything in the most ambitious compositions yet recorded. The Fender bass was not a background instrument; it was worthy of a lead role in the Beach Boys and the brilliant works of Motown, and its players had finally grabbed one.

A lead role had been something unimaginable for the bass just a decade earlier. The men and women who played acoustic bass had often been anonymous, ostracized with their quiet instruments in the back of ever-louder groups. The adoption of the Fender bass did not make its players public stars. But it pushed music in a direction that allowed their instrument, their linking of rhythm and melody, to become perhaps the most important single component of a pop song after the vocals. The bass groove would soon grow into the vital core of music. In future years, through the evolution of funk, disco, and hip-hop, the electric bass subsumed nearly every other sound in music except the drums with which it conspired. There would be hits without great singers (or any singer), hits without guitar solos (or any guitar). But in the wake of Carol Kaye and James Jamerson, there were fewer and fewer hits—at least in forward-looking styles of music—without the groove of an electric bass.

40.

"HERE WAS THE REAL THING"

LONDON, FALL 1966

Eric Clapton's new band, Cream, was booked to play at Regent Street Polytechnic on October 1, 1966. The band had formed surreptitiously, with Clapton still publicly pledged to John Mayall but seeking a trio of his own—a simple group, with bassist Jack Bruce and drummer Ginger Baker, that would give them all room to explore on their instruments, that would play a style of rock still blues based but more psychedelic and experimental. Cream was heralded from its first announcement in *Melody Maker* as a supergroup, but even supergroups need to find their footing, and Cream's hunt was still under way on the fall evening when Clapton, Bruce, and Baker were lounging in their dressing room at Regent Street Polytechnic, preparing to go onstage.

A familiar face walked in. It was Chas Chandler, the bassist of the Animals, whom all of Cream knew well. A friend of the band. He'd come that night not as a fellow musician, however, but as a manager.

Accompanying Chandler was a person none of them had seen before: a thin black American wearing outrageous clothes, with a cloud of Afro surrounding a dreamy face and huge brown eyes. He seemed distant— not in a cold way, as Clapton could, but pleasantly aloof. This figure wandered silently over to the dressing room mirror and began toying with his hair, poufing it out with a comb to maximum diameter.

Chandler, meanwhile, chatted amiably. He asked his friends in Cream if this newcomer could go onstage with them and jam at the show, just for a few songs. It was a common practice for friendly musicians to venture up during one another's sets, but no one had yet asked to jam onstage with Cream. Who, after all, would dare try to outmatch God and his chosen archangels? The result was almost certain embarrassment.

Chandler insisted, however, that his unprepossessing companion was an accomplished guitarist. He pestered Clapton and his lads to allow this newcomer a moment onstage, just a short one. Hesitantly, the members of Cream agreed. Sure, they'd let this unknown American jam with them— live, in public, at a major gig of theirs. Sure. God had a funny feeling about it.

JACK BRUCE TOLD Jimi Hendrix that he could plug into the massive Marshall bass amp. Jimi unpacked his Stratocaster and got ready. The lights in the auditorium at Regent Street Polytechnic went down. Someone probably muttered a few words of introduction—the sudden arrival of a fourth musician onstage, especially one who looked like Jimi Hendrix, could hardly go unremarked upon—and then Jimi called the song: "Killing Floor," an old blues tune made famous by Howlin' Wolf. Bruce and drummer Ginger Baker didn't know it. Eric Clapton did—mostly the slower version recorded by Albert King—and thought it was particularly tough, with a rhythm hard to get right at any tempo. Live recordings from this time suggest what happened next.

Jimi unfurled one descending, fluid lick on his Stratocaster: a flash of notes to stretch out those fingers, showing just a glimpse of his ability.

Then the American newcomer took off, shooting up the neck to splatter out a bright phrase, falling back down to the lower registers, pumping a chord to set the tempo, and launching into the song proper as the members of Cream lumbered to life behind him. This was not Albert King's "Killing Floor," or Howlin' Wolf's, but a jet blast, absurdly fast, beyond 130 beats per minute. But Hendrix's chording still clutched the subtleties of Wolf's original call-and-response rhythm, kept it all together through the verses, those spidery hands accenting the beat here, adding a little trill or a commenting phrase there, playing lead and rhythm at the same time, gliding around the whole guitar neck and talking through the instrument in two or three different voices as if doing so was the easiest thing in the world.

On the other side of the stage, Eric Clapton's hands fell off the neck and body of his Gibson Les Paul. His jaw followed them toward the floor. Clapton realized immediately that he'd made a serious miscalculation. He'd been expecting this newcomer to hold back, as he thought was customary, but Jimi, given his largest audience yet in this foreign country, was throwing out everything he had. What Clapton had imagined would be a friendly jam was suddenly, he realized, a cutting contest. He was God, and this American was coming with everything to take his throne.

Over on his side of the stage, Jimi had no effects, no fuzz, no wah-wah— but then, he'd had none with Curtis Knight or Little Richard, either. With just his guitar plugged into Bruce's amp, Hendrix fired into a solo, long fingers ripping sounds out of the Stratocaster that no one in the hall had ever heard before: tremolo dive-bombs, yawning string bends, electric slashes of the pickup selector switch. Jimi had now hijacked the Cream concert, and he began to reveal the full extent of his powers, the flamboyant exhibition that would become the talk of everyone who saw it over the next two years: he played the Strat behind his head, he played the Strat with his teeth, he fell to the floor at the climax of a solo, he did the splits, he flicked his tongue. It was outrageous, but also frighteningly skillful. Some would get distracted by Jimi's theatrics, overlook his skills and dismiss him as a mere showman. But to many observers, Hendrix exhibited a degree of expressiveness and personality, a combination of pure guitar athleticism and deep-running soulfulness, that had never been seen before.

Clapton knew immediately that there was nothing he could add to this. He'd never been a showman, and even in terms of pure ability, he'd met his match. By the time Jimi slashed out his first solo, Clapton had shuffled backstage into the dark, to watch in semiprivate as this unknown American committed deicide. Chas Chandler hurried back to assess the lordly damage his client had wrought. "Eric was standing [there], trying to light a cigarette, and his hands were shaking," Chandler recalled. "And he just says, 'Is he *really* that good?' "

It was a rhetorical question. Clapton knew the audience had been "completely gobsmacked" by Jimi's impromptu performance. Word quickly got around in the press that God had been unseated, that there was a new power on the scene. "They loved it, and I loved it, too, but I remember thinking that here was a force to be reckoned with," Clapton recalled. "It scared me, because he was clearly going to be a huge star, and just as [Cream] were finding our own speed, here was the real thing."

By "the real thing," of course, Clapton meant that Jimi was an American black man—a musician who could play the blues with a credibility and authenticity unattainable for a white Englishman. Jimi hadn't been born in the South, but he'd learned his craft there; he'd made the pilgrimage to Chess Records in Chicago to meet Muddy Waters; he'd played with Ike Turner and copped licks directly from B. B. King. He embodied a tradition that Clapton could only study. To anyone who knew the history, Jimi Hendrix represented the legacy of the black American guitarist-geniuses who'd come before him: players like Charlie Christian, T-Bone Walker, Lonnie Johnson, Son House, Robert Johnson, Memphis Minnie, Muddy Waters, Elmore James, Sister Rosetta Tharpe, B. B. King, Albert King, Freddy King, Otis Rush, Buddy Guy. These were the players who'd first elevated the electric guitar into the most humane and compelling instrumental voice of the twentieth century, the artists whose music enabled everything the London and San Francisco hippies were gushing over in 1966 and '67. But when they were doing it in the 1930s, '40s, and '50s, most of the outside world couldn't have cared less. Symbolically, Jimi Hendrix was now carrying their torch, claiming credit where credit was long overdue. His mere presence in blues-besotted London reminded the scene's fans and players (at least the cannier ones) that this music was borrowed from a far less fortunate race and generation, and his arrival gave them the chance to atone for this unfairness and claim allegiance to a convenient embodiment of "the real thing."

But of course, no one was born knowing how to play guitar like Jimi Hendrix, and to think of him as a world-shattering guitarist by divine right—as many did—was to ignore the true scope of his achievement. Perhaps more than any other person in London, Eric Clapton could understand the intensity of the commitment that had gotten Jimi here, the innumerable hours of practice, the years of dehumanizing poverty. He'd lived something like it. And blues guitar was also not the only experience they shared. Both men had mastered their music in spite of early lives in which a mother's love and attention was largely or completely withheld. Clapton thus found a deep commonality with Jimi, even as he watched this newcomer's race and biography bestow a credibility he could never attain.

After October 1, 1966, Clapton was no longer the unquestionable leader of the London scene, no longer the sole deity of English guitar worshippers. There was a period of tension between Eric and Jimi, a sort of sniffing out, a testing of the poses of rivalry and friendship over several encounters. Yet by being immediately, publicly bested by Jimi, and then getting to know him, Clapton found a companion and equal, another person who felt the same ambitions and yearnings he did, and who shared a similar past. As he spent time with Jimi, Clapton realized that this wildly talented American was just as wracked by insecurity as he was, just as subject to the destructive (and joyful) whims of partying and decadence. After he discovered a kinship with Jimi, the angry boy from Ripley saw some of his old loneliness abate.

There was another symbolic rift between these two men besides white and black, English and American—a division missed by few of their close followers, and one that would have great consequence for the future of their instrument. In the flurry of enthusiasm that followed Hendrix's arrival in London in the fall of 1966, anyone paying close attention would have noted that this flamboyant newcomer had overthrown Clapton and his all-powerful Gibson Les Paul with, of all things, a Fender Stratocaster—a guitar seen at that time and place as a meager and old-fashioned tool.

41.

"THE GUITARS NOWADAYS PLAY JUST AS GOOD"

ENGLAND AND THE UNITED STATES, 1966–1968

In the early 1960s, the curvy shapes and bright colors of Fender guitars had rendered competing Gibson models conservative and stodgy. Half a decade later, the resurgence of the Les Paul Model's natural wood finishes made those swooshy Fenders seem equally out of date, redolent of a bygone age of Formica and tail fins. Some of this was purely the rotations of fashion, but there'd been a major shift in the culture after 1965, a growing disillusionment with authority, government, and the beneficence of the modernist drive. The civil rights movement and the Vietnam War now called persistent attention to injustices and hypocrisies at the core of American society. Music responded by getting louder, more serious, even angry. Self-satisfaction was out—more afflicted sounds were called for, and the high output of Gibson's dual-coil, humbucking pickups pushed amplifiers into thick, aggrieved distortion, while the guitar's heavy body and glued-in neck produced a crying, mournful sustain.

There'd been inklings of these sounds before John Mayall's *Blues Breakers with Eric Clapton*, but the album convinced players on both sides of the Atlantic that the sonic qualities of this guitar matched especially well their distressed and tumultuous historical moment.

The Fender Stratocaster, meanwhile, was what Buddy Holly and Ike Turner had played, what the surf rockers had used—a workaday instrument out of step with the times. "They were so unfashionable, Stratocasters," Eric Clapton recalled. "As far as the new blues-rock hotshots were concerned, it was a guitar for skinny, bespectacled nerds," wrote rock historian Charles Shaar Murray. The Strat carried the baggage of association with a previous rock 'n' roll era, and sonically, it seemed unable to issue the tormented sounds of the new blues rock. Those skinny little single-coil pickups and that bolt-on neck got a clear, spanking, upbeat tone, too weak to drive amps into torrents of distortion.

Then came Jimi Hendrix, and the right-handed white Stratocaster he brought to England. Hendrix had tried (and would try) practically every guitar on the market, but he was adamant about which model he preferred. "I use a Fender Stratocaster," Jimi later told the *Los Angeles Free Press*.

> Everyone's screaming about the seven-year-old Telecaster, and the 13-year-old Gibson, and the 92-year-old Les Paul [guitar]. They've gone into an age bag right now, but it's nothing but a fad. The guitars now[a]days play just as good. . . . The Stratocaster is the best all around guitar for the stuff we're doing. You can get the very bright trebles and the deep bass sound. I tried [a] Telecaster and it only has two sounds, good and bad, and a very weak tone variation. A Guild guitar is very delicate but it has one of the best sounds. I tried one of the new Gibsons, but I literally couldn't play it at all, so I'll stick with Fender.

For those watching Jimi's arrival on the London scene, his ability to conjure otherworldly sounds from the Stratocaster bordered on the mystical. While most players sought the old Gibsons they thought were essential, Jimi took a shiny new Fender off the rack and wrangled ridiculously entrancing sounds out of it—sounds that seemed all his own. But of course it wasn't mysticism that made these sounds. It was technology.

Upon his arrival in England, Chas Chandler had outfitted Jimi Hendrix and his new bassist Noel Redding with small amplifiers suitable for rehearsals, amps that to most people would have seemed plenty loud. Jimi, however, quickly saw that the local rock vanguard preferred massive, hundred-watt Marshall stacks with high distortion, heavy bass, and overwhelming volume. He and Noel Redding wanted Marshalls desperately, but at that moment, no one had the money for new amps—Chandler was then selling off his personal bass guitars to fund the unsigned group. Heedless, Jimi and Noel began a campaign to destroy their original amps and have them replaced with Marshalls. "We tried everything to break them," remembered Mitch Mitchell, drummer in the newly formed Jimi Hendrix Experience. "They got dropped down flights of stairs, we nearly threw them out of the windows. It took about three days, but in the end we managed it." By the time the Experience headed off to play their very first gigs in France, Chandler had sold a few more basses, and Jimi and Noel had gotten matching hundred-watt Marshall stacks, each about the dimensions of a full-size refrigerator. Jimi turned his up to full, chest-pounding, ear-shattering volume—but even at those levels, his Stratocaster couldn't attain the nuclear distortion a Les Paul could.

More circuitry was necessary. And in the fall of 1966, the very season that Jimi Hendrix arrived in London, the Arbiter company of London released a silvery metal disc called the Fuzz Face. Numerous other fuzz pedals had arrived on the market beforehand—both Keith Richards and Eric Clapton had used them—but the Fuzz Face was unique for two reasons. Its circuitry emitted a warm, natural tone distinct from the buzzing-bee artificiality of most stomp boxes. And the Fuzz Face could produce anything from cascades of thick distortion to absurdly inchoate noise, no matter what kind of guitar was run through it. It transformed the Stratocaster's spanky thinness into a heaving rumble, and Jimi Hendrix adopted it immediately. He relied on this pedal all through that fall and winter, as he and the other members of the Jimi

Hendrix Experience wrote and recorded their debut album. It was the Fuzz Face—wreaking havoc on Jimi's Strat and Marshall—that painted the tones of his follow-up single to "Hey Joe," the incomparable "Purple Haze." It was the Fuzz Face that gave "Foxey Lady" the aspect of a steam kettle boiling over, about to burst. And when the pedal was turned off, the Strat's single-coil pickups chimed with a clarity that Gibsons couldn't match, producing the glassy tones heard on songs like "Hey Joe" and "The Wind Cries Mary."

In Jimi's hands, with his preferred tools, even the modest and old-fashioned Stratocaster could summon gobsmacking torrents of fuzz. This three-part wonder—the guitar, the amp, the pedals—was essentially a single instrument to Jimi, no part of it optional, and he would employ it consistently onstage and in the studio. The Stratocaster became a core feature of his presence, along with the tantalizing clothes, lethal sex appeal, and supernatural abilities, the totality of the package inspiring fans and critics to salute him as "the Black Bob Dylan," "the Black Elvis," or just "the best guitar-picker in the world." The fact that Hendrix—slayer of gods, embodiment of black American blues genius, purported inspiration for the term "heavy metal"—chose a *Stratocaster* was something every future electric guitar player would have to reckon with. Initially, though, it seems Hendrix's peers saw his choice of guitar as just another sign of his near-madness. "There was something about the way he played the Stratocaster that made it seem like it was off-limits," Clapton recalled. "I thought, 'Well, I'm not going to get involved in all that. It's just too crazy.'"

Though the Gibson Les Paul wasn't strictly necessary anymore to produce heavy distortion, many players still felt it produced the thickest, most saturated sounds and handled them uniquely well. Even after Hendrix's arrival, the preferred tool for rockers wasn't a bright, sharp Fender razor blade, but a heavy, growling Gibson hammer. The Les Paul Model continued to see a tremendous surge in popularity—but, of course, the original guitars, always rare, grew only more expensive and harder to find. Even Eric Clapton, after his cherished 1960 Les Paul Model was stolen, switched to the more commonly available SG.

Around 1967, Les Paul, who by that point believed he was retired, found himself discussing this issue with Arnie Berlin, head of Gibson's parent company in Chicago. "They're showing up at my house and pounding on my door trying to buy them from me," Les said of his old Gibson signature model. Arnie Berlin was the son of M. H. Berlin, who, with Ted McCarty, had pushed Gibson to build a solid-body electric almost a decade after its earlier leaders had laughed Les and his Log out the door.

"Well, maybe that's just because they're hard to get, maybe it's just the status of having a rarity," Arnie told Les.

"Oh, I'm sure of it," Les said. "They're hard to get because we've quit making them, and the people who already have them are hanging on to them."

Whether due to Les's persuasion—or, more likely, Gibson execs discovering on their own the growing market for 1950s Les Pauls—the company soon realized that it couldn't ignore the surging demand for this discontinued model. If players were dying to have that chunky old guitar, Gibson would have to give it to them.

So seven years after Les Paul had declined to renew his contract with the company, at the summer trade shows of 1968, Gibson displayed a line of Les Paul guitars based on the originals. There was the reissued Les Paul Standard—in gold, just like the original models—and the Les Paul Custom, in gloss black with gold hardware. There were minor differences in the new versions, and their arrival would not stop values for the old ones from eventually climbing into the hundreds of thousands or even millions of dollars. But starting in 1969, the Gibson single-cutaway solid-body would be available brand-new to any guitarist who could pay $395 for a Standard or $545 for a Custom. The Les Paul Model would from then on remain in continuous production, with Les himself getting a 5 percent royalty on the wholesale price of every single instrument.

And so the long-simmering rivalry between Leo Fender and Les Paul bubbled up again on stages and in recording studios and rehearsal rooms everywhere. Years earlier, neither man could have imagined the sounds these guitars now made. Eric Clapton had elevated the Gibson into the choice battering ram of hard rock, soon to be adopted by Led Zeppelin's Jimmy Page. Meanwhile, Jimi Hendrix had transformed the Stratocaster into an incomparably eloquent voice for his soulful psychedelia. Fenders and Les Pauls were twins, opposites, companions—rivals that were remarkably complementary. Through the odd meanderings of time and fashion and technology, two musical instruments born largely in 1940s Hollywood had risen to become the cherished tools of an unfathomably louder age. The guitars of Leo and Les had far outlived the dreams of their makers—and yet, to the current generation of players, and to future ones, they were just being born.

42.

"YOU FINALLY HEARD WHAT THAT SONG WAS ABOUT"

BETHEL, NEW YORK, AUGUST 1969

On Monday morning, a stillness settled over the farm. The August sun murmured through overcast skies, illuminating a brown hillside, strewn with debris, where the crowd had been. Ankle-swallowing mud had overrun every blade of grass. Floating on the mud was a sea of wreckage: shoes, skirts, cushions, sandals, bottles, butts, entire vehicles empty of fuel, their occupants crouched on their roofs like marooned sailors. The epic freak show had come and mostly gone, and what it left behind could easily have been mistaken for a battlefield.

It was not yet over. Some thirty or forty thousand people still watched as, down on the stage, what seemed to be a random band of hippies—bell-bottoms, headbands, poufy hair—jammed loosely in the wan light. He stood there on the left of that monstrous skeletal platform, leather fringes trailing his arms as they flew around the neck of a white Stratocaster—one held, as usual, upside down.

Jimi Hendrix, illuminated in haze: now the highest-paid player in rock music, the de facto headliner of this three-day gathering. The Woodstock festival was so far behind schedule that its biggest draw only appeared on a Monday morning, eight hours after the event was supposed to have ended. At the start of the set, Hendrix announced that he'd be trying something new.

"We got tired of 'the Experience,' and every once in a while we was blowing our minds too much," he said into the mic, "so we decided to change the whole thing around and call it 'Gypsy Sun and Rainbows.'" This was a larger group: five musicians, including a second guitar player. The Experience had crumbled after two years aboard the rocket of success, and Jimi himself was now miserable: fighting a proxy war with his managers, growing bored of the persona he'd built in his first years of stardom, melancholy as ever. So at Woodstock Jimi was starting over, performing with a mostly new band. They hadn't had much time to rehearse or finish new songs, and that morning, the ensemble sounded loose and out of tune. Many of the festival's remaining attendees were hiking out under the murky sky, exhausted, hunting for gas or food. Jimi watched them trudge away from the stage as his band roared through a thirteen-minute version of "Voodoo Chile (Slight Return)," one of the set's better numbers. He saw Woodstock ending before his eyes.

"You can leave if you want to," he said. "We're just jamming, that's all. Okay? You can leave, or you can clap."

And as the currents of feedback from "Voodoo Chile" wafted out into the dwindling audience, Jimi began to pluck out the first notes of another melody. A tune that nearly everyone—everyone down there in the mud, everyone behind him on that massive stage, every one of the millions who watched it on film years later—knew by heart.

The first notes were knifelike, deep, slashing. *O say can you see*, serrated by the cutting pickups of the Stratocaster and the blaring cabinets of the Marshall stacks. They arrived not as language but as pure, roiling sound, reverberating around the Woodstock mud bowl. Jimi Hendrix was recasting the patriotism and pride of "The Star-Spangled Banner," that old barroom melody Francis Scott Key made into a national anthem, right onstage in the dull Monday glow. He was going to make the song *his*.

Out in the fields, all activity came to a halt as listeners realized what was happening. Eyes widened and jaws fell open at the exhilarating tumult of those first few notes, at the very notion of such an attempt. The morning stillness in a moment became a hard freeze. "Everything just stopped," one Woodstock photographer remembered.

Initially it was almost reverent: the Strat gleamed through the tarnish of the Fuzz Face and some custom-built electronic effects that all seemed to be turned on. Jimi carved the song's proud melody out of an enveloping mass of noise, the walls of whistling feedback and distortion raw marble for his sonic sculpture. Waves of howling fringed *the dawn's early light*. The first vowel in *proudly we hailed* came as a long, anguished upward note. Yearning swirled around *the twilight's last gleaming* and *the perilous fight*. Each phrase arrived slowly and deliberately, the original melody still amazingly legible in the din, though Jimi was sometimes not even plucking guitar strings. With everything in his rig turned up so loud, the sounds just shot off the fingers of his right hand like lightning bolts.

He stepped on his wah-wah pedal to give a nasal bite to *the rockets' red glare*, and as soon as the phrase left his fingers, there came a soaring cry, then a fall—a single note pulled up and then cut down by the whammy bar—that signaled the song's descent into total chaos. What came next wasn't melody but a terrifying evocation of war: planes buzzing, bombs exploding, helicopter blades chopping, ambulance sirens wailing, mothers shrieking, men howling in pain, and amid it all the unanswerable scream of *why*, a childlike yowl against the very existence of such senselessness. Jimi up there seemed to lose himself, forget the crowd, the morning, the mud; his face became an elastic rictus of feeling, his fingers fluttering winglike across the maple fretboard, conjuring the military cacophony that he, a former paratrooper, knew well.

The chaos paused for a clear phrase: *the bombs bursting in air*. And then his guitar exploded again, the Stratocaster conjuring strafing and napalm, grenades and carpet bombs, the rumble of a jet just overhead. On the drum kit, Mitch Mitchell detonated his own explosions and crashes, but this was unmistakably Jimi's show, a chance to display all of the theatrics and technique he'd acquired, and to push his electric guitar to produce sounds only he knew it could. He used every aspect of his Stratocaster: the tremolo arm, which he yanked and pounded, pulling the strings out of tune; the cutaway body, which allowed him to reach the very highest notes on the fretboard; the single-coil pickups that issued sharp, stinging bites. He depended on those gigantic Marshall amplifiers for obliterating volume, along with the Fuzz Face and a box called a Uni-Vibe that gave his guitar a whooshing, sloshing character. The guitar, that wooden box with strings, long too quiet for its own good, was in his hands an electric orchestra that could describe even the complexity and horror of war.

The crying and grinding from the Woodstock stage quieted into a familiar phrase, a few lonely high notes: *Gave proof through the night . . .* There, the onetime army boy snuck in a few bars of "Taps," the mournful old bugle call, respect for the departed. Then he sped into a lope, racing along, his tone rounded off by the wah-wah: *O say does that star-spangled banner yet wave.* After that, a massive crest of feedback rose and then broke apart, dissipating into ever-smaller torrents that radiated outward.

Stop. He cut off the feedback and paused.

Then, Jimi Hendrix began to moan out the final line—slowly, confessionally, as if to someone he knew intimately rather than nameless thousands.

O'er the land of the free . . .

The song moved to its close with another moan of monstrous feedback, the void roaring in, freedom as beauty, but freedom denied to so many. And then, in a quick spasm, brightly, immaculately: *and the home of the brave.*

The last notes trilled and rang in golden, liquid glory, and before they could feed back into acid, Jimi underscored them with a few broad, shining chords, the pride and the anguish all shimmering there in the humid morning, his performance conjuring truths about the United States of America that so many previous renditions of the song had failed to express.

IT HAD LASTED three minutes and forty-three seconds. Jimi Hendrix didn't stop to await applause for what he'd just done, to see if it was greeted with approbation or indifference. He rode the swell of feedback straight into "Purple Haze" and went on playing.

To the thousands standing agape on the mud fields of Woodstock, it was clear that something important had just occurred—the most unforgettable moment of the festival, perhaps of the era: "A quintessential piece of art," as Woodstock organizer Tom Law remembered it, that "hooked us up with Vietnam, with the devastation and the sin and the brutality and the insanity."

"Before that," said witness Roz Payne, "if someone would have played 'The Star-Spangled Banner,' we would have booed. After that, it became our song."

"It was probably the single greatest moment of the Sixties," said the music critic Al Aronowitz. "You finally heard what that song was about, that you can love your country, but hate the government."

A patriotic melody, rendered in a distorted electronic voice, cleaved in half by a sonic evocation of the horrors of war: By playing "The Star-Spangled Banner" that day, Hendrix cemented his reputation as the most vital American performer in rock after Bob Dylan. He gave a generation of Americans a new connection with their national anthem, showing that even this most patriotic of songs could embody their painfully conflicted views.

Jimi also elevated the electric guitar into a fully mature and capable voice, an instrument that could speak not only to young people but *for* them on the largest stages of the world.

A simple technology, radio equipment screwed into a wood-shop project, had become a tool for the most personal and most public yearnings. Nothing could be at once louder, more vivid, more chaotic, more *human*. When Jimi's soul cried, when that Stratocaster transformed his voice into a piercing electric wail, the whole world had to listen.

EPILOGUE

Eric Clapton was browsing through guitar shops in London on September 17, 1970, when he ran across a white Stratocaster. Its curves and color matched those of the guitar Jimi Hendrix had brought with him to London from New York almost exactly four years earlier, as well as the instrument he'd played at Woodstock the previous summer. Clapton knew he'd be seeing Jimi that very night: Sly and the Family Stone was due to headline the Lyceum Theatre on Wellington Street, and Jimi would certainly catch the show. So Clapton bought the guitar as a gift—a symbol of friendship toward the man who'd once dethroned his lordliness with a plain, pale Fender.

Clapton brought the guitar to the Lyceum, intending to give it to Jimi after the show. But Hendrix never appeared. He'd been spending time with a new German girlfriend that week, and had been behaving rather strangely, as friends would recall: showing up to jams too zonked on wine or speed or heroin to play, and forgetting his guitar besides. That very night, Jimi was scheduled to meet Sly Stone and others for an after-hours jam at the Speakeasy Club—a rare treat he wouldn't usually miss. But he never came to that, either.

The next morning, Clapton learned that Jimi Hendrix was dead. Instead of seeing Sly the previous evening, he'd gone to a party and spent the night at the apartment of his new girlfriend. Exhausted and desperate for rest, but riding a tumultuous mix of substances, Hendrix had taken a heavy dose of prescription sleeping pills, and the combination of drugs caused him to throw up in his sleep—but also kept him from waking up and gagging. Jimi had lain there and choked, dying of asphyxiation while his girlfriend slept beside him, sometime in the early morning hours of September 18, 1970.

Friends and fans were devastated by the loss of such a prodigious talent and such a warm, kind, and shy man. Eric Clapton felt the pain especially deeply, finding himself that Friday morning "filled with a feeling of terrible loneliness." In his presence, Hendrix had diminished some of Clapton's solitude; in his tragic and needless death, he reinforced it.

Inspired by Hendrix, countless future individuals would express themselves through the electric guitar, many in ways that couldn't be imagined in 1970. Yet there'd never be another guitar player quite like him, someone who seemed to find new possibilities for the instrument with every flick of his fingers. From that day on, listeners could only ponder the vast and thrilling recorded legacy Hendrix left behind, and imagine the surprises and revelations he might have concocted had he lived past the age of twenty-seven. Would he have gone into jazz with his friend Miles Davis? Prog rock with the English virtuosos? Punk metal, even?

Perhaps some glimpse of his project lived on through the career of Clapton, who continues to perform past his seventieth birthday, exploring many genres of music but always circling back to the blues. In the early seventies, only a few years after Jimi died, Clapton switched loyalties from various Gibson models to a Fender Stratocaster. Since then, he has played the double-cutaway Fender model almost exclusively among electric guitars. There is some irony in the fact that the man who resurrected the Gibson Les Paul Model in the midsixties became an icon inextricably linked with what is arguably Leo Fender's most beloved design. But it shows, perhaps, the inherent worthiness of each of these instruments—and the towering eminence of their namesakes.

IN THE YEARS when Jimi Hendrix was elevating the Stratocaster into the most iconic silhouette in rock music, CBS seemed to be doing everything possible to ruin the company that made it.

Leo Fender had believed in selling tools that would give a lifetime of service, knowing this meant fewer sales and less profit but more loyal customers. Under his leadership, the company strove to uphold strict standards of quality, and often (though not always) succeeded. Amps were made excessively sturdy; only the best cuts of wood were used for guitars; even the wiring for pickups was carefully selected and handled.

But in the new factory building CBS had erected next to the old Fender plant, workers struggled with cheaper components, a tolerance for poor build quality, and shoddy product designs. The consultants who'd written in 1964 that a staff of college-trained engineers could surely develop new products as well as Leo Fender were proven spectacularly wrong. After the CBS takeover, not a single new product from Fullerton achieved anything close to the reputation of the Fender classics. Leo's Telecaster, Stratocaster, Precision and Jazz basses, and virtually every amplifier he made between 1952 and 1965 would endure for decades as coveted vintage trophies or reissued models in near-continuous production. Later guitar designs, like the Jazzmaster and the Jaguar, would remain cherished underdogs, also in production.

The same couldn't be said of CBS-Fender's first major post-Leo product line, a prototype from which had appeared on Forrest White's desk in 1966. The more that White, then director of manufacturing, had looked at the new amplifier—a large, silvery box with futuristic details straight out of *The Jetsons*—the less he'd liked it. For one thing, there was no easy way to repair the amp. Ease of maintenance had been a Fender hallmark since the days of Leo's radio shop, because out on the road, in the hands of musicians, everything eventually breaks.

The more urgent problem with the prototype on White's desk was that it sounded awful. This amp, unlike any previously made by Fender, was solid state—that is, it relied not on old-fashioned glass vacuum tubes for power, but on transistors, the tiny semiconductors that would become an integral part of radios, calculators, and computers. Transistors were lighter, were cheaper, ran cooler, and to some ears, offered greater sonic fidelity than the 1920s vacuum tube technology. Leo had wanted to get out of Fender in part because he thought that more complex, transistor-driven amps would render his technical skills obsolete.

Well, *this* one sure wouldn't. CBS engineers had rushed out designs for the solid-state models, and in their haste had forgotten to make them sound good. White found the tone of this prototype flat and dull compared to the tube amps rolling out of Fullerton. Where a Deluxe Reverb or a larger Twin Reverb projected a lush, three-dimensional sonic image, adding so much character to the guitar that it qualified as an instrument on its own, this solid-state amp emitted just a dry brittleness. Pleasing character—not necessarily high fidelity—was what players wanted in a guitar amplifier, and this one didn't have it at low volumes or high ones.

White refused to approve the solid-state amp for production, declaring the amps unworthy of Leo Fender's name. According to his memoir, the resulting spat with CBS executives led to his resignation from Fender on December 6, 1966, ending his twelve-year run in Fullerton. White then went to work for the parent company of Gibson. CBS, meanwhile, released the hurried new solid-state amps to an icy reception from players and such abysmal sales that it abandoned the entire line a short while later. The company's first major research-and-development effort in Fullerton had proven a complete failure.

In these years, nearly every factory employee witnessed an episode in Fender's decline. Charlie Davis, a longtime worker in the plant and the service center, shuddered over the cheaper bridge CBS designed for the Stratocaster, which couldn't hold the whammy bar without its threads getting stripped, and, due to its lighter weight, didn't sound as good as the old one. Davis shook his head at the too-large drill bit CBS insisted on using on a hole for one component. He had to insert a toothpick in the hole to make sure the part stuck, and recalls four years of wrangling the corporate bureaucracy before that one drill bit was changed.

Abigail Ybarra continued winding the pickups for which she'd eventually become famous, having left her initials on some of the best-sounding Fender guitars of the fifties and sixties. She too was flabbergasted by the new mandate. Parts came to her workbench and pickups left her care that would never have passed quality standards before. "And CBS came and said use it, use everything," she recalled. "We had to get used to doing things like that."

Under Leo's management, Fender employees had expected to stay at the company for their entire working lives. Now that the founder was out of the picture, many started to question that assumption, especially given that few of their bosses felt the same way. Babe Simoni, who as a hotheaded new arrival had unknowingly yelled at Leo Fender back in the early fifties, took bets with his coworkers on how long each new CBS-installed department head would last. It became a belief at Fender that the parent company would send executives out to Fullerton to work as punishment, exiling them from the real action in New York.

Even Don Randall was struggling: trying to live in California, work in New York City, and run the sole manufacturing arm of a company whose real expertise lay in radio, television, and recording. The ruthless Ivy Leaguers who oversaw CBS pressed him for cost savings, and his once-loyal salesmen grew disgruntled. Randall had been forced to lower the commissions of the Fender jobbers he'd relied on for so long—some of whom had earned more per year than CBS chairman William Paley himself—and this led to a near-revolt. As usual, Randall answered the jobbers' complaints with a firm hand, writing in a letter of June 1967: "I am sure you all realize that the 'fairyland' in which you were living some day had to revert into something approaching reality." Though there was nothing Randall could do for his salesmen, the reality hit hard.

Randall began to wonder if perhaps he wasn't an organization man at heart, if he lacked the necessary cunning to climb a corporate ladder. At Fender, he'd made all the big decisions himself, with almost no one to second-guess him. Running the CBS musical instruments division was

entirely different: the commuting to the East Coast, the endless meetings, the corporate politics, the decisions-by-committee, the demands of
the bean counters. All these guys with PhDs who thought they knew the
guitar business but had no idea of what the average pro musician or teenage garage rocker really wanted. Leo Fender had certainly been cranky
and difficult to work with, but he'd valued his customers above all else.

One day in April 1969, Randall's oldest son, Don Jr., returned home
on a day when he thought his father was at work to find a brand-new
gold Cadillac parked in the driveway. Don Jr. thought it was the ugliest
car he'd ever seen—metallic paint and wheel skirts hanging under the
fenders; a typically gaudy late-sixties land yacht. He went inside to find
a beaming grin stretching across his father's square face. That morning,
Don Randall had told CBS to shove it. After four years as an underling
of William Paley, Randall had requested a release from his contract, quit
the corporate behemoth for good, and gone straight out to buy himself
a flashy new car.

The Caddy was only the latest symbol of Randall's remarkable success. The poor boy from a family of struggling Idaho farmers now owned
a collection of airplanes, and kept avocado and lemon trees on the spacious lands of his Tustin home. Still tanned and fit at fifty-one, Randall
felt himself ill suited for permanent retirement after leaving CBS. Aching
for a return to the business he loved, he founded his own eponymous
amplifier company the very next year, and ran it until 1987. Randall
Amplifiers still operates today, supplying formidable equipment to players like Metallica's Kirk Hammett.

Don Randall spent the rest of his life living comfortably in Orange
County, surrounded by his wife, Jean, and his three children—Don Jr.,
Kathy, and Tim—until he passed away on December 23, 2008, at the age
of ninety-one. Within the musical instrument industry, Randall became
widely recognized as a pioneer, a man whose genius for marketing and
gregarious personality rocketed a California upstart into the lead role
in its industry. Working with Fender ad man Bob Perine, Randall had
changed the image of the guitar in the popular mind, transforming it
from a specialized tool for professionals to an everyday consumer prod-

uct, a shapely and lively addition to the average American living room. Whether or not Leo fully appreciated his enormous and essential contribution to Fender's success—and it's likely he didn't—the company, the electric guitar, and popular culture wouldn't be what they are without Don Randall.

TWO YEARS AFTER selling his instrument business to CBS, Leo Fender visited a different doctor than the one who'd been treating his strep infection. This one tried something new. Leo later said it was a massive dose of antibiotics; other acquaintances recall that the treatment skirted the edge of legitimate medicine. Either way, after briefly making him very sick, this new fix did something the carrot juice, soup diets, and prior doctoring never had. It killed the strep.

Thus, within a few years of selling Fender, Leo had regained good health. In 1969, he turned sixty years old. He was now stunningly wealthy, with no growing factory to oversee anymore. Many years of life lay ahead, and Leo would make the most of them.

After the sale, Leo bought land around Southern California, eventually developing his own eighteen-acre business park along the newly named Fender Avenue in Fullerton. He became a private lender to close friends and associates. He was still under contract to develop instruments for CBS, but the company showed no interest in the new ideas he came up with. So he tried out retirement, ordering a new yacht from Stephens Brothers in Stockton almost every year until 1974, when he took delivery of a fifty-one-foot cruiser called the *Aquafen IX*. He and Esther traveled to China, Egypt, Hawaii, Alaska, and elsewhere; with his beloved Nikons, Leo photographed countless vacations and cruises, though usually training his lens on some mechanical device that would be invisible to anyone else, like the anchor winch on the bow of a ship.

Leo had known almost nothing else in his life besides work, and soon, it seems, he was bored with relaxation. He still ached to answer musicians' needs with the best possible equipment. He felt guilty about handing off his factory employees—whom he cared for and who had adored him—to the cold corporate atmosphere of CBS. And although he never quite said it himself, Leo almost certainly regretted selling the little company he'd founded in the back of a radio repair shop so many years earlier. Especially once he saw the lousy products CBS started to churn out under his name. Almost as soon as his noncompete clause with CBS expired, he leapt right back into making instruments.

Leo didn't want to run another large enterprise. Instead, he wanted, as the Fender historian Richard Smith put it, "a place to tinker and some friends around to have lunch with." In 1972, Leo Fender and Forrest White founded a new instrument company, bringing in former Fender veterans like George Fullerton and Babe Simoni. This outfit would eventually become Music Man, a Southern California enterprise that continues today. Though Leo funded the company and designed the instruments, he kept his involvement quiet. His Music Man StingRay electric bass would prove a classic design, and musicians loved the rich, tube-driven tone of Music Man amplifiers. A rift among the managers and financial problems eventually led to the sale of Music Man to a guitarist and entrepreneur named Ernie Ball, but by then, Leo had started another company.

"G&L" stood for "George and Leo"—Fullerton and Fender—although once again, Leo designed the instruments and put up most of the money. He and George worked closely together through the 1970s and '80s—so closely, in fact, that according to George's son, Geoff, Fullerton's house once had a private phone line to which only Leo knew the number, so he could call at any hour of the day and run ideas by the partner he'd had since 1948. Even when Leo was out on a cruise, it wasn't unusual for George to get calls from his friend late at night and, once he got on the line, to hear Leo pitch a new idea for a guitar pickup or bridge.

Leo and Esther traveled extensively, but by the end of the 1970s, their adventures ceased. Esther had fallen ill with lung cancer. To make life easier on her, the couple moved out of their spacious ranch house and into a mobile home on the north side of town. Leo might have been the only local yacht-owning millionaire who lived in a trailer park. But after a three-year battle with lung cancer, on August 1, 1979, Esther Fender died at the age of sixty-five. The vibrant, teetotaling party girl was still listed on her death certificate as a telephone operator—the steady job that had helped cover the paychecks at the Fender factory back in the 1940s and '50s, and had also likely encouraged her habit of smoking. She'd been an essential piece of the Fender project, not only with the financial support she'd given Leo, but in the bottomless confidence she placed in him.

Esther's passing shattered the normally stoic Leo Fender far more than many expected, or perhaps even realized. He felt loneliness and profound guilt at all the years he'd left her alone, especially those while she was ill with cancer. Seeing their close friend wracked with grief and guilt, George and Lucille Fullerton asked a friend from church, a divorcee named Phyllis, to come talk to him. Left alone with this kind, gregarious younger woman, Leo poured out his feelings. Phyllis became a regular at dinners with George, Lucille, and Leo, and the Fullertons soon saw Leo's spirits improve—indeed, they saw a chatty, even flirtatious side emerge from their laconic friend. Apparently, Leo only needed to be seated next to a cute blond woman to open up.

Only a year after Esther's death, Leo and Phyllis married, moving into a comfortable hillside house in Fullerton. The newlyweds honeymooned on a cruise boat, where, on the first night, Phyllis entered their stateroom bathroom to find a small, elegant black box on the counter. She thought it was a gift Leo had slyly left behind, a little extra present to celebrate their nuptials. She opened it, and found instead a shiny brown glass eye. In all the time they'd known each other, all through their courtship and wedding, Leo Fender hadn't said a word about his childhood accident.

When he and Phyllis weren't taking cruises, Leo's life followed the same pattern it had for decades. Each day he awoke, dressed, drove for ten minutes in his cushy white Lincoln down to the plant, and went in to work in a windowless office where he spent the day designing components for new guitars. Even as his reputation grew dramatically with the popularity of rock music, Leo rejected the idea that the models he'd designed in the 1950s and '60s were superior to what he made in the present. G&L produced a full line of electric guitars and basses, many of them packed with innovative new features, and, as much as he could, Leo resisted copying the old shapes and designs of classic instruments like the Telecaster and Stratocaster.

Although G&L was minuscule compared to Fender, Leo's new firm came into conflict with his old one. There was sniping about the shape of its headstocks, just as there'd been in the mid-fifties with Paul Bigsby, and legal action over G&L's use of the name Leo Fender, rights to which CBS had purchased in 1965.

Most intriguing, though, was a 1970s CBS-issued trade magazine article asserting that Freddie Tavares, who'd worked in Leo's lab during the fifties, actually designed several of Fender's classic instruments. Several Fender employees would later make such arguments in interviews and memoirs, claiming credit for certain features, but this one particularly enraged Leo. He'd apparently been scratching out a diagram for a new circuit and calculating some figures on a yellow legal pad when he saw the story. He quickly began writing out a response, addressing it to CBS president William Paley himself.

"Fred Tavares was employed in late 1953 as a laboratory assistant and handyman," Fender wrote. "He did not design the amplifiers, the Telecaster guitar, the bass, the Stratocaster, the various steel guitars . . . Nor did he design the tooling to produce the foregoing. This can be verified." The article, Fender wrote, was "untruthful and defamatory," and "could cause [him] several million dollars damage." There's no evidence that this note, with the calculations and circuit diagram above the text, was ever sent. But it shows that Fender was keenly aware of the need to protect his growing reputation.

In the new guitar magazines sprouting up in the seventies, and among collectors of vintage instruments especially, Fender was seen as almost the founder of a new religion. But in the letter, Leo revealed the more earthly concerns in his mind: the designs he wanted credit for, and the more than fifty patents under his name that he sought to protect. Perhaps even more than the instruments themselves, those patents were Leo's truest legacy, documents of the workings of his peculiar mind in the language of the engineer and industrial designer. According to the present owners of G&L, who kept Leo's handwritten letter to William Paley in their files, Freddie Tavares later apologized to Leo in person and retracted any claim that he'd designed Fender instruments.

The episode nonetheless points to a lingering question about Leo's work and legacy. There were numerous musicians around at all stages of Fender's development, suggesting ideas, rejecting them, demonstrating through their crude modifications to the instruments what changes they wanted. And Leo Fender rarely started from scratch with any of his designs. His first solid-body guitar borrowed key ideas from Paul Bigsby and Rickenbacker, as well as some inspiration from Les Paul. The most original instrument Leo created—his proudest achievement—was the Precision Bass. Everything else had had a clear ancestor, and all Fender products had benefited from the input of the guinea-pig players hanging around the factory. Yet no matter the extent of any other contributions—contributions that can be hard to judge given the distance of years—Leo's name alone ended up on the patents.

Too, the products were ultimately his responsibility. He had final say over everything the company designed and released from 1946 to 1964; he invested his funds and years of his life—and Esther's—in making them a success. Thinking up ideas for an instrument wasn't the same as wagering one's future on it. That certain features or details came from George Fullerton, Bill Carson, Jimmy Bryant, Freddie Tavares, Noel Boggs, or dozens of other Fender factory denizens is true and shouldn't be discounted; in some ways, Fender instruments were a team effort. Without Doc Kauffman getting Leo interested in building electric steel guitars and amps during World War II, the laconic radio repairman likely never would have founded an instrument company, as he himself admitted. But the importance of the notions that bubbled up from Fender employees or Leo's acquaintances pales next to the achievement of building the ideas into a mass-produced instrument that millions of people could afford and enjoy—one that changed the sound and look of popular music. That achievement was Leo's alone.

Almost immediately after Fender's success became clear in the late fifties, competitors began copying its designs. By the 1970s, any instrument with three single-coil pickups, two cutaways, and a blotchy white pickguard was, in the public mind, *just* an electric guitar, something almost every manufacturer made—not specifically a Fender Stratocaster. Leo took a certain pride in seeing the way other firms, especially those from Asia, copied his designs down to the last detail, even if that detail had been added by mistake and served no purpose. By the early 1980s, with CBS-Fender at its nadir of quality and reputation, the immaculate Stratocaster and Telecaster copies coming from Japan found more favor with players than the American models. In 1985 CBS, running deeply in the red, finally decided to get out of the instrument business and sold the Fender brand to a group of private investors. It did *not*, however, sell the Fullerton buildings—so for about a year, while the new owners built a manufacturing facility in Corona, California, and sold only imported instruments, Fender ceased to exist as an American company. By the late eighties, under the new management of William Schultz, Fender Musical Instruments was rising to become the industry leader it is today, producing a vast line of models and running a custom shop that turned out museum-worthy new guitars.

Meanwhile, Leo and George persisted at G&L. They built some great products, though never anything as revelatory as the Stratocaster or the Precision Bass. Times had changed in manufacturing and in music, and Leo Fender couldn't relate to the headbangers or New Wavers of the eighties as he had to the cowboys and jazzmen of the forties and fifties. Neither he nor many other veterans of the Fender company much liked where guitar music was going, but Leo toiled on, seeing himself, as Phyllis Fender recalls, as a servant of musicians. As guitar culture grew, Fender earned wider recognition for the enormous contributions he'd made. He'd been given an award by the Country Music Association in 1965 and later earned a technical Grammy for his work. More acclamation would come, but as always, Leo preferred to remain outside of the spotlight. Apart from sometimes chatting up the members of cruise ship bands, Leo didn't rush to tell strangers who he was, and he found it uncomfortable to be recognized in public. Except perhaps to tweak an amplifier, he'd never been one for going onstage.

In 1984 or 1985, Leo was diagnosed with Parkinson's disease, and its onset made it increasingly difficult for him to interact with others or make himself understood. Nonetheless, he continued to go to work every day at G&L, having lunch with George Fullerton and working on designs late into the evenings at the home he shared with Phyllis.

On the morning of March 21, 1991, Phyllis noticed that she didn't hear the usual snoring from Leo's side of the house. She went into the room where Leo worked and saw his body lying on the floor where he'd fallen. She called the paramedics, but it was no use. Parkinson's and work had finally exhausted the tireless radio repairman, and he was pronounced dead at St. Jude Medical Center in Fullerton. After patenting more than fifty inventions and designs, creating a handful of iconic instruments and amplifiers, and making his name beloved by players around the world—after eighty-one years of life, spanning from the age of the horse and buggy to the age of the Space Shuttle—the humble, quiet, glass-eyed Leo Fender had died. He'd achieved more than he could have imagined, more than he ever expected, more than perhaps he even knew. Leo himself had gone silent, but the instruments that bear his name won't cease to make music any time soon.

THE OPEN BAR was stocked and ready. Buffet tables stretched out in a long line, stacked with ribs, chicken, and shrimp. Inside the Hard Rock Cafe on Fifty-Seventh Street in Manhattan, organizers decided to move Les Paul's seventy-second birthday party from an upper balcony to the entire place, shutting down the restaurant to the public. Later that night, June 9, 1987, it became clear why. Arriving guests included guitar heroes Jeff Beck and Jimmy Page, both of whom had flown in from London. Robbie Krieger of the Doors showed up. So did Chic guitarist Nile Rodgers and rockabilly pioneer Duane Eddy. Tony Bennett arrived. MTV, *Rolling Stone*, WNBC, the New York *Daily News*, *People*, and *USA Today* all sent reporters. The Hard Rock Cafe faced twice the number of scheduled attendees as fire marshals would allow inside. Partiers stood shoulder to shoulder, pouring sweat on that warm Manhattan evening.

And finally there arrived the birthday boy himself, stepping out of a long black limo: Les Paul, his thinning frame sheathed in a baby-blue turtleneck, his boyish blue eyes glowing in joy at this magnificent party, these famous guests—all for *him*. Twenty years earlier, or even ten or five, such a resplendent tribute wouldn't have seemed possible.

Les Paul had learned that having your name on a popular guitar isn't the same as being popular yourself. Gibson had reissued the Les Paul Model in 1969, and it became the cornerstone of the company's solid-body line. As Led Zeppelin, Black Sabbath, and other bands transformed blues rock into hard rock, and then hard rock into heavy metal, the Les Paul guitar became ubiquitous. By the 1980s, MTV showed Aerosmith's Joe Perry and Guns N' Roses' Slash strutting around, their bare chests exposed, sunburst Les Pauls hanging at a conspicuous distance below their waist. Even the rock underground favored the smallish body and overpowering tone of the Gibson: the Sex Pistols' Steve Jones played a Les Paul, as did the Stooges' James Williamson, demonstrating the power of those dual humbucking pickups for punk. After its revival in the mid-1960s, the original Gibson solid-body reigned superior in hard rock.

Yet through the 1960s and early 1970s, Les himself remained an obscure figure, working quietly at his rural New Jersey home, retired from the stage. How did he, the boy who'd come of age on a Waukesha bandstand, endure this? Painfully, it seems. Like his old friend and rival Leo Fender, Les Paul didn't enjoy the music of the time. He could see the theoretical appeal of distorted electric guitars, but after spending decades pursuing a resplendent, muscular, clean tone on the instrument, he wasn't about to trade it away for the sake of fashion.

He also endured a period of extremely bad luck. In 1969, a friend jokingly slapped Les on the right side of the head, accidentally cupping his hand over the ear and damaging the eardrum. Les underwent several surgeries to try to fix the problem, but, as he writes in his memoir, none proved successful. Incredibly, almost the same thing happened to Les's left ear in 1972. After five surgeries altogether to improve his hearing, Les still relied on a hearing aid, finding himself unable to assess his playing with the same clarity he once had.

As if losing his audience and then his ears wasn't bad enough, Les began losing his fingers, too. His arthritis, which he'd struggled with since 1961, worsened. Known for playing complex, frilly leads, and for the careful precision with which he could issue even the fastest, most demanding passages on the guitar, Les now bore witness to the slow decline of his abilities as his fingers painfully refused to execute their commands.

Les never stopped tinkering with electronics at his home studio in Mahwah and was still developing the gadgets and designs that produced the guitar and recording sounds he wanted. He had essentially invented multitracking, which came of age with the huge recording budgets of the 1970s. He'd pioneered the sound of the solid-body electric guitar. And yet, of course, he still wasn't satisfied. In these years, Les worked on developing a new style of pickup he believed would revolutionize his instrument once again.

A surprising thing had happened in the years after 1965, when Les retired from the road: he and Mary Ford had rekindled a close friendship. It wasn't a romantic relationship, as Mary had already remarried, but she and Les would spend hours together on the phone, talking about their past, their children, their music. She too eventually gave up performing in favor of family life. But unfortunately, its joys didn't alleviate her depression or help cure her alcoholism. After years of heavy drinking, Mary had developed diabetes, but she still didn't quit the bottle. Les writes that Mary would call him late at night through the early and mid-seventies to reminisce about their past. On one of these calls, in the late summer of 1977, she complained to Les about having blurred vision—a symptom of her diabetes. Les told her to go immediately to a doctor, but she didn't. A couple of weeks later, according to biographer Mary Shaughnessy, Mary Ford fell into a diabetic coma and was rushed to the hospital.

Though the family played her old records and soothed her with conversation, Mary Ford never woke up. She passed away on September 30, 1977, at Methodist Hospital in Arcadia, east of Pasadena, California, at fifty-three years old: a singer and guitarist who was as famous in her time as a musician can get. Mary Ford had played an essential role in attaining the celebrity she and Les had enjoyed, the stature that led to his endorsement deal with Gibson, and thus she helped bring about the birth of that iconic instrument. But Mary had also stood onstage as a gifted player and singer in her own right, a woman who showed herself to be at least her husband's equal when it came to entertaining an audience, and a ready match for him on the guitar. Though discounted by many men—including Les himself—Mary Ford pioneered a starring role as the guitar-playing female singer, a role ever more women would follow. By the time of her death, a generation of female rockers in bands like the Runaways, the Pretenders, and the Go-Go's were starting down the path that Mary Ford, the pretty Pasadena girl who sang country-style and tore up an electric fretboard, had blazed for them.

Though Les didn't attend Mary's funeral, he was shattered by her death. Only upon losing her, it seems, did he truly come to appreciate the close bond they'd had—a bond broken more by the demands of performing than by true incompatibility. "What stayed with me was a very deep appreciation for how fortunate Mary and I were," Les wrote in his autobiography. "Very few in this world are that lucky. There were things between us, regrettable things we both did that hurt, but with a love like ours, the bad things go with time, and the good things are there forever."

The pain of her loss was compounded by the passing of Les's friend Bing Crosby only two weeks later, cementing the feeling that the end of an era had come. For Les himself, though, a brighter new age was beginning—a slow resurgence that would ultimately bring him to a crowded and opulent party at the Hard Rock Cafe in Manhattan.

His return to public notice began with an album he recorded with country wizard Chet Atkins. *Chester and Lester* featured the two guitarists trading licks over a subdued background, chatting and ribbing each other between tunes, showing off their easygoing virtuosity. To everyone's surprise, the album—tracked live in a Nashville studio over two days, during which Les and Chet bickered constantly—proved a tremendous hit. It was a thrill to have such talents in such a low-key setting, to hear not just their playing but their attempts to one-up and belittle each other. In addition to finding commercial success, the album won Les Paul his first Grammy Award. (The awards weren't bestowed until 1959, well after Les's first popular peak.) The two veteran artists performed live at the Grammy Awards ceremony in February 1977: a couple of aging white guys flicking around their shiny guitars, all alone on a stage. With Les back in the public eye, players like Peter Frampton approached him to issue informal tributes. Here was the man whose name graced the guitars every young rocker loved. He was still alive, and despite the arthritis, he could still play. More awards, for recording and songwriting, soon followed.

But what really changed things for Les was his rediscovery of public performance. He'd been appearing before crowds almost since he got that first harmonica at age eight, and in retirement, he'd forgotten how much he needed it, how badly he craved a chance to jam and tell the jokes he'd collected and filed on index cards. After the Grammy Awards and a few other public performances, Les decided to put a small group together for a run of shows in New York. The first one took place on Monday, March 26, 1984, at Fat Tuesday's, a cramped club on Third Avenue. Monday night is not usually a popular night for live music, but Les drew such an enthusiastic crowd that his run was extended, then extended again. Soon, it became a standing engagement: the Les Paul Trio performing live, every Monday night in New York City. Les's regular shows became a draw for musicians all over the world, from every generation. Guest players ran the gamut from old jazz friends like Tal Farlow and George Benson to eighties stalwarts like Eddie Van Halen and Billy Idol, and of course, the illuminati of the sixties rock scene: Jeff Beck, Jimmy Page, and Keith Richards.

With Les returned to prominence, paying tribute to him became almost a national pastime. That, in part, is what led to the blowout at the Hard Rock Cafe for his seventy-second birthday, but it wasn't only a celebration. The event was intended to soothe the frayed relationship between Les and Gibson, the guitar company he felt was paying insufficient attention to the namesake of one of its most popular models.

Like its rival Fender, Gibson had stumbled along a difficult path after

278 ~w~ THE BIRTH OF LOUD

its golden years in the 1950s and early '60s. In 1969, the company was sold to a conglomerate called Norlin, which treated Gibson much as CBS treated Fender, penny-pinching its instruments into low-quality shadows of their former glory. The arrival of Asian imports in the seventies further decimated Gibson's bottom line until, in 1986, Norlin sold the brand to a group of private investors. New CEO Henry Juszkiewicz soon made the company profitable, but he had a major endeavor on his hands. He would lead the new Gibson to more than two decades of success, selling new and reissued models that were widely adored. But as computerized instruments (samplers, drum machines, especially laptops) came to play an ever-greater role in pop music, Juszkiewicz invested in expensive companies and technologies many players saw as tangential, at best, to Gibson's line of guitars. In the middle of 2018, the Gibson company, squirming under mountains of debt from these acquisitions, filed for Chapter 11 bankruptcy to refocus on making musical instruments. Its guitar line—led by the Les Paul Models—is now regarded as its core asset.

Back in 1987, Juszkiewicz had appeared on the brink of losing that famous name, with other manufacturers lurking, hoping to get the legend's endorsement. So that summer, despite having more pressing things to do, Juszkiewicz had no choice but to show some public appreciation. A party—a huge one—was necessary to win back Les Paul's favor.

The event proved bigger than anyone expected, with the crowd in the Hard Rock Cafe swelling likely beyond capacity. Jimmy Page and Jeff Beck held court at a VIP table near the stage. Paul Shaffer's band had come up from David Letterman's TV studio to provide backing for the night. Everyone was sweaty and excited, riding high on gratis cocktails. And with the lords of forty years of pop music assembled in one room, the tributes to Les poured forth. Les's Gibson guitar had kept his name in circulation, but many testified to the influence of his work as a pop star, the mind-blowing multitracked records he'd made with Mary Ford. "I had an LP at a very early age, when I was about fifteen or sixteen, and I was just totally mesmerized by it," Jimmy Page told a reporter. "The pure imagination of it, its arrangements . . . it's just in a total world of its own, and obviously it was a total inspiration." Page was among the most iconic devotees of the Les Paul, but to hear the genius behind Led Zeppelin's thunderous sound express his appreciation for Les and Mary's sweet, swirling little melodies showed just how deeply the couple's records had cut.

At eleven p.m., Henry Juszkiewicz went onstage to introduce Les, who beamed through the entire evening. The Hard Rock Cafe staff presented Les with an onyx-and-marble model of his signature guitar, and then the jamming began: First with a few instrumental jazz numbers, the kind of stuff Les played with his trio every Monday night. Soon, Page went up and, along with jazz whiz Al Di Meola, turned the proceedings into a raucous blues jam. Les's shiny Gibson had to fight through the noise of Page's crunchy distortion, but somehow it did—you could hear him loud and clear, his guitar punchy and thick but still purely clean, twiddling out runs with almost the same precision he'd always had. Arthritis had sapped some of his flash, but Les had adjusted his playing in response, reducing his reliance on technical passages and emphasizing single, powerful notes.

The party didn't end until after three a.m. Reports of it appeared in the national media over the coming days and weeks. Les Paul, the technical genius and forgotten pop star, had been restored to household-name status in the world of American music.

More tributes and awards would follow in future years, along with numerous documentaries and interviews. Les's arthritis continued to worsen, and he continued to need (and tinker with) his hearing aids—but nothing kept him from the regular Monday-night performances he gave in New York City. When Fat Tuesday's closed in 1995, Les moved his trio's gig uptown to Times Square, to the more comfortable Iridium, where his shows—an intimate mix of music, comedy, storytelling, and famous guests—remained a strong draw.

As ever, the stories Les told onstage and in countless interviews were deeply embellished, sometimes to the point of absurdity, making the task of sorting out the facts of his life incredibly difficult. Les would go on to make all sorts of assertions about being in various impossible places at impossible times; he would allow himself to get credit for things he hadn't done—a strange habit, as if he feared what he had done was somehow not enough. But for Les, facts were never to get in the way of a good story.

Most egregious were the claims that Les "invented" the solid-body electric guitar—claims he never exactly made himself, but also never quite denied. Usually, those arguing the point cite the Log he made in 1940–41 as evidence, and indeed, the Log was a vital step in the electric guitar's development. But it was a proving ground, an experiment, rather than a viable instrument. It was a one-off attempt that Les built for himself and only seldom used.

Tracing the electric guitar to one single designer or inventor is impossible. Like many modern inventions, it developed in numerous different places in numerous different hands. Solid-bodied electric steel guitars were invented for Hawaiian-style playing in 1931. Other standard electric guitars were built in tiny numbers in the 1930s and '40s, and though none attained much influence, several absolutely predated the Log. It was Paul Bigsby who built the prototype for the modern electric solid-body in 1948, based on a picture Merle Travis drew for him. After Leo Fender saw this instrument, he borrowed its ideas to design his Telecaster, which was released in 1951 as the first true production solid-body electric guitar.

Les Paul also gets credit for designing his Gibson signature model, when the work of guitar researchers like Robb Lawrence (and the testimony of former Gibson president Ted McCarty) shows that in fact a team of Gibson staff members created the instrument. Les left his mark on the guitar in several ways, and he obviously helped make it famous. But he didn't sketch it out, prototype it, or do any of the true design work. It appeared very close to its final form when McCarty presented it to Les in the fall of 1951, asking for his endorsement.

What Les deserves far more credit for is his guitar playing—his pioneering of the instrument as a lead tool for pop music, and his seduction of American listeners with flashy tricks and solos many had never heard before. He truly *did* make the electric guitar into a new instrument, as *DownBeat* wrote back in 1953.

The greatest piece of Les Paul's legacy, when seen from the second decade of the twenty-first century, is what he accomplished in the studio. Not only did Les first recognize the artistic possibilities of layering different recordings on top of one another, but he pioneered a style of music-making that is ubiquitous today, in an age in which almost every musician—guitarists, bassists, drummers, singers, keyboardists, DJs, whoever—owns and controls their own studio, whether in the form of sophisticated hardware or a basic computer program like Apple's Garage-Band. Les Paul was the first player to claim the studio as an instrument, a move so common today that we often forget to remark on it. Les aimed to control not only the music that went onto the canvas of recorded sound, but everything about the canvas itself: the framing, the immaculateness of the background, the depth and layering of the sounds, and where it hung on the viewer's wall. Today, music-making is almost inseparable from production; with the rise of hip-hop and electronic music, it's virtually impossible to think of most songs apart from their recordings. This path was first cut by Les Paul, inside the garage of that little Hollywood bungalow, in the years immediately following World War II.

Yet as much as he was a genius in the studio, Les was, at heart, a creature of the stage. After starting his Monday-night trio dates at Fat Tuesday's in 1984, he continued them through the 1990s, and then past the turn of the millennium, giving countless thousands of fans a chance to see the legend and pay tribute. Arthritis sapped the spryness from his fingers, his hearing deteriorated, but Les Paul returned to Times Square every week to sit on his high stool and tell jokes and stories to his fans. The weekly ritual continued until August 12, 2009, when the Wizard of Waukesha passed away at a hospital in White Plains, New York, finished off not by a car accident, or heart troubles, or electrocution, but complications from pneumonia. At age ninety-four, the man born Lester Polsfuss had lived until the very end at his comfortable country manse, surrounded by stacks of recording equipment and hundreds of electric guitars, most of which bore his name.

The world since has been a little quieter.

ACKNOWLEDGMENTS

I started planning this book as a graduate student in Samuel G. Freedman's Book Seminar at Columbia University, during the first winter I lived on the East Coast, over a sprint of sleepless weeks that in some ways feels like a lifetime ago. Over almost four years, I've traveled thousands of miles on planes, trains, buses, on foot, and in a fleet of rental cars; spent hundreds of hours poring through file boxes in various libraries; shared breakfast with sources I thought I'd never meet; and got turned down by others I thought would be no problem. A number of people I was hoping to talk to for this book—the singer Kay Starr, the guitarist Tommy Allsup—sadly passed away while I was in the midst of arranging to meet them.

But I had some idea of what I was getting into, thanks to the support, patience, information and occasional admonishment given in the Book Seminar, that greatest of graduate courses. (Or whatever amalgam of boot camp and literary indoctrination program it best resembles.) Thank you, Sam Freedman, for all your help in making real this contribution to the cause of cultural literacy. May it please the ancestors.

The early days of this project benefited greatly from the wisdom of a few great writer-teachers in Columbia's graduate nonfiction writing program. Directional guidance came from Lis Harris, Richard Locke, Brenda Wineapple, and, although I doubt he knew it back then, Daniel Bergner. The great Patricia O'Toole was a model of dedication and a vital help when it came to research methods. Clifford Thompson and Mark Rotella read some of this story in the form of a thesis, and offered helpful ideas on how to improve it. I'm still awed by the expansive knowledge and generosity of these folks, and thankful for their encouragement in pursuing what must have seemed, in New York City in 2015, a pretty obscure subject.

Many previous writers and researchers laid the groundwork for this book, and a few personally helped my efforts along. Richard R. Smith shared not just his vast archive of documents covering the history of the Fender company, but his intimate knowledge of the personalities involved. His book, *Fender: The Sound Heard 'Round the World*, remains the essential source for in-depth knowledge about Fender and its instruments. Richard, it was incredible fun becoming your friend, and I can never thank you enough.

Everywhere you go in the world of guitar history, you find the name Tom Wheeler—he published a shelf of terrifically well-researched and well-written volumes on the subject, several of which I referenced frequently during this project. I spoke with Tom early on in my research, gleaned a bit of his wisdom, and got some vital help. I was saddened by his passing in February 2018.

On the Les Paul side of the story, my efforts were enabled by the dogged research of biographer Mary Shaughnessy, who was kind enough to share some of her thoughts on Les and Mary and their era. Robb Lawrence also helped, both with an interview and with his enthusiastic books on Les. Deke Dickerson was another friend to the project and helped greatly in clarifying the Bigsby-Fender debate. Andy Babiuk has written several gorgeous, informative volumes about the instruments of the Beatles, the Rolling Stones, and Paul Bigsby, and was kind enough to think through some of the thornier issues with me. John Blair lent some of his vast knowledge of the history of surf music. Writer and historian Rich Kienzle helped this project through countless articles, liner notes, and an interview. Ron Middlebrook offered context, photographs, and encouragement.

Contributing new information and insight to the story of the electric guitar was always my goal, and I couldn't have achieved it without the help of the employees, friends, and family members who sat for multiple long interviews. Tim Randall, Don Randall Jr., and Chelena Grimshaw all made a huge contribution by sharing memories, papers, and photographs, and by allowing me access to the files of their father, Don. I am deeply grateful.

I will remain ever in debt to Phyllis Fender, Leo Fender's second wife, for her enthusiasm for this book from its earliest days, and for her willingness to be interviewed by a stranger from New York. Phyllis, I'd love to buy you lunch at Polly's, if you'll ever let me.

Many thanks are also owed to Gary and Alan Gray, Leo Fender's nephews, for their vivid recollections of their uncle, his wife, his workplace, and the various characters who careened through it. Charlie Davis spent hours telling me firsthand what it was *really* like to work at Fender, as did Bob Trujillo and Christine Aguirre and their families, as did Bob Rissi. Roger and Robert Kohlenberger helped me find a recording of their father, Bill, talking about working at Leo Fender's radio shop. John Neal told me about his father's construction projects for Fender. The great steel guitarist Herb Remington told me how he came to meet Leo and play with Bob Wills. Shorty Robbins did the same. Dick Stephens, the Stockton boatbuilder, drew a verbal portrait of Leo I couldn't have found elsewhere. Geoff Fullerton, George's son, sat for a very long interview in which he relayed a ton of useful information. Thank you, Geoff, and I eagerly await your book about Fender. Dannielle Robertson, aka Sandy Boggs, daughter of the great steel guitarist Noel Boggs, shared details on Leo and Esther that became essential to telling their story.

Bob Summers and his wife kindly invited me into their home one long afternoon to talk about Mary Ford (aka Colleen Summers), Les Paul, and more. Drew Berlin helped me think through the legacy of Les

Paul, and shared great details about the auction of his instruments. Buddy McPeters, Mary Bigsby, Terry Tavares, John Hall, and Chris Montez all helped clarify various pieces of this story. Carol Kaye welcomed me into her home and spoke candidly about her life and her music for hours on several different occasions, providing essential color and detail. Thank you so much, Carol.

I also came to depend on the knowledge of several guitar builder-experts, most notably Lynn Wheelwright, Steve Soest, and the amplifier guru Paul Morte, who helped me understand various details and claims. The vintage guitar expert George Gruhn weighed in on several issues relating to the book, and though we interpret some things differently, I'm grateful for his thoughtfulness. To all of the experts I met at the Wichita-Sedgwick County Historical Museum's Electric Guitar Symposium—including John Troutman, Eric Cale, Matthew Hill, and Arian Sheets—thank you for the kindness and the education.

One of the many pleasures of doing a book like this is befriending librarians and research assistants around the country who vibrate with enthusiasm for their subject. Cheri Pape, at the Fullerton Public Library's Local History Room, directed me not just to everything Fender but everything Fullerton. And I owe a giant debt of gratitude to Dan Del Fiorentino, Katie Wheeler, and Bethany Gilbert at the National Association of Music Merchants Library and Oral History Program, for making available the full recordings of NAMM interviews with many of the key subjects in this book. I'd also like to thank the research staffs at the Rock and Roll Hall of Fame Library and Archives (especially Jennie Thomas), the Country Music Hall of Fame, the New York Public Library for the Performing Arts, the Los Angeles Public Library, the Santa Monica Public Library, the UCLA Center for Oral History Research, the Rutgers University Institute of Jazz Studies, the Costa Mesa Historical Society, the Santa Maria Historical Society, and Jane Ishibashi at Fullerton College. I'm sure I've forgotten some, so if you liked this book, hug a librarian.

A number of people were elemental to turning this idea into a book. My agent, Chris Calhoun, believed in a proposal about a bunch of guitar-building weirdos on the West Coast, and saw to it that I was able to concentrate on researching and writing their story for a blessedly long period. At Scribner, the brilliant Rick Horgan shared a vision for what this tale could be and pushed me hard to realize it. Emily Greenwald provided helpful insights and shepherded the book through its many phases. Aja Pollock saved me from a number of embarrassments. So many others helped, too—thank you all for your excellence and patience.

You have to feel sorry for writers' friends: the generous ones get buried by drafts and then blasted by their friends' insecurities. Among the readers I could count on for sympathy and brutality were Sean Hurley (who probably has read more of this book than anyone but its author); Noah Gallagher Shannon (who cheerfully persisted through two drafts and made brilliant suggestions); and my former *SF Weekly* colleagues and friends Anna Roth and Brandon Reynolds, who read and pondered along with me. Thanks to Katie Zanecchia, who gave support and guidance about the world of publishing. Matty Van Meter and Constanza Martinez, my writing workshop family from Columbia, encouraged me to go down this path. You're all the best, and I'll read the shit out of those manuscripts you all goddamn better write.

One strange thing about writing a book about other people is that some essential part of yourself ends up in their story. So this book is in some ways a product of the people who made me: my parents and family, who contributed ideas, criticisms, and memories to this project, as well as meals, transportation, and bedrooms. Thank you to the Innerest Circle: Blake Criswell, Chloe Gates, Michael Mullan, Peter Feytser, and Sean Hurley. Thanks to Cody Nabours for telling me about all kinds of great music. Thanks to Auntie T and Fred for their love and humor. Thanks to my wife's parents, Brent and Marcy, who believed in this book and talked it up to everyone they knew, and did so much more. The deepest gratitude to Mom (Perrin Krumbuegel), Dad (Thomas Port), Judy Thomas, and Marco Krumbuegel for encouraging me to be who I am, and for believing in the wisdom of this path. I love you all. (Dad, next time I need a book idea, let's just drive up to Napa.)

Gratitude is not a big enough word for what I owe my companion in life, Lindsay Criswell, whose kindness and patience resemble those of a saint, but whose sense of humor thankfully does not. This project was often difficult and sometimes deeply discouraging, but I always found comfort in having someone so brilliant, fierce, and lovable in my corner. Without her, it never could have happened. We got guns hidden under our petticoats, lady. I love you.

And lastly, thanks to the heroes of this book, Leo Fender and Les Paul and the others, who helped make the sound of the music that has made my life.

NOTES AND SOURCES

This book is built from hours of interviews with firsthand witnesses to these events, as well as leading historians of them; private documents of which I was granted use; public records; oral histories (some never previously accessed); memoirs, biographies, and autobiographies of those involved; archival materials; films, photographs, and recordings and their liner notes; museum exhibits; newspaper and magazine articles; and about a hundred other books. I was fortunate to be granted access to the original Fender company documents collected by guitar historian Richard R. Smith, and to the private papers of Don Randall, as well as to a cache of never-before-used oral histories captured on video by the archivists of the National Association of Music Merchants. (A complete accounting of the many favors I received in assembling this book is in the acknowledgments.)

As all writers of history do, I came to rely on the work (both published and not) of prior authors and researchers, and I have tried to mention the names of the most important ones in the text itself. Among the authors and researchers without whose dedicated efforts this book could not have been written are Richard R. Smith, Mary Alice Shaughnessy,

Tom Wheeler, Robb Lawrence, Andy Babiuk, Geoff Fullerton, Robert Gordon, A. R. Duchossoir, Philip Norman, and Charles Cross.

In a handful of places, I have extended the details of a scene slightly beyond the spoken or written accounts of it, or drawn reasonable conclusions from the available information. In these constructions, no verifiable fact was ever ignored or changed. If conflicting views or details exist, they are given. In places where I discuss a character's unspoken thoughts, those thoughts were recorded elsewhere.

PROLOGUE

2 *just after Christmas 1964: The T.A.M.I. Show* opened in Austin on December 29, 1964, according to the *Austin American-Statesman*; in Los Angeles December 26, according to the *Los Angeles Times*; and in Washington, DC, on December 26, according to the *Washington Post*.

2 *frivolous teen movies:* See, for instance, Ann Bordelon, "Who Goes to Movies? Teenagers," *Austin American-Statesman*, December 31, 1964.

2 *"Adults, unaware of the differences":* "Rock 'n' Roll: Shrieks at the Center Indicate Popular Film," *Boston Globe*, December 31, 1964.

2 *pursuit of such:* The *Los Angeles Sentinel*, a black newspaper, noted on November 5, 1964, that "the rollicking inter-racial dance group appearing throughout the flick might anger some Southern Whites."

4 *completely different competition:* In his autobiography, *Life* (New York: Little, Brown, 2010), Keith Richards writes of listening to the Beach Boys: "There was no particular correlation with what we were doing, so I could just listen to it on another level."

CHAPTER 1

7 *apartment in Queens:* Les Paul and Michael Cochran, *Les Paul in His Own Words* (San Francisco: Backbeat Books, 2005, 2016), 89.

7 *allergic to mornings:* Les was well-known for his nocturnal habits and dislike of mornings, as Mary Alice Shaughnessy writes in many places in her authoritative biography *Les Paul: An American Original* (New York: William Morrow, 1993).

7 *jazz jam sessions:* Paul and Cochran, *Les Paul in His Own Words*, 109; Shaughnessy, *Les Paul*, 88–89.

7 *barrel back across:* According to Shaughnessy in *Les Paul*, 85, Les once got caught driving seventy-five miles per hour on the bridge in his Buick and talked his way out of a ticket.

8 *a proud Renaissance Revival building:* The Epiphone factory was located at 142 West Fourteenth Street, in a building that now is occupied by the Pratt Institute.

8 *made an arrangement:* Paul and Cochran, *Les Paul in His Own Words*, 102.

8 *torn apart and reassembled:* Ibid., 18–19 and 22–23.

8 *a crippling weakness:* Ibid., 21.

8 *At fourteen:* Shaughnessy, in *Les Paul*, 14, credibly dates this event to the summer of 1929, although it may have been earlier. In one interview (Oral History of American Music, Yale University, interviewer Joan Thomson, side 207 a–b, April 3, 1978), Les claims it was the summer of the so-called Long-Count Fight between boxers Jack Dempsey and Gene Tunney, which would have made it around September 1927, when Les would have been twelve.

9 *a Troubadour model:* Robb Lawrence, *The Early Years of the Les Paul Legacy, 1915–1963* (New York: Hal Leonard Books, 2008), 5.

9 *jammed it into the top panel:* Interview with Les Paul, Oral History of American Music, side 207 a–b.

9 *"the electric guitar spelled money":* Shaughnessy, *Les Paul*, 14.

10 *Eleven years later:* Les sometimes dated his work on the instrument he was creating, which he would call the Log, to 1940, and sometimes to 1941. Since Les was electrocuted in May 1941 and left Waring and New York that summer with numb hands, it seems to me that work on the Log most likely began in 1940.

10 *forty-five-piece jazz orchestra:* A photo of Waring's group in Paul and Cochran, *Les Paul in His Own Words*, 96–97, shows forty-eight people, including the members of the Les Paul Trio and Waring himself.

10 *had championed:* Leonard G. Feather, "Waring's Social Club Is Unique in Music Circles . . . ," *DownBeat*, October 1, 1940.

10 *appeared on the market in 1932:* Electro String's amplified Hawaiian guitar, made by the Ro-Pat-In Corporation and later known as a Rickenbacker, was developed in 1931 and first sold in 1932, according to Richard Smith, *The Complete History of Rickenbacker Guitars* (Fullerton, CA: Centerstream Publishing, 1987), 11.

10 *"miniature orchestra":* This quote is somewhat disputed, though it appears in Spanish virtuoso Andrés Segovia's "The Romance of the Guitar," *Etude* 48, no. 5 (May 1930), accessed at http://www.icoldwell.com/robert/music/etude/XLVIII_05.html.

10 *considered state-of-the-art:* With Waring, Les often played what he called his "Gibson Cheapie": an ES-150, the company's first electric Spanish model, introduced in 1936, which he continuously modified.

11 *purely electric tone from a purely electric guitar:* Paul and Cochran, *Les Paul in His Own Words*, 102. The emphasis on purity here is in debt to Steve Waksman, *Instruments of Desire: The Electric Guitar and the Shaping of Musical Experience* (Cambridge, MA, and London: Harvard University Press, 1999), 39–46.

11 *crisp electric signal:* Paul and Cochran, *Les Paul in His Own Words*, 102.

12 *none seemed to care one bit:* Ibid., 103.

12 *"listen with their eyes":* Paul Burch, "Les Paul: The Wizard in His Own Words," Epiphone.com, June 1, 2016, http://www.epiphone.com/News/Features/2016/Les-Paul-The-Wizard-In-His-Own-Words.aspx.

13 *Les got a meeting:* This meeting, assuming Les was truthfully recounting it, most likely occurred in 1942, although other sources date it to 1943 or even 1946. See Shaughnessy, *Les Paul*, 105.

13 *broomstick with pickups:* Shaughnessy, *Les Paul*, 105; Paul and Cochran, *Les Paul in His Own Words*, 116.

CHAPTER 2

14 *almost perfectly still:* This scene is a reconstruction based on facts from author interviews, photographs, music recordings, and various histories of Fender, Bob Wills, and western swing. Bob Wills and His Texas Playboys performed regularly at the Aragon Ballroom on Lick Pier in the 1940s, and it is widely known that Leo Fender supplied equipment and operated the public address systems at these concerts. Leo was also known then for venturing onstage to repair his equipment in the middle of performances. Sources include:

- Richard R. Smith, *Fender: The Sound Heard 'Round the World* (New York: Hal Leonard, 2003).
- Bill Carson, *My Life and Times with Fender Instruments* (Bismarck, ND: Vintage Guitar Books, 1998).
- Charles Townsend, *San Antonio Rose: The Life and Music of Bob Wills* (Urbana: University of Illinois Press, 1976).
- "Sage Brush OK with Aragon," *Billboard*, July 8, 1944.
- "American Folk Tunes," *Billboard*, November 15, 1947.
- Author interview with Sandy Boggs, March 27, 2016.
- Various photographs from the collection of the Santa Monica Historical Society.
- A discography of Wills's Tiffany Transcriptions recordings at http://www.tiffany transcriptions.com/discography/, showing that for a period in 1946, Wills's band included both Noel Boggs on steel guitar and Junior Barnard on lead electric guitar. Barnard's playing on the essentially live Tiffany recordings is likely how he would've performed for an audience.

15 *metallic wail:* "They'd yell their heads off," Leo Fender recalled of the feedback of early acoustic-electric guitars in "Fender the Founder: A Low-Decibel Chat with the Henry Ford of the Solid Body," *Rolling Stone*, February 1976, 59.

15 always *wanted to play loud:* Buddy McPeters, "Junior Barnard: Hard-Driving Soloist of Western Swing," *Guitar Player*, September 1983, 44.

16 *worked on that guitar:* Leo added a pickup to Barnard's guitar in late 1947, according to Tom Walzem and Mike Newton, "When Do You Absolutely Know You're Looking at the Work of Leo Fender," *Fretboard Journal*, November 2011. It's almost certain he did other work and repairs prior to that.

16 *prone as it was to producing feedback:* Leo had added an electronic pickup to a radio shop customer's acoustic guitar during the war (Smith, *Fender*, 11) and thus would have known about the volatility of such a combination.

16 *back in 1919:* This is an estimate of Leo's age based on the author's March and July 2016 interviews with Gary Gray, Leo's oldest nephew.

17 *out onto the fields:* Tom Wheeler, "Leo Fender: One of a Kind," *Guitar Player*, May 1978, 32.

17 *carry over a whole town:* Smith, *Fender*, 7.

17 *listen to the maritime communications:* Forrest White, *Fender: The Inside Story* (San Francisco: Backbeat Books, 1994), 4.

17 *Arizona and New Mexico:* Author interview with Gary Gray, March 16, 2016, and July 27, 2016.

17 *date the establishment:* Fender Radio Service ad in *Fullerton News Tribune*, January 27, 1948.

18 *"he couldn't keep a beat":* Smith, *Fender*, 7.

18 *crude acoustic guitar:* "Pro's Reply: Leo Fender," *Guitar Player*, September 1971, 9.

18 *pattern of harmonics:* "Fender the Founder," 60.

18 *come out to see Wills play:* In the small Central Valley town of Tulare, for example, Wills drew 2,300 in a single night, *Billboard* reported on September 30, 1944.

18 *rolled up to Leo's radio repair shop:* Smith, *Fender*, 48, recounts how Leo's Fullerton shop was often the Playboys' first stop on their way into Southern California. Former Playboy steel guitarist Herb Remington recalled in a NAMM (National Association of Music Merchants) Oral History interview (November 16, 2015) that Leo gave new instruments to the band when they stopped by, knowing the Playboys would take them all over the country and influence others to use Fender equipment.

18 *booze, reefer, other things:* Rich Kienzle, *Southwest Shuffle: Pioneers of Honky-Tonk, Western Swing, and Country Jazz* (New York and London: Routledge, 2003), 188.

19 *nothing but his equipment:* Smith, *Fender*, 48.

19 *"lemonade":* Ibid., 65.

20 *running her hand up his trousers:* Peter La Chapelle, *Proud to Be an Okie: Cultural Politics, Country Music, and Migration to Southern California* (Berkeley and Los Angeles: University of California Press, 2007), 108.

20 *plopped himself onto the stage:* As described in Carson, *My Life and Times*, 9, and author interview with Sandy Boggs, March 27, 2016.

20 *"He's the reason you can hear us tonight":* Author interview with Sandy Boggs, March 27, 2016.

CHAPTER 3

21 *third-largest metropolis:* Kevin Starr, *Embattled Dreams: California in War and Peace, 1940–1950* (New York: Oxford University Press, 2002), 230.

21 *was from Pasadena:* Summers was born July 7, 1924.

22 *two palm trees:* From pictures of the house in Paul and Cochran, *Les Paul in His Own Words*, 152.

22 *Summers found:* Shaughnessy, *Les Paul*, 145–46; Paul and Cochran, *Les Paul in His Own Words*, 164–66.

22 *outdoor fireplace:* Paul and Cochran, *Les Paul in His Own Words*, 152–63.

22 *"There's Les now":* Ibid., 165–66; Shaughnessy, *Les Paul*, 144–45.

23 *leading the Sunshine Girls:* Details on Summers's background and early days with Les from Shaughnessy, *Les Paul*, 147–52.

23 *his wife, Virginia, and his two young sons:* Lester Paul Jr. ("Rusty") was born in June 1941 in New York City; the couple's second son, Gene Paul, was born in August 1944 in California.

24 *as soon as Les had arrived in LA:* Les left his job in Chicago in June 1943, was drafted in the fall of 1943, and reported for army duty January 27, 1944, according to letters in the Les Paul Papers, Rock and Roll Hall of Fame, box 5, folder 1; Paul and Cochran, *Les Paul in His Own Words*, 136; and Shaughnessy, *Les Paul*, 113.

24 *another bit of conniving:* Les had idolized Crosby and hankered to play with him since childhood. Paul and Cochran, *Les Paul in His Own Words*, 148–49; Shaughnessy, *Les Paul*, 120–21.

24 *best solo:* Jazz critic Gary Giddens, in the *American Masters* documentary "Les Paul: Chasing Sound" (PBS, aired July 11, 2007), says, "Les never played a better chorus in his life."

24 *Decca Records had released:* Shaughnessy, *Les Paul*, 123, and Les Paul Papers, box 5, folder 1, letter dated October 24, 1945. According to Joel Whitburn, *Pop Hits 1940–1954* (Menomonee Falls, WI: Record Research, 1994), it debuted on the *Billboard* charts on October 13, 1945.

24 *Crosby had helped persuade:* Paul and Cochran, *Les Paul in His Own Words*, 151–53, and Shaughnessy, *Les Paul*, 123.

24 *unending stream of visitors:* Paul and Cochran, *Les Paul in His Own Words*, 161.

25 *sharply turned him down:* Shaughnessy, *Les Paul*, 151.

25 *out to see his trio perform:* Les name-drops a number of Hollywood stars in Paul and Cochran, *Les Paul in His Own Words*, 169. Some of them are confirmed in Shaughnessy, *Les Paul*, 152–53.

26 *as Les recalled:* Les told this story, and many other stories, several different ways, though the basic details in Paul and Cochran, *Les Paul in His Own Words*, 174, remained consistent.

CHAPTER 4

28 *back in 1943:* Smith, *Fender*, 18; "Leo Fender: One of a Kind," *Guitar Player*, May 1978.

29 *only how to build steel guitars:* Research by Richard Smith, Lynn Wheelwright, and Deke Dickerson has shown that Fender and Kauffman collaborated on a line of very early steel guitars and amps during the war, which they named Vibro.

29 *eager to trade:* Leo had been seeking ideas for products to manufacture for many years, according to author interviews with Richard Smith.

29 *precipice of ruin:* Author interview with Geoff Fullerton, March 21, 2017; "Pro's Reply: Leo Fender."

30 *years of sacrifice:* Details on Esther's career, attitude, and marriage to Leo come from author interviews with Gary Gray, Alan Gray, Richard Smith, Geoff Fullerton, and Phyllis Fender, as well as Smith, *Fender*, 8–9, and the National Register of Historic Places registration form for Fender's Radio Service, 107 South Harbor Boulevard, Fullerton.

30 *corrugated steel sheds:* The infamous working conditions of the original Fender factory sheds are recounted in George Fullerton's two books, *Guitar Legends: The Evolution of the Guitar from Fender to G&L* (Fullerton, CA: Centerstream Publishing, 1993), 10–15, and *Guitars from George & Leo: How Leo Fender and I Built G&L Guitars* (Milwaukee: Hal Leonard, 2005), 16–24; White, *Fender*, 32; and Smith, *Fender*, 30–32.

30 *so terrified:* White, *Fender*, 13.

30 *into his groin:* Smith, *Fender*, 34.

30 *upright businessman:* Author interviews with John Hall (August 13, 2015) and Don Randall Jr. (January 2, 2016, and September 7, 2016), and Smith, *Fender*, 26.

31 *infested with termites:* Smith, *Fender*, 31.

31 *termite came boring:* Different versions of this story abound. White tells one in *Fender*, 17–18.

32 *rush to the bank:* Author interview with Geoff Fullerton, March 21, 2017.

32 *"He could sell you a set of false teeth":* NAMM Oral History interview with Dale Hyatt, March 20, 2007.

32 *a schmoozer and a prankster:* Author interview with Don Randall Jr.

32 *kept an apartment:* Author interview with Don Randall Jr. and Kathy Randall, September 7, 2016.

32 *a request Charlie Hayes made to Leo:* Smith, *Fender*, 63.

33 *whole new sound:* Paul and Cochran, *Les Paul in His Own Words*, 176–78.

34 *Les shook hands:* Andy Babiuk, *The Story of Paul Bigsby: Father of the Modern Electric Solidbody Guitar* (Savannah, GA: FG Publishing, 2008), 32.

35 *"He talks a lot":* Author interviews with Richard Smith.

35 *"Leo was a person [who] learned what to do":* Jim O'Donnell, *Les Paul: The Lost Interviews* (North Charleston: CenterStage Media, 2013), 114.

35 *"'I'm gonna do something about it'":* Ibid., 71.

CHAPTER 5

36 *who brought him over:* Babiuk, *Story of Paul Bigsby*, 32.

36 *a decade older and perhaps half a foot taller:* Merle Travis, "Paul A. Bigsby: Merle Travis Remembers . . . the Man Who Could Make Any Damn Thing," *Guitar World*, September 1980; and Tom Wheeler, "Paul Bigsby, Part III," "Rare Bird" column, *Guitar Player*, December 1980.

37 *not to be reminded:* White, *Fender*, 34.

37 *wayward youth:* Babiuk, *Story of Paul Bigsby*, 9–18.

37 *"any damn thing":* Travis, "Paul A. Bigsby," 56.

37 *grown indignant:* Babiuk, *Story of Paul Bigsby*, 19.

37 *a group of country-western sidemen:* Author interview with Andy Babiuk, June 9, 2016; Paul and Cochran, *Les Paul in His Own Words*, 162–63.

38 *listened carefully:* Paul and Cochran, *Les Paul in His Own Words*, 162–63; Babiuk, *Story of Paul Bigsby*, 32–33; O'Donnell, *Les Paul*, 71, 112–13; Jon Sievert, "Les Paul," *Guitar Player*, December 1977, 50; Fullerton, *Guitar Legends*, 18; and author interviews with Richard Smith and Phyllis Fender.

38 *teetotaling Leo:* Leo Fender did not drink alcohol. It appears not to have been a religious conviction, but being around so many well-lubricated musicians certainly acquainted him with drinking's ill effects.

39 *installed it on one of his main guitars:* Babiuk, *Story of Paul Bigsby*, 33–35; Deke Dickerson, BigsbyFiles.com.

39 *Merle Travis asked Bigsby about it:* Dickerson's website quotes Les Paul in an interview with Andy Babiuk: "Merle Travis asked about the pickup, which he called 'the big guy in the back.'"

39 *Chet Atkins . . . requested one, too:* Country Music Foundation Oral History Project, interview with Chet Atkins, interviewer Douglas B. Green, July 5, 1977.

40 *grabbed a roll of KXLA script paper and sketched out his design:* Travis, "Paul A. Bigsby" and "Recollections of Merle Travis, 1944–1955, Part 2," *John Edwards Memorial Foundation Quarterly* 15, no. 55 (Fall 1979); NAMM Oral History interview with Bigsby friend and protégé R. C. Allen.

CHAPTER 6

41 *"clunkers," as Les called them:* Paul and Cochran, *Les Paul in His Own Words*, 117–22.

41 *"headless monster":* Shaughnessy quotes Les calling it this in *Les Paul*, 134; in Paul and Cochran, *Les Paul in His Own Words*, 172–75, Les refers to it simply as "the headless guitar."

42 *"It was like something from Mars":* Les's friend Vic Schoen, quoted in Shaughnessy, *Les Paul*, 134.

42 *"undisputed finest, clearest tone quality":* Country Music Foundation Oral History Project, interview with Jim Atkins, interviewer Bill Ivey, March 1975.

42 *The room was filled:* Paul and Cochran, *Les Paul in His Own Words*, 180–81; Shaughnessy, *Les Paul*, 141.

43 *"All hell broke loose":* Paul and Cochran, *Les Paul in His Own Words*, 180.

43 *wrote out the basic conditions of a contract:* Ibid., 181; Shaughnessy, *Les Paul*, 142–43.

44 *half living room:* This description is based on photos of the bar at the time of its 1948 grand opening, on display during a visit in early 2016.

44 *"roughneck":* Shaughnessy, *Les Paul*, 173.

44 *As they headed south:* Paul and Cochran, *Les Paul in His Own Words*, 184–87; Shaughnessy, *Les Paul*, 155–56; and documents from the Les Paul Papers, box 5, folders 2–5,

including "Les Paul Doing Fine, but Fear Arm Injury May Hinder Guitarist," undated press clipping.

CHAPTER 7

46 *The barnlike building:* From photos of the American Legion post in the collection of the Placentia Library History Room, Placentia, California.

46 *a band of western musicians convened there:* This account assembled from Travis, "Paul A. Bigsby" and Travis, "Recollections of Merle Travis"; "Luck and Persistence, 'Not Talent'—Are Key" (interview with Placentia dance promoter Cliffie Stone), *Los Angeles Times*, May 6, 1993; Kienzle, *Southwest Shuffle*, 103; Babiuk, *Story of Paul Bigsby*, 44–60; NAMM Oral History interview with R. C. Allen; and research by Deke Dickerson posted at BigsbyFiles.com.

47 *a flowing, avian shape:* The guitar was first built with no cutaway and with an almost beaklike headstock shape (visible in a picture at BigsbyFiles.com), and then modified within a few months after Leo first saw it to the shape it has today.

47 *"newfangled guitar":* Travis, "Paul A. Bigsby."

47 *mostly solid-wood body:* Though it had no sound holes, the Bigsby-Travis guitar was not a true solid-body—its back was hollow and covered over.

47 *Fender couldn't have missed this last detail, but he was too fascinated to be polite:* Travis, "Recollections of Merle Travis." Leo certainly would have recognized the Bigsby name on the headstock.

48 *although he would deny these events:* Tom Wheeler, in "Merle Travis and Paul Bigsby," wrote that "Mr. Fender disagrees with the story in all significant respects." Leo Fender always denied that these events occurred but was well-known to have a selective memory. Given the many conflicting accounts and physical signs of Bigsby's influence, his denials are simply impossible to believe.

48 *all kinds of attention:* Smith, *Fender*, 95.

48 *had to be cajoled into coming on board:* Author interview with George's son Geoff Fullerton, March 21, 2017. This account conflicts with what George Fullerton wrote in his two books, but Geoff heard this story from his father, and, as he put it, "My dad is a Southern gentleman, and what he says and what happened is two different things."

49 *Leo shared with George his nascent vision for a new electric standard guitar:* Author interview with Geoff Fullerton; Fullerton, *Guitar Legends*, 8; Fullerton, *Guitars from George & Leo*, 19.

50 *To answer these questions:* Fullerton, *Guitars from George & Leo*, 20–21; Fullerton, *Guitar Legends*, 10–11; Smith, *Fender*, 66–68.

51 *instead of him, depriving him of any formal education in engineering or electronics:* White, *Fender*, 5.

52 *In 1917:* Phyllis Fender with Randall Bell, *Leo Fender: The Quiet Giant Heard Around the World* (Leadership Institute Press, 2018), 11; Smith, *Fender*, 6–7; author interviews with Phyllis Fender, August 4, 2015, and December 9, 2015.

52 *To earn extra money:* Author interview with Geoff Fullerton, March 21, 2017.

52 *high perch of the farm wagon:* Phyllis Fender in *Leo Fender*, 29, writes that it was a truck Leo fell off, but it seems unlikely that the Fender family owned a truck in 1917, when Leo was only seven or eight. Their wagon is shown in Fullerton, *Guitar Legends*, 29.

53 *sketched outlines of a body:* Smith, *Fender*, 65.

53 *hooked up a gas hose to a steel drum:* Fullerton, *Guitar Legends*, 11.

CHAPTER 8

54 *close to death:* Paul and Cochran, *Les Paul in His Own Words*, 186–89; Shaughnessy, *Les Paul*, 156–65; and various documents in the Les Paul Papers, box 5, folder 2.

54 *wouldn't survive:* Referenced in Shaughnessy, *Les Paul*, 165.

55 *"Paul goes one-man guitar band":* Both reviews from *Billboard*, February 21, 1948, 31.

55 *"Iris Watson":* Undated United Press news clipping in Les Paul Papers, box 5, folder 2.

55 *lingering fever:* Paul and Cochran, *Les Paul in His Own Words*, 190.

55 *Les heard two doctors arguing about it:* Les Paul, "The Best Advice I Ever Had," *Reader's Digest*, June 1957, 212.

56 *"so I can play":* Quoted in Shaughnessy, *Les Paul*, 167.

56 *"I finally got so ornery":* Letter from Les on his personal letterhead, undated, in Les Paul Papers, box 2, folder 25.

57 *"When my trio and I would come out":* Paul and Cochran, *Les Paul in His Own Words*, 195.

57 *"lightweight":* Shaughnessy, *Les Paul*, 170.

57 *Paul Bigsby came over with something:* Evidence strongly dates the small Les Paul–Bigsby guitar to the period of Les's recovery, as Dickerson explains at BigsbyFiles.com.

58 *Babiuk confronted Les:* Dickerson, BigsbyFiles.com.

59 *"I let myself be talked into it":* Paul and Cochran, *Les Paul in His Own Words*, 220.

59 *"Four weeks later":* Shaughnessy, *Les Paul*, 168.

CHAPTER 9

60 *In the summer of 1949:* Paul and Cochran, *Les Paul in His Own Words*, 195–98; Shaughnessy, *Les Paul*, 171–73.

61 *should also be his costar:* Paul and Cochran, *Les Paul in His Own Words*, 197.

61 *$150 per weekly, fifteen-minute episode:* Ibid., 199. The show was originally called *Les Paul at Home*, but the name changed shortly to include Mary Ford.

61 *Ampex Model 300:* Ibid., 203–7.

62 *almost as soon as he'd heard about it:* Les often claimed credit for introducing Crosby to the idea of magnetic tape recording (Ibid., 200–201), but independent sources tell a different story. (See "History of the Early Days of the Ampex Corporation," as recalled by John Leslie and Ross Snyder, published by the Audio Engineering Society Historical Committee at AES.org.)

62 *"all but stunned":* "Paul's Comeback," *Newsweek*, September 5, 1949, 64.

63 *married, with two friends as witnesses:* Shaughnessy, *Les Paul*, 178. The witnesses were Dr. George and Bertha Miller—Milwaukee friends and the parents of future rock star Steve Miller, who would be Les Paul's godson.

CHAPTER 10

64 *Little Jimmy Dickens:* Jim Washburn, "Leo Fender: His Contribution Struck a Chord Around the World," *Los Angeles Times*, March 23, 1991.

65 *were waiting for the band to take a break:* Fullerton, *Guitar Legends*, 15; Fullerton, *Guitars by George & Leo*, 23; Kienzle, *Southwest Shuffle*, 193–204, and liner notes to Speedy West and Jimmy Bryant, *Flamin' Guitars*, CD box set (Bear Family Records, 1997); and author interview with Kienzle, March 8, 2017.

65 *"Well, could I try it?":* Fullerton, *Guitar Legends*, 15.

65 *"money green":* Kienzle, *Flamin' Guitars* liner notes.

67 *had a section of the body cut away:* The Bigsby-Travis guitar did not have this shape originally, but it had this shape well before any Fender prototypes appeared.

67 *"I designed the Fender guitar":* "Merle Travis: The Man," *Guitar Player*, September 1976, 20.

67 *hours shaping by hand:* Author interview with Deke Dickerson, March 15, 2016.

67 *two blocks of pine:* Smith writes in *Fender*, 66, that the first Fender prototype was not a solid-body, but consisted of two pine pieces with a closed-off resonating cavity in the middle.

67 *ordered by none other than Jimmy Bryant:* Babiuk, *Story of Paul Bigsby*, 70–77.

68 *"I have done everything I know":* F. C. Hall, letter to Don Randall, August 8, 1949, in the Don Randall Private Collection.

68 *exactly the same tuners:* Babiuk, *Story of Paul Bigsby*, 51–52, 60–63.

68 *adopting a good idea:* One more smoking gun in the case of the Bigsby-Fender influence comes in a letter from Don Randall to F. C. Hall from July 1950, in which Randall writes: "Merle Travis is on the program and he is one of the country's foremost guitar stylists. He is playing the grandaddy of our Spanish guitar, built by Bigsby—the one Leo copied." From the Richard Smith Files.

69 *returned from a Hawaiian vacation:* Musical Merchandise, February 1952, 16.

69 *At thirty-two:* Don Randall was born in Kendrick, Idaho, on October 30, 1917.

69 *"definitely the high moral type":* F. C. Hall, letter to Army Air Force Redistribution Station No. 4, Santa Ana Army Air Base, California, November 16, 1945, in support of a discharge for Don Randall to resume work at Radio-Tel, shared with author by Don Randall Jr.

69 *taught himself electronics:* Author interviews with Don Jr. and Kathy Randall, March 11, 2016; family documents shared with author; and documents in the Don Randall Private Collection.

70 *"canoe paddle":* Smith, *Fender*, 78; "The Strat at 60," *Music Trades*, October 2014.

70 *"toilet seat with strings":* "Fender the Founder," 61.

70 *"That thing'll never sell":* Tom Wheeler, *The Fender Archives: A Scrapbook of Artifacts, Treasures, and Inside Information* (Milwaukee: Hal Leonard, 2014), 12.

70 *"It really looks hot"*: Don Randall, letter to F. C. Hall, undated (summer 1950), in Don Randall Private Collection.

71 *"I really believe that this should be carefully considered"*: Don Randall, letter to F. C. Hall, July 13, 1950, in Don Randall Private Collection and Richard Smith Files.

71 *"Francis,"* . . . *"I don't believe you realize the gravity"*: Don Randall, letter to F. C. Hall, undated (August 1950), in Richard Smith Files.

CHAPTER 11

72 *June 28, 1950*: Kienzle, *Flamin' Guitars* liner notes, 16–17.

72 *even more notice*: Ibid.; Kienzle, *Southwest Shuffle*, 193–204; and "Jimmy Bryant: An Unsung Hero," *Guitar World*, September 1980, 15–65.

73 *based on a classic old blues*: Kienzle, *Southwest Shuffle*, 115.

73 *an astounding success*: Joel Whitburn, *Joel Whitburn Presents Hot Country Songs 1944–2008* (Menomonee Falls, WI: Record Research, 2008).

74 *"I hope they start shipping the Spanish guitar soon"*: Handwritten note from Fender salesman Dave Driver to F. C. Hall, August 15, 1950, in Don Randall Private Collection.

74 *Hyatt drove a truckload of Fender equipment*: Tony Bacon, *Six Decades of the Fender Telecaster* (Milwaukee: Hal Leonard, 2005), 21; Smith, *Fender*, 81–82.

75 *he appreciated elegant hollow-body guitars*: Author interview with Rich Kienzle, March 8, 2017.

75 *to try to match the sound of Gibson's grandest hollow-body*: Author interview with Buddy McPeters, February 20, 2016.

75 *"I believe that Leo is very much concerned"*: F. C. Hall, letter to Don Randall, August 16, 1950, in Don Randall Private Collection.

76 *a channel was cut in the back of the neck*: Author interview with Geoff Fullerton, March 21, 2017.

76 *Randall decided to call it the "Broadcaster"*: Smith, *Fender*, 84.

76 *the difference in names and specs would confuse many*: Fender salesman Mike Cole, letter to Don Randall, January 16, 1951, in Don Randall Private Collection.

77 *received a telegram*: Western Union telegram, February 20, 1951, in Richard Smith Files and Don Randall Private Collection.

77 *"It is a shame that our efforts . . . are lost"*: Don Randall, letter to all Fender salesmen, February 21, 1951, in Don Randall Private Collection.

77 *bearing no model name at all*: Smith, *Fender*, 88.

78 *"This guitar can be played at extreme volume"*: Fender 1950 catalog, Broadcaster entry.

CHAPTER 12

79 *matched the success of the first*: Whitburn, *Pop Hits 1940–1954*.

79 *did nothing exciting*: Paul and Cochran, *Les Paul in His Own Words*, 193–94.

79 *Les felt was borrowed, or stolen, from him*: Ibid., 224.

79 *confused buyers:* Shaughnessy, *Les Paul,* 187.

80 *dismissed as soon as she heard it:* Paul and Cochran, *Les Paul in His Own Words,* 224.

80 *steadfastly refused to release it:* Shaughnessy, *Les Paul,* 186–88; Paul and Cochran, *Les Paul in His Own Words,* 229–30.

80 *recorded it on the Ampex:* Shaughnessy, *Les Paul,* 185–86; Les tells a more elaborate version in Paul and Cochran, *Les Paul in His Own Words,* 226–28.

81 *he relented:* Shaughnessy, *Les Paul,*188.

81 *among the bestsellers:* St. Louis Post-Dispatch, March 28, 1951. Clip in Les Paul Papers, box 1, folder 18.

81 *recording hit no. 1 . . . higher echelons of the rhythm and blues charts:* Whitburn, *Pop Hits 1940–1954.*

81 *four million records:* Walter Winchell column, October 5, 1951, in Les Paul Papers, box 1, folder 18.

81 *six million wax platters:* Walter Winchell column, June 18, 1952, in Les Paul Papers, box 5, folder 9.

81 *held strong just below it:* Whitburn, *Pop Hits 1940–1954;* Shaughnessy, *Les Paul,* 188.

81 *"So far this year":* Time, October 29, 1951, 71, in Les Paul Papers, box 1, folder 18.

81 *"risen to the top of the ladder":* Cash Box, August 11, 1951, in Les Paul Papers, box 1, folder 18.

82 *"Dear Les and Mary congratulations":* Telegram from Jim Conkling to Les Paul, September 18, 1951, in Les Paul Papers, box 5, folder 1.

82 *"This 'New Sound'":* Duluth Herald, April 14, 1953, in Les Paul Papers, box 1, folder 18, clippings 1949–53.

82 *to make the song ubiquitous:* Shaughnessy, *Les Paul,* 192–93.

82 *only artists in history:* "Disks by Duo Sell 4 Million," Billboard, August 25, 1951, 1.

CHAPTER 13

83 *three or four nights every week:* Don Randall, letter to salesman Don Patton, March 20, 1951, in Don Randall Private Collection.

83 *"Our Spanish guitar is selling in quantity":* Don Randall, letter to Don Patton, May 24, 1951, in Don Randall Private Collection.

83 *relative bargain:* Fender Electric Instrument Company Price List, 1951, in Don Randall Private Collection.

84 *where Fender was already popular:* Smith, *Fender,* 84–85.

84 *"I was up in Los Angeles":* Don Randall, letter to salesman Dave Driver, June 21, 1951, in Richard Smith Files.

84 *its neck inscribed with the date 5-10-51:* "Property from the Estate of Les Paul," Julien's Auctions catalog, 2012, 382–87.

84 *thought the guitar was a prototype:* Paul and Cochran, *Les Paul in His Own Words,* 236.

85 *"to look at [the guitar] and think about it":* Ibid.

85 *"This is where I'm going"*: O'Donnell, *Les Paul*, 114.

85 *"first hit me as a swell idea"*: Paul and Cochran, *Les Paul in His Own Words*, 236.

85 *"There was no Fender then"*: O'Donnell, *Les Paul*, 114.

85 *Les also decided that he didn't really like Leo's Telecaster very much*: Author interviews with Andy Babiuk, June 9, 2016, and Drew Berlin, March 27, 2017.

86 *"I told Leo"*: Paul and Cochran, *Les Paul in His Own Words*, 236.

86 *"I believe the solid-body guitar"*: Ibid., 236–37.

86 *developing a rival solid-body electric guitar immediately*: Lawrence, *Early Years*, 52.

86 *staff of experienced artisans*: Ted McCarty, NAMM Oral History interview, June 20 or March 6, 2000.

87 *"We didn't think it took a lot of skill"*: Shaughnessy, *Les Paul*, 200.

87 *a small shape would work well*: Lawrence, *Early Years*, 53–54.

87 *"I said, 'Look, if we are going to make a guitar'"*: Ibid., 55.

87 *"needed an excuse"*: Ibid., 60.

87 *reader's poll in that year's* DownBeat *magazine*: Les was voted top guitarist in the annual reader's poll, *DownBeat*, December 28, 1951, 1.

88 *holed up in a hunting lodge*: Shaughnessy, *Les Paul*, 201–2; Lawrence, *Early Years*, 62; Paul and Cochran, *Les Paul in His Own Words*, 204–11.

88 *classic rounded shape with a single cutaway*: Lawrence, *Early Years*, 58–59.

89 *a guitar for tuxedos*: Waksman, *Instruments of Desire*, 49.

89 *"They're getting awfully close to us"*: Shaughnessy, *Les Paul*, 201.

89 *fueled by pots of coffee . . . risk losing his earnings*: Ibid., 201–2.

89 *Gibson nameplates*: Lawrence, *Early Years*, 62.

CHAPTER 14

90 *The guitar players who hung around*: White, *Fender*, 77–78; Carson, *My Life and Times*, 42.

90 *hear of gigs playing upright bass*: David Gans, "Electric Guitar Pioneers Leo Fender and George Fullerton: An Interview with Two Gentle Giants of the Music Industry," *BAM*, August 29, 1980, 35.

91 *leaning over to put their ears against their instruments*: Ibid.

91 *put their instrument in a canvas bag and tied it to a car roof*: Smith, *Fender*, 100; Philip Norman, *Rave On: The Biography of Buddy Holly* (New York: Fireside Books, 1996), 126.

91 *they came to a head one night*: Smith, *Fender*, 103; Randy Lewis, "Electrically Charged: Author Amplifies Role of O.C.'s Fender and the Sound 'Heard Round the World,' " *Los Angeles Times*, April 30, 1996.

92 *Leo realized what his competitors hadn't*: The Seattle musician and tinkerer Paul Tutmarc had produced a solid-body electric bass under the Audiovox name in 1936 and 1937, but it never had any great success, and it's unlikely Leo ever saw one. Scott Malandrone and Mikael Jansson, "Jurassic Bass: Was There Electric Bass Before Leo," *Bass Player*, July 1997.

93 *"something wrong with the band"*: Leonard Feather, "Hamp-lified Fiddle May Lighten Bassists' Burdens," *DownBeat*, July 30, 1952.

94 *"The neck is fretted like a guitar"*: Don Randall, letter to salesman Mike Cole, November 30, 1951, in Richard Smith Files.

94 *"Obviously, the new bass is a big departure"*: "Portable String Bass Really New," *Musical Merchandise*, April 1952, 35.

95 *Leo had wanted its weight to balance horizontally*: Gans, "Electric Guitar Pioneers," 35.

95 *"Yes, it IS a bass"*: Caption in *Musical Merchandise*, August 1952.

95 *"those who were not sure if Leo was crazy"*: White, *Fender*, 52.

95 *"dealers really rushed the guitar room"*: A. R. Duchossoir, *Gibson Electrics: The Classic Years* (Milwaukee: Hal Leonard, 1994, 1998), 44.

96 *the wildly incorrect statement*: See, for example, Guy Gugliotta, " 'The Log' Puts Paul in Ranks of Top Inventors," *Washington Post*, May 15, 2005.

96 *"Ted, how could you do this?"*: Lawrence, *Early Years*, 60.

96 *McCarty saw that a fully electric design*: Duchossoir, *Gibson Electrics*, 40.

96 *"He's cutting into the market"*: Lawrence, *Early Years*, 60.

CHAPTER 15

97 *"They don't listen to that kind of old blues"*: Robert Palmer, *Deep Blues: A Musical and Cultural History, from the Mississippi Delta to Chicago's South Side to the World* (New York: Penguin Books, 1981), 135.

98 *folks like Big Bill Broonzy*: Robert Gordon, *Can't Be Satisfied: The Life and Times of Muddy Waters* (New York: Little, Brown, 2002), 72–73.

98 *"Dreamy Eyes"*: Ibid., 130.

98 *the simple acoustic guitar*: Ibid., 79.

98 *four-room apartment*: Palmer, *Deep Blues*, 143.

98 *"he was almost like a bum"*: Gordon, *Can't Be Satisfied*, 88.

98 *stools at a half-circular bar*: Description from ibid., 88–89, and various photographs of Muddy and others at the Zanzibar.

98 *Muddy would sit in a chair . . . pigs' feet and corned-beef sandwiches*: Ibid.

99 *only three other musicians up there*: Muddy's band would later grow to five or six, but at this stage consisted of only two guitars, harmonica, and drums.

99 *now an electric lamentation*: "I Feel Like Going Home" is, as Gordon points out in *Can't Be Satisfied*, 93, likely a mishearing of the lyrics "I feel like blowing my horn." As a blues standard, the song's style and Muddy's performance, more than its lyrics, would have reminded these listeners of home.

99 *They called themselves the Headhunters*: Gordon, *Can't Be Satisfied*, 89.

99 *found himself inside a downtown recording studio*: Ibid., 189; Nadine Cohodas, *Spinning Blues into Gold: The Chess Brothers and the Legendary Chess Records* (New York: St. Martin's Press, 2000), 43–44.

100 *"What's he saying? What's he saying?"*: Cohodas, *Spinning Blues into Gold*, 44.

100 *three thousand copies*: Sandra B. Tooze, *Muddy Waters: The Mojo Man* (Toronto: ECW Press, 1997), 83.

100 *Muddy could find only a single copy*: Gordon, *Can't Be Satisfied*, 94; Palmer, *Deep Blues*, 159; Tooze, *Muddy Waters*, 84; Cohodas, *Spinning Blues into Gold*, 44.

100 *"Poor recording distorts vocal and steel guitar backing"*: *Billboard*, July 10, 1948, 104.

100 *refused to bring Muddy's full group into the studio*: Cohodas, *Spinning Blues into Gold*, 52; Tony Glover, Scott Dirks, and Ward Gaines, *Blues with a Feeling: The Little Walter Story* (New York: Routledge, 2002), 56.

100 *covert session for the Regal label*: Gordon, *Can't Be Satisfied*, 96.

101 *More hits came*: Ibid., 104–10.

101 *"They even named it the Muddy Waters blues"*: Ibid., 113.

101 *"the first to use amplification to make their ensemble music rawer"*: Palmer, *Deep Blues*, 16.

101 *rewrote the lyrics*: John Collis, *Ike Turner: King of Rhythm* (London: The Do-Not Press, 2003), 35.

102 *fallen out of the trunk of the car*: Peter Guralnick, *Sam Phillips, the Man Who Invented Rock 'n' Roll: How One Man Discovered Howlin' Wolf, Ike Turner, Jerry Lee Lewis, Johnny Cash, and Elvis Presley, and How His Tiny Label, Sun Records of Memphis, Revolutionized the World!* (New York: Little, Brown, 2015), 104.

102 *no way to get it fixed*: Palmer, *Deep Blues*, 222.

102 *liked to record musicians as they presented themselves*: Guralnick, *Sam Phillips*, 165–66.

102 *wad of paper*: Ibid., 105; Palmer, *Deep Blues*, 222.

102 *early March day*: Guralnick, *Sam Phillips*, 106; Cohodas, *Spinning Blues into Gold*, 58.

102 *distortion was doubtless part of why "Rocket 88" found even more success*: Palmer, *Deep Blues*, 223, notes that while "there was nothing particularly startling about the way 'Rocket 88' moved," other, similar records "weren't as electric."

103 *then, suddenly, they did*: See Palmer, *Deep Blues*, 224; Guralnick, *Sam Phillips*, 106; and Collis, *Ike Turner*, 36, on the song's transformative appeal.

103 *Haley decided to change his entire direction*: Collis, *Ike Turner*, 38; Palmer, *Deep Blues*, 224.

103 *a white singer might find*: Palmer, *Deep Blues*, 224.

103 *nightly violence*: Eileen Sisk, *Buck Owens: The Biography* (Chicago: Chicago Review Press, 2010), 21–23; Gerald W. Haslam, *Workin' Man Blues: Country Music in California* (Berkeley: University of California Press, 1999), 116.

104 *A few lamps cast a wan glow*: Scott B. Romar, Randy Poe, and Robert Price, *The Bakersfield Sound* (Nashville: Country Music Foundation Press, 2012), 26; Country Music Foundation Oral History Project, interview with Joe and Rose Lee Maphis, interviewer Douglas Green, January 15, 1975, tape 2, side A; various photographs.

104 *decent white people didn't dance*: Country Music Foundation Oral History Project, interview with Joe and Rose Lee Maphis, tape 2, side A.

104 *His yellowish guitar sounded electric*: Haslam, *Workin' Man Blues*, 116.

104 *purchased his Fender Telecaster:* Sisk, *Buck Owens,* 17–18.

104 *could be handy in a fight:* "You had to learn to defend yourself with a Fender guitar," Carl Perkins is quoted as saying in Haslam, *Workin' Man Blues,* 116. "I love them solid-body guitars."

104 *so stunned . . . they portrayed it in a song:* Country Music Foundation Oral History Project, interview with Joe and Rose Lee Maphis, tape 2, side A.

105 *driving back to Los Angeles:* Romar, Poe, and Price, *Bakersfield Sound,* 26.

CHAPTER 16

106 *She tensed:* Shaughnessy, *Les Paul,* 198–99, recounts one of many instances of Mary's stage fright.

106 *ferried into the city across Lake Michigan:* Paul and Cochran, *Les Paul in His Own Words,* 271.

106 *Les Paul and Mary Ford Day:* Ibid.

107 *"Vote for Les Paul and Mary Ford" . . . little pendants:* From an image in Paul and Cochran, *Les Paul in His Own Words,* 272–73.

107 *The major downtown music stores:* From a brief in *Music Dealer,* October 1952, in Les Paul Papers, box 4, folder 23.

107 *You know, this new Gibson guitar:* This is the folksy way Les would explain his gadgets. See *The Les Paul Show with Mary Ford,* episode 1, https://www.youtube.com/watch?v=ev-_UbM0Zfc.

107 *A few reporters would note:* Uncorrected proof for *Morristown Daily Record,* February 28, 1952, in Les Paul Papers, box 1, folder 18, clippings 1949–53; Shaughnessy, *Les Paul,* 205.

107 *"If people didn't realize it was a hoax":* Paul and Cochran, *Les Paul in His Own Words,* 268–69.

107 *The couple took up "There's No Place Like Home":* Author interview with Bob Summers, January 10, 2017; a version of this act can be viewed at https://www.youtube.com/watch?v=awjTKeS9Wvo ("Les Paul & Mary Ford Absolutely Live," published June 7, 2014).

107 *Les plucked out a fancy little run:* From "Les Paul & Mary Ford Absolutely Live" and from a description in *Melody Maker,* September 20, 1952, review of performance at London Palladium, in Les Paul Papers, box 5, folder 9, scrapbook 1951–52.

108 *"It sounds obvious in conception":* Ibid.

108 *"Gal, incidentally, is a nicely gowned looker":* *Variety* review of Les Paul and Mary Ford at Paramount Theatre, October 24, 1951, in Les Paul Papers, box 1, folder 18, clippings 1949–53.

109 *"I still dread going onstage":* From undated article (likely 1951 or '52) in *Woman,* 51–53, in Les Paul Papers, box 1, folder 22.

109 *breaking all previous attendance records . . . taking in more than $37,000:* Les's manager Gray Gordon, letter to Hal Cook at Capitol Records, August 4, 1952, in Les Paul Papers, box 1, folder 25, correspondence 1952–53.

109 *microphone over the sink:* Dena Kleiman, "Mary Ford Dies; Sang with Les Paul," *New York Times,* October 2, 1977, 42.

109 *began to wear Mary out:* Shaughnessy, *Les Paul*, 212.

110 *"[She] kept saying, 'We have more money than we can ever spend' ":* Paul and Cochran, *Les Paul in His Own Words*, 266.

110 *discovered and hounded:* Ibid., 247.

110 *thirteenth consecutive hit:* Shaughnessy, *Les Paul*, 214.

110 *Listerine contract worth $2 million:* Ibid., 216.

110 *"He was tighter than the bark on a tree":* Ibid., 213.

110 *resisted buying Mary new clothes:* Ibid.

110 *resting in a St. Paul hotel room:* Ibid., 214–15.

111 *more than fifteen million copies:* Undated advertisement/handbill in Les Paul Papers, box 2, folder 25, correspondence of Les and Mary, 1951–1957.

111 *referred to her husband as a slave driver:* Shaughnessy, *Les Paul*, 217.

111 *"What Benny Goodman did for the clarinet":* George Simon, "Les and Mary Bring Back the Guitar," *Metronome*, November 1953, 15.

112 *When Les and Mary made promotional visits:* Documents in Les Paul Papers, box 5, folder 12, scrapbook, various dates.

112 *"I am sure more man hours were devoted to the manufacture":* Ted McCarty, "Fretted Instrument Volume Up 25%—New Record Set," *Music Trades*, December 1953, 26.

CHAPTER 17

113 *"Because for the difference in price":* Tom Wheeler, *The Stratocaster Chronicles: Celebrating 50 Years of the Fender Strat* (Milwaukee: Hal Leonard, 2004), 26.

113 *employed thirty-three people:* Counted in photo in Smith, *Fender*, 114. Leo himself likely took the picture.

114 *sole indulgence:* Leo's 1952 Dodge sedan, which George later purchased, is pictured in Fullerton, *Guitar Legends*, 30.

114 *scrawling tallies:* As seen on various documents in Richard Smith Files.

114 *exacerbated by material shortages:* Randall discussed the effects of the war in several places, including a March 16, 1951, letter to salesman Don Patton in the Don Randall Private Collection.

114 *saw the Les Paul Model as an existential threat:* Wheeler, *Stratocaster Chronicles*, 54; Smith, *Fender*, 122–23.

114 *In 1952, Paul Bigsby began selling:* Dickerson, BigsbyFiles.com.

115 *vibrato designed for the Fender Telecaster:* Babiuk, *Story of Paul Bigsby*, 119–20.

115 *largely friendly:* Author interview with Andy Babiuk, June 9, 2016.

115 *best source of a feature:* NAMM Oral History interview with George Fullerton, October 11, 2003; NAMM Oral History interview with Bill Carson, July 21, 2001.

115 *players had been telling Leo what was wrong:* Carson, *My Life and Times*, 15.

115 *"two-by-four":* Author interview with Buddy McPeters, February 20, 2016.

115 *started to hear complaints about the tuning of his guitar:* Carson, *My Life and Times*, 7.

115 *dug painfully into a player's chest:* Ibid.

116 *took a hacksaw to his first:* Ibid., 15.

116 *"wasn't very pretty":* Wheeler, *Stratocaster Chronicles*, 60.

116 *he got the point:* Carson, *My Life and Times*, 15.

116 *"the place looked like a complete mess":* White, *Fender*, 63.

116 *just outside the uninsulated wall:* Ibid., 72.

116 *cold—even sociopathic:* Author interview with Geoff Fullerton, March 21, 2017; Carson, *My Life and Times*, 34.

117 *mountain of empties:* Kienzle, *Southwest Shuffle*, 213.

117 *mercilessly booted the Fender endorser:* White, *Fender*, 78.

117 *"What makes you think you can come in here":* Ibid., 71–72.

117 *four or five pickups:* Carson, *My Life and Times*, 17.

117 *"fit like a good shirt":* Ibid.

117 *George Fullerton wanted a recessed jack . . . Don Randall wanted a sunburst finish:* Wheeler, *Stratocaster Chronicles*, 52–54.

118 *Carson wanted a headstock:* Carson, *My Life and Times*, 18.

118 *Jimmy Bryant wanted the new guitar to be called:* Ibid., 43–44.

118 *"Carson's guitar":* Ibid., 19.

118 *"Crazy Man, Crazy":* Charlie Gillett, *The Sound of the City: The Rise of Rock and Roll* (New York: Da Capo Press, 1970, 1983, 1996), 3.

118 *"Mary is taking a little time off":* Full-page ad in *Billboard*, July 17, 1954, seen in Les Paul Papers, box 5, folder 10, scrapbook 1953–54.

CHAPTER 18

119 *"was another instrument entirely":* Ellis Amburn, *Buddy Holly: A Biography* (New York: St. Martin's Press, 1995), 11.

119 *not much else to do besides pick:* John Goldrosen and John Beecher, *Remembering Buddy: The Definitive Biography of Buddy Holly* (New York: Da Capo Press, 1996), 11.

120 *hillbilly classics:* Norman, *Rave On*, 37–38.

120 *"We'd been hillbillies, but after the Cotton Club":* Amburn, *Buddy Holly*, 36.

120 *unleashed a new energy in Buddy:* Norman, *Rave On*, 59.

120 *nice kit for a teenager from a struggling family:* Ibid., 52.

120 *a 1952 model:* Dated by Walter Carter in John Thomas, "Buddy Holly's Les Paul: A Guitar That Changed the Course of Music History by Not Being Played," *Fretboard Journal*, April 2017.

120 *listening obsessively to Muddy Waters:* Goldrosen and Beecher, *Remembering Buddy*, 16.

120 *Buddy's love for Les Paul's guitar work:* Norman, *Rave On*, 52.

121 *Buddy and his crew followed:* Ibid., 62.

121 *complained about the weight of his new guitar:* Amburn, *Buddy Holly*, 38.

121 *"he was an average hard-on good ol' American boy":* Norman, *Rave On*, 70.

121 *felt his image was too plain:* Ibid., 73.

121 *asked his oldest brother, Larry, for a loan:* Ibid.; Amburn, *Buddy Holly*, 42; Bill Griggs, *The Words and Music of Buddy Holly: His Songs and Interviews (The Technical Stuff)* (Lubbock, TX: Rockin' '50s Magazine, 1995), 5.

121 *"Why don't you ask for the moon?":* Amburn, *Buddy Holly*, 42.

121 *sliced the "E" off his last name:* Norman, *Rave On*, 75.

121 *put the loan in a different context:* Griggs, *Words and Music*, 5, writes that the second owner of Buddy's Les Paul purchased it used, after Buddy had recently traded it in, on April 23, 1955.

122 *The store touted:* "Adair's Now Offering Guitar, Ukulele Instruction," *Lubbock Evening Journal*, April 23, 1956.

122 *that the instrument was too plain:* Norman (*Rave On*, 73), Amburn (*Buddy Holly*, 42), and other Holly biographers cast the Les Paul this way, when in fact the opposite was true: the Les Paul Model was a known quantity from the leading guitar maker; the Stratocaster would have been a dazzling but untested newcomer.

123 *felt not elation, or admiration, but rage:* Babiuk, *Story of Paul Bigsby*, 120; author interview with Andy Babiuk, June 9, 2016; author interviews with Mary Bigsby, April 7, 2016, and September 27, 2016.

123 *It worked better:* The first Bigsby vibratos used a hard rubber bushing, rather than a spring, to return the lever to its place, and were clearly inferior to the Fender design. Bigsby's addition of a spring made the two comparable.

124 *an old Croatian instrument:* Audio interview with Leo Fender on CD included with Wheeler, *Stratocaster Chronicles*, track 7.

125 *"I told Leo I wanted a large, fancy headstock":* Carson, *My Life and Times*, 18.

CHAPTER 19

126 *looked out at the lights of Las Vegas:* Paul and Cochran, *Les Paul in His Own Words*, 289.

126 *mother and daughter "were doing fine":* "Les Paul Reveals Birth of Daughter," *Austin American-Statesman*, November 26, 1954.

127 *wasn't breathing normally:* Shaughnessy, *Les Paul*, 219.

127 *at one fifteen a.m. . . . first child died:* Ibid., 220; "Les Paul's Baby Dies," *New York Times*, December 1, 1954, 22.

127 *wasn't told right away:* Shaughnessy, *Les Paul*, 220.

127 *Mary Ford shattered:* Paul and Cochran, *Les Paul in His Own Words*, 289.

127 *Papers nationwide:* News items ran in the *New York Times*, the *Los Angeles Times*, the *Hartford Courant*, and elsewhere.

127 *music columnists still gushed:* Fred Reynolds, "Platter Chatter," *Chicago Daily Tribune*, December 4, 1954.

127 *until the very day Mary gave birth:* Shaughnessy, *Les Paul*, 219.

127 *the flood from her eyes unceasing:* Ibid.

128 *"You know, we're up here, and we work so hard"*: Paul and Cochran, *Les Paul in His Own Words*, 289.

128 *drove their hotel neighbors crazy:* Ibid.

129 *Les dismissed them:* "I enjoy a lot of rock 'n' roll music, but the majority is not good," Les said, according to the *Clearwater Sun*, April 10, 1960.

129 *made his and Mary's live performances only more important:* Shaughnessy, *Les Paul*, 224.

129 *what skilled musicians could do:* Les drew this distinction, for example, in Fred Fiske, "The Pros Are Coming Back," *Washington Daily News*, September 19, 1958, 81.

129 *Also calling was the White House:* Shaughnessy, *Les Paul*, 231; Paul and Cochran, *Les Paul in His Own Words*, 292.

130 *He could be so cold sometimes:* Harris Nelson, "Entertainer Finds Les Paul Not All Sweetness and Light," *Richfield News* (Minnesota), January 13, 1955, 10.

130 *How far . . . could she stand to go with him?:* "Is never going onstage an acceptable answer to the problem," Les recalled wondering on 294 of Paul and Cochran, *Les Paul in His Own Words*. "That's what she wanted me to agree to, and it was going to be very difficult."

CHAPTER 20

131 *submitting to this grouchy old man, about to play at an intolerably low volume:* Norman, *Rave On*, 151.

133 *rumble to more national success:* Cohodas, *Spinning Blues into Gold*, 117–18.

133 *hybrid of various styles:* Chuck Berry, *The Autobiography* (New York: Fireside, 1988), 88–89.

133 *based on "Ida Red":* Ibid., 143.

134 *"There was something in many of those youngsters":* Memphis Press Scimitar, April 29, 1959, 1, quoted in Cohodas, *Spinning Blues into Gold*, 145.

134 *a harder, whiter diction:* Berry, *Autobiography*, 90–91.

134 *"photos of black faces":* Ibid., 135.

134 *"It's a country dance and we had no idea":* Ibid., 136.

CHAPTER 21

136 *wondered whether Hayes's pretty new wife, Dorothy, knew what she was in for:* Author interview with Don Randall Jr. and Kathy Randall, March 11, 2016.

137 *addressing White as "kid":* White, *Fender*, 91.

137 *"two donkeys on each end of a rope":* Ibid., 92.

137 *a new house in Tustin . . . and a dealer-fresh Cadillac:* Fullerton, *Guitar Legends*, 38; White, *Fender*, 91–92; Smith, *Fender*, 151–52.

137 *Hall was hedging his bet:* Smith, *Fender*, 115.

137 *longest lunch . . . "So long, kid":* White, *Fender*, 91.

138 *Racing in the opposite direction:* Details from "Two Die in Three-Car Collision," source unknown but likely *Los Angeles Times*, June 10, 1955; "Head-On Smashup Kills Two,"

Long Beach Press-Telegram, June 10, 1955, B1; Fullerton, *Guitar Legends*, 38; and Smith, *Fender*, 152.

138 *was getting ready for bed:* Author interview with Don Randall Jr., January 2, 2016.

138 *"Uncle Charlie isn't here anymore":* Ibid.

138 *leveled Don Randall:* Author interview with Don Randall Jr. and Kathy Randall, March 11, 2016.

139 *pull his car off the road and vomit:* Smith, *Fender*, 11.

140 *"We told Francis either you sell to us or we sell to you":* Ibid., 152.

140 *"The parties have encountered differences of opinion":* Draft of "Agreement for Sale of Stock and Interest in Corporation," to be signed by F. C. Hall, Donald D. Randall, and Clarence Leo Fender, November 7, 1955, in Don Randall Private Collection.

140 *less than half of what his lawyer claimed it was worth:* Notes from Hall's lawyer attached to a separate copy of the above sale agreement in Richard Smith Files calculates the cash price for Hall's stock at $92,843 as of October 31, 1955.

140 *It seems he did feel betrayed by Randall:* Author interview with John Hall, August 13, 2015.

140 *didn't hold Fender or musical equipment in any special regard:* Ibid.

140 *too distracted by his golf game:* Smith, *Fender*, 148, 154.

141 *so infuriated:* Author interview with Don Randall Jr. and Kathy Randall, March 11, 2016.

141 *believed in linear technological progress:* Sales figures and assessment of Leo's thinking from Smith, *Fender*, 145.

141 *above $1 million for the first time . . . a net profit of $100,884:* Fender sales balance sheet, May 31, 1957, in Don Randall Private Collection.

142 *he needed to take his mind off the plant:* Author interviews with Gary Gray, March 16, 2016, and July 27, 2016.

142 *The Chris-Craft:* Ibid., July 27, 2016.

142 *"It was kind of like being in a rocket ship on water":* Author interview with Sandy Boggs, March 27, 2016.

CHAPTER 22

143 *a lover of distortion:* Guralnick, *Sam Phillips*, 133.

144 *"If we're going over well, our guitars weigh less than a feather":* St. Petersburg Times, April 12, 1960, clipping in Les Paul Papers, box 1, folder 21, 1958–1960 clippings.

144 *preferred to pick up Les's old hollow clunkers:* Paul and Cochran, *Les Paul in His Own Words*, 245.

144 *had peaked in 1953:* Shipping totals from Duchossoir, *Gibson Electrics*, 218.

144 *at the direction of president Ted McCarty, an engineer at Gibson named Seth Lover:* NAMM Oral History interview with Ted McCarty, 2000; Duchossoir, *Gibson Electrics*, 63–66.

145 *retained the largest market share:* From "Evaluation of the Guitar Market," confidential 1965 study prepared for Kay Musical Instrument Company by Marplan/Chicago, in Don Randall Private Collection, showing market share pre-1961 and after.

145 *got the company to send out two new guitars and amplifiers:* Norman, *Rave On*, 210.

145 *a more crucial Fender player:* Merrill appeared with a Stratocaster in Fender ads as early as December 1956.

146 *no more than a passing fad:* For example, Carson, in *My Life and Times,* 64, reproduces a 1965 conversation in which he describes rock 'n' roll as "a primitive series of musical mistakes."

CHAPTER 23

147 *were outright blockbusters:* Goldrosen and Beecher, in *Remembering Buddy,* 198, report that "That'll Be the Day" hit no. 1 in England, but only no. 3 in the US; "Oh Boy" hit no. 3 in the UK but only no. 10 in the US.

147 *regarded as a giant:* Norman, *Rave On,* 173–74.

148 *"At that moment"* . . . *"I realized it was all over for musicians like me":* Ibid., 185.

148 *"It showed that to play rock 'n' roll you did not have to be":* Ibid., 171.

149 *That same night:* Amburn, *Buddy Holly,* 144.

149 *neither Lennon . . . nor McCartney . . . could afford tickets:* Norman, *Rave On,* 191.

149 *a new attitude toward his spectacles:* Amburn, *Buddy Holly,* 147.

150 *"He didn't like it, 'cause it was thin and real heavy":* Tooze, *Muddy Waters,* 113.

151 *even playing bargain nights when he had to:* Gordon, *Can't Be Satisfied,* 154–55.

151 *bad cut on his left hand:* Tony Standish, "Muddy Waters in London: Part II—Conclusion," *Jazz Journal,* February 1959, 4; Gordon, *Can't Be Satisfied,* 147.

151 *a little less confident:* Gordon, *Can't Be Satisfied,* 162–63.

151 *"Screaming Guitar and Howling Piano":* Ibid., 159.

151 *"this is not the voice of the 'old-time' American Negro":* Iain Lang, "Really the Blues," *Sunday Times Magazine,* October 12, 1958, 20.

152 *"[Muddy] fiddled with the knobs":* Review by Les Fancourt, quoted in Gordon, *Can't Be Satisfied,* 161.

152 *"Electric guitar had not really been heard":* Ibid.

152 *"By the time the spellbinding 'Blues Before Sunrise'":* Standish, "Muddy Waters in London."

152 *"It was tough, unpolite, strongly rhythmic music":* Max Jones, "This World of Jazz," *Melody Maker,* October 25, 1958, 11.

153 *"I didn't play guitar until about two months ago":* Standish, "Muddy Waters in London."

153 *"Now I know,"* . . . *"that the people in England like soft guitar and the old blues":* Jones, "This World of Jazz," 11.

153 *Among those who saw Muddy Waters:* Gordon, *Can't Be Satisfied,* 163.

CHAPTER 24

154 *"Like many adults, I've been in the habit":* Bing Crosby, as told to Bob Willet, "My Kind of Music Is Coming Back!," *New York: The Sunday Herald Tribune Magazine,* April 24, 1960, 15.

156 *playing local talent shows, and showed enough ambition:* John Blair, *Images of America: Southern California Surf Music 1960–1966* (Charleston, SC: Arcadia Publishing, 2015), 12–13.

156 *working in metallurgy:* Tom Titus, "Menagerie, Tax Bracket Set CM's Dick Dale Apart," *Daily Pilot,* undated clipping in files of Costa Mesa Historical Society, likely 1963.

156 *Hamptons of Los Angeles:* Kevin Starr, *Embattled Dreams: California in War and Peace, 1940–1950* (New York: Oxford University Press, 2002), 16.

156 *clogged the street outside:* Blair, *Images of America,* 14.

156 *spilled into the parking lot:* Ibid., 15.

157 *swelled from dozens to hundreds:* Kent Crowley, *Surf Beat: Rock 'n' Roll's Forgotten Revolution* (New York: Backbeat Books, 2011), 58.

157 *A box of ties was even kept at the door:* Author interview with John Blair, December 1, 2016.

157 *setting them on fire:* A typical Dale exaggeration; Crowley, *Surf Beat,* 76.

157 *fried the capacitors inside:* Author interview with Paul Morte, March 22, 2017.

158 *Marty Robbins country records:* Tom Wheeler, *The Soul of Tone: Celebrating 60 Years of Fender Amps* (Milwaukee: Hal Leonard, 2007), 236.

158 *Inside the concrete bunker of Leo's lab . . . Yet at the end of every weekend:* Creative Worx Motion Media, "Dick Dale Talks About Leo Fender & Guitars Part 2," 1996, published February 4, 2015, https://www.youtube.com/watch?v=RAnYTlQGWHs.

158 *Tavares finally told Leo:* Wheeler, *Soul of Tone,* 237.

158 *line of cars three miles long:* Author interview with John Blair, December 1, 2016.

159 *"Now I know what Dick is trying to tell me":* Wheeler, *Soul of Tone,* 237.

160 *"This is you":* Ibid.

160 *one of the first so-called stacks:* Another Southern California amp company, Standel, claims to have offered a "piggyback" design before Fender. Smith, *Fender,* 195.

160 *Tavares holding the JBL cone in his hands:* Wheeler, *Soul of Tone,* 237.

160 *Leo felt his eardrum crumble:* Ibid., 196.

161 *"Dick Dale Showman":* Robert J. Dalley, *Surfin Guitars: Instrumental Surf Bands of the Sixties* (Ann Arbor: Popular Culture, Ink, 1996, second edition), 189.

161 *Brian Wilson, who brought the group of boys he was singing with:* Timothy White, *The Nearest Faraway Place: Brian Wilson, the Beach Boys, and the Southern California Experience* (New York: Henry Holt, 1994), 137.

161 *"On entering the building, you could hear the shock waves":* Patrick Ganahl, "Dick Dale," *Guitar Player,* July 1981, 38.

161 *A title was born:* White, *Nearest Faraway Place,* 138, plausibly claims that "Let's Go Trippin,'" widely considered Dale's first surf single, was recorded in a small Hollywood studio.

CHAPTER 25

164 *a button to induce artificial reverberation:* Crowley, *Surf Beat,* 79.

164 *"was able to sing and sound like Elvis":* Ibid.

164 *licensed from Hammond:* Smith, *Fender,* 197.

164 *somehow obtained Dick Dale's very own Fender Reverb:* Dalley, *Surfin Guitars,* 69.

165 *the most successful surf music recording yet made:* Blair, quoted in Crowley, *Surf Beat,* 118.

165 *none of the saxophones or horns:* Ibid., 117.

165 *Don Randall's sales team laughed it off:* Fullerton, *Guitars from George & Leo*, 32.

165 *never succeeded as a jazz guitar:* Smith, *Fender*, 176–77.

166 *readers of the national music magazine* DownBeat: NAMM Oral History interview with Robert Perine, interviewer Dan Del Fiorentino, November 17, 2003.

166 *while the image of bandleader Lawrence Welk gazed down from a billboard:* Art Seidenbaum, "Spectator, '64: The Teen Fair Is Jumping," *Los Angeles Times,* March 25, 1964, D1.

167 *totaled more than $2.2 million:* "Fender Sales, Inc., Statement of Earnings and Retained Earnings, for 3 Months Period Ended December 31, 1963," 3, in Don Randall Private Collection.

167 *Fender claimed 26 percent of the national electric guitar market:* "Evaluation of the Guitar Market 1965," 10.

167 *not everyone could surf, not everyone looked good at the beach:* Crowley, *Surf Beat*, 146–47 and 165, and Elijah Wald, *How the Beatles Destroyed Rock and Roll* (New York: Oxford University Press, 2009), 228–29, both address the limitations of surf music culture.

167 *Rather than touring, he preferred to stay home:* Titus, "Menagerie, Tax Bracket."

167 *went onstage before Dale's set at the Rendezvous:* White, *Nearest Faraway Place*, 147–48.

168 *"the boom of the barrel and the hiss of the lace":* Crowley, *Surf Beat*, 149.

168 *"run its course":* Crosby and Willet, "My Kind of Music."

CHAPTER 26

169 *ready to give up the stage for years:* Shaughnessy, *Les Paul*, 245.

170 *take custody of a newborn baby girl . . . gave birth to a boy named Robert:* Ibid., 236.

170 *Jack Paar would still have him and Mary:* Ibid., 247.

170 *their electric Gibsons blew out the speakers:* Ibid., 236.

170 *"You bet your ass I was tough to work for":* Paul and Cochran, *Les Paul in His Own Words*, 294–95.

171 *view the Les Paul Model itself as a failure:* Duchossoir, *Gibson Electrics*, 88.

171 *"I didn't like the shape":* Wheeler, *Soul of Tone*, 156–57.

172 *Mary snuck out and boarded a flight to Los Angeles:* Shaughnessy, *Les Paul*, 249.

172 *"I just don't understand him at all":* Ibid., 247.

172 *she escaped . . . filed for legal separation:* Ibid., 250.

172 *"openly, publicly, and notoriously consorted":* UPI, "Les Paul Suing Mary for Divorce," *Boston Globe*, November 8, 1963.

172 *juicy, illusion-puncturing gossip:* For example, Alfred Albelli and Lester Abelman, "Les Paul Says His Mary Played Not Only Guitar but the Field," *Daily News* (New York), November 8, 1963, 4.

173 *a settlement worth more than half a million dollars:* UPI, "Guitarist Les Paul Divorces Mary Ford," *Los Angeles Times*, December 18, 1964.

173 *fear that Mary might try to claim some of his future income:* Les was candid about not wanting to renew in the midst of a divorce; see Wheeler, *American Guitars*, 157, and Paul and Cochran, *Les Paul in His Own Words*, 296.

CHAPTER 27

174 *He stood up on the bridge of his yacht:* This scene from author interview with Sandy Boggs, March 27, 2016.

175 *"Where you going, Leo?":* Ibid.

176 *"You were correct, they were a bit off":* Handwritten note to Leo Fender from Rod Swift at Stephens Marine Inc., December 30, 1965, in the archives of the Haggin Museum, Stockton, California.

176 *first Leica cameras, later Nikons:* Author interviews with Leo's nephews Gary Gray, March 16, 2016, and Alan Gray, April 25, 2017.

176 *thousands of rolls of film:* Author interviews with Gary Gray, March 16, 2016, and July 28, 2016.

176 *helping those of the other seem less unusual:* Author interview with Sandy Boggs, March 27, 2016.

177 *"Well, hell, Leo":* Author interview with Geoff Fullerton, March 21, 2017.

177 *"Leo said there's not much point in being married":* Author interview with Gary Gray, July 28, 2016.

177 *"He didn't know how to have polite conversation":* Author interview with Sandy Boggs, March 27, 2016.

178 *"Don't you think you could probably handle that a little bit better":* NAMM Oral History interview with Babe Simoni, May 25, 2010, interviewer Dan Del Fiorentino.

179 *hardly any rules:* NAMM Oral History interview with Abigail Ybarra, August 19, 2009, interviewer Dan Del Fiorentino.

179 *wheelbarrow filled with candy bars and gum:* Ibid.

179 *whole hams and three-pound boxes of See's Candies:* Author interview with former Fender employee Charlie Davis, March 23, 2017.

CHAPTER 28

180 *earned less than $35,000 . . . by about 600 percent:* Rough draft of Fender internal history dated May 26, 1964, in Don Randall Private Collection, 11.

181 *fourteen to sixteen weeks . . . estimated at $1.5 million:* Ibid.

181 *not to take orders for more amps and guitars:* Smith, *Fender*, 246–47.

181 *"Are you sure everything's locked?":* Fullerton, *Guitar Legends*, 59.

181 *forty-seven employees . . . a thousand electric guitars every week:* Rough draft of Fender internal history, 3–14.

182 *$242,000 each:* Ibid., 17.

182 *largest maker of electric guitars and amplifiers:* In 1963, according to "Evaluation of the Guitar Market 1965," 10.

182 *he felt that he didn't belong:* Smith, *Fender*, 243.

182 *would become irrelevant soon:* Ibid., 245.

182 *didn't figure he'd live very long:* Gans, "Electric Guitar Pioneers," 36.

182 *expanding meant borrowing money:* Smith, *Fender*, 245.

182 *"Prone to loose talk":* Ibid.

183 *everyone who wanted a Fender instrument by now had one:* Author interview with Geoff Fullerton, March 21, 2017.

CHAPTER 29

184 *"He played all the time":* Ernie Isley, quoted in David Henderson, *'Scuse Me While I Kiss the Sky: Jimi Hendrix: Voodoo Child* (New York: Atria Books, 1978, 1981, 2008), 73.

185 *seized by homosexual tendencies . . . discharged from the army:* Charles R. Cross, *Room Full of Mirrors: A Biography of Jimi Hendrix* (New York: Hachette Books, 2005), 93–94.

185 *Hendrix would often ask to hold Jones's guitar:* Ibid., 100.

185 *Hendrix's amp couldn't match Jones's:* Ibid., 101.

186 *"That man just done wiped you up":* Ibid.

186 *pawn or lose numerous guitars:* Michael Heatley, *Jimi Hendrix Gear: The Guitars, Amps and Effects That Revolutionized Rock 'n' Roll* (Minneapolis: Voyageur Press, 2009), 34, 44–50.

186 *"Five dates would go by beautifully":* Cross, *Room Full of Mirrors*, 105.

186 *"I am Little Richard!":* Henderson, *'Scuse Me*, 78.

186 *"He'd turn his git-tar down but he would still overshadow a person":* Charles Shaar Murray, *Crosstown Traffic: Jimi Hendrix and the Rock 'n' Roll Revolution* (New York: St. Martin's Press, 1989), 162–63.

CHAPTER 30

188 *and wearily open the trunk:* Author interviews with Carol Kaye, December 21, 2015; July 31, 2016; and January 7, 2017.

188 I can't believe I have to play this shit: Ibid., July 31, 2016, and January 7, 2017.

188 *storied R & B producer Bumps Blackwell:* Ibid., January 7, 2017.

189 *shuttered or transformed into rock clubs . . . accepted starvation as a way of life:* Ibid.

189 *live with the fear that there might not be enough to eat:* Ibid.

189 *Carol Kaye had died:* Ibid.

190 *that fall of 1963:* Carol Kaye, *Studio Musician: Carol Kaye, 60s No. 1 Hit Bassist, Guitarist* (self-published, 2016), 106.

190 *who loathed the fact . . . were often black men:* Author interview with Carol Kaye, January 7, 2017.

190 *bought two Fender Precisions:* Kaye, *Studio Musician*, 71; author interview with Carol Kaye, December 21, 2015.

191 *"bus driver":* Author interview with Carol Kaye, December 21, 2015.

191 *a few months after Carol's first encounter:* Kaye, *Studio Musician*, 134.

192 *$104 per three-hour session:* Ibid.

192 *free to lay down all the Fender bass grooves:* Author interview with Carol Kaye, July 31, 2016.

CHAPTER 31

193 *reached Francis Carey Hall in the fall of 1963:* Andy Babiuk, *Beatles Gear: All the Fab Four's Instruments from Stage to Studio* (San Francisco: Backbeat Books, 2002), 108.

193 *set technical specifications . . . himself:* Smith, *Complete History of Rickenbacker*, 62.

194 *NBC News: The Huntley Brinkley Report,* NBC News, November 18, 1963, accessed at https://www.youtube.com/watch?v=wVjuKaJjsNA&t=29s.

194 *the* New York Times: "Liverpool Cellar Clubs Rock to Beat Groups: Long-Haired Youths with Guitars Take Charge as Cult," *New York Times,* December 26, 1963, 34.

194 *"pudding-bowl haircuts":* Huntley Brinkley Report.

194 *refusing to issue music:* Philip Norman, *Shout!: The Beatles in Their Generation* (New York: Simon & Schuster, 1981), 225–26.

194 *"We'll need samples of both these models":* Babiuk, *Beatles Gear,* 108.

194 *"We think it would be an excellent idea":* Ibid.

194 *"Buck, this is the hottest group in the world today":* Smith, *Complete History of Rickenbacker,* 69.

195 *"To keep them on Rickenbacker":* Ibid.

195 *"Please do not mention [the meeting] to a soul":* Babiuk, *Beatles Gear,* 108.

196 *singing Buddy Holly's vocal harmonies:* Norman, *Rave On,* 22–23.

196 *he'd meant to buy a Stratocaster:* "The Leo Fender Story," DVD video in Herb Staher collection, Rock and Roll Hall of Fame Archives, box 9.

197 *arranging a miniature trade show:* Smith, *Fender,* 77.

197 *shuttled the Beatles out of the Plaza Hotel:* Smith, *Complete History of Rickenbacker,* 77; Babiuk, *Beatles Gear,* 108–10.

197 *may have brought a right-handed model:* Alan Ohnsman, "Guitar Made Famous by the Beatles Is Still in High Demand," Bloomberg News, August 21, 2008.

197 *McCartney refused the Rickenbacker:* Babiuk, *Beatles Gear,* 113.

198 *snuck across Central Park back to the Plaza:* Brad Tolinski and Alan DiPerna, *Play It Loud: An Epic History of the Style, Sound, and Revolution of the Electric Guitar* (New York: Doubleday, 2016), 159–60.

198 *a 24/7 chaos machine:* Norman, *Shout!,* 248–49.

198 *"Yes . . . It's a Rickenbacker":* Smith, *Complete History of Rickenbacker,* 77.

198 *shipped to him later in the month:* Babiuk, *Beatles Gear,* 113.

199 *a new song called "A Hard Day's Night":* Ibid., 120–22.

199 *radically expand his little Rickenbacker factory:* Author interview with John Hall, August 13, 2015; Smith, *Complete History of Rickenbacker,* 66.

CHAPTER 32

201 *was going to kill him:* Gans, "Electric Guitar Pioneers," 36.

201 *twenty-seven buildings . . . Leo could hardly recognize it:* Wheeler, *Fender Archives,* 69.

201 *missed the point of its cheaper and simpler competitor:* Smith, *Fender,* 207–8.

201 *posting an antiunion screed:* White, *Fender,* 128–29.

202 *yet another sign ... far too large:* NAMM Oral History interview with Abigail Ybarra.

202 *Doubt now filled Leo:* Smith, *Fender*, 245.

202 *sell the company to him:* Ibid.

203 *number had risen to $2 million:* Ibid.

203 *a million dollars in pretax profit:* Untitled financial document in Don Randall Private Collection showing annual net sales and pretax profits for all Fender companies except Squier from 1960 to 1967.

203 *"If I bought it now":* Smith, *Fender*, 245.

203 *"It was a huge amount":* Babiuk, *Beatles Gear*, 138–39.

203 *pegged Fender's offer at $10,000:* "Leo Fender Story."

203 *his firm never paid artists:* Author interview with Gary Gray, March 19, 2016.

204 *Randall sent Jim Williams:* Babiuk, *Beatles Gear*, 138.

204 *was likely past the point:* Ibid.

204 *"the boys had been successful with what they were playing":* Ibid.

204 *Beatles looked upon its products favorably:* McCartney and Harrison had both sought Fenders before becoming famous but couldn't afford or find them; in 1965, Lennon and Harrison both purchased Stratocasters.

204 *"I felt I'd broken my cardinal rule":* Babiuk, *Beatles Gear*, 138.

CHAPTER 33

205 *something closer to $10 million:* Baldwin president Lucien Wulsin Jr., letter to Don Randall, July 6, 1964, in Don Randall Private Collection.

205 *had yet earned a dollar in profit:* "Fender-Rhodes, Inc., Statement of Income and Expense, Year Ended Sept. 30, 1964," and "Fender Acoustic Instrument Co., Inc., Balance Sheet," July 31, 1964, in Don Randall Private Collection.

206 *some $470,000:* Smith, *Fender*, 246.

206 *The deal even included:* Unsigned draft letter from Lucien Wulsin to Don Randall, August 17, 1964, in Don Randall Private Collection.

206 *instead put Randall in touch:* Smith, *Fender*, 246.

206 *"synergy became the byword":* Clive Davis, *The Soundtrack of My Life* (New York: Simon & Schuster, 2013), 41.

207 *that the company employing them might soon change hands:* Smith, *Fender*, 246–49.

207 *Leo seemed quieter than usual:* White, *Fender*, 144–45.

207 *"Unquestionably, Fender's name ranks very high":* Arthur D. Little report for CBS, in Richard Smith Files, 23.

207 *"Fender amplifiers can be kicked, dropped":* Ibid., 26.

207 *"virtually all of the engineering talent":* Ibid., 28–29.

207 *"The men we met were presentable":* Ibid., 20.

208 *"rather substantial compensation":* Ibid., 8.

208 *White was basically guessing:* White, *Fender*, 151.

208 *"Randall's enthusiastic services are secured"*: Little report, 19.

208 *"his leadership as the factor"*: Ibid., 9.

208 *"He has the successful, practical inventor's genius"*: Ibid., 18.

208 *"Mr. Fender finds it hard to believe"*: Ibid., 17.

209 *"a sharp diminution"*: Ibid., 8–9.

209 *"it would be highly desirable"*: Ibid., 9.

209 *changed the tenor*: Smith, *Fender*, 246.

209 *take all the orders they could possibly get*: Ibid.

210 *"Everything afterward was anticlimactic"*: Ibid., 246–47.

210 *on October 16, 1964*: Ibid., 247.

211 *"Sit down, I have something to tell you"*: White, *Fender*, 145–46.

CHAPTER 34

212 *Check number 8339*: Leo Fender and Don Randall check copies, in Don Randall Private Collection.

212 *Randall went alone*: Smith, *Fender*, 247.

212 *a dark winter day*: Wheeler, *Fender Archives*, 66.

213 *asking about a strange story they'd seen . . . "You know as much as I do"*: Carson, *My Life and Times*, 56–60.

213 *Ybarra was frightened*: NAMM Oral History interview with Abigail Ybarra.

213 *"We have an important announcement"*: Wheeler, *Fender Archives*, 66.

213 *"Which is worth more"*: "CBS Plucks West Coast Guitar Firm," Associated Press, January 6, 1965.

214 *"It wouldn't surprise us if CBS split the Yankees"*: Bill Irvin, "CBS Strumming a Different Tune," *Chicago American*, January 8, 1965, in Don Randall Private Collection.

214 *"the largest cash transaction in music industry history"*: "Fender Guitars Bought by CBS for $13 Million," *Music Trades*, January 1965.

215 *a favorite tool of Leo's father*: Author interview with Sandy Boggs, March 27, 2016.

215 *"I don't know what I would have done without you"*: White, *Fender*, 146.

CHAPTER 35

218 *Dylan himself had no idea what was happening*: Elijah Wald's masterful history of this event, *Dylan Goes Electric!* (New York: Dey Street, 2015) reports on page 271 that "Dylan was startled by the audience's response."

218 *go back to* The Ed Sullivan Show: Lee Zhito, "Newport Folk Festival Hit as Artistic and Financial Success," *Billboard*, August 7, 1965, 7.

218 *"We want the old Dylan"*: Wald, *Dylan Goes Electric!*, 263.

218 *"I thought Dylan was abandoning us"*: Ibid., 265.

219 *assaultive, quite literally terrifying*: Ibid., 259.

219 *Dylan's electric set felt like a silencing*: Ibid., 283, 304–5.

219 *"What he used to stand for"*: Ted Holmberg, "A Triumph to the Final Note," *Providence Journal*, July 26, 1965, quoted in Wald, *Dylan Goes Electric!*, 273.

CHAPTER 36

221 *reintroduced to something he already knew*: Eric Clapton, *Clapton: The Autobiography* (New York: Broadway Books, 2007), 33.

221 *playing to the same aging, all-black audiences*: Charles Keil, *Urban Blues* (Chicago: University of Chicago Press, 1966), 118.

222 *had seen Keith Richards of the Rolling Stones playing*: Richards played his 1959 Les Paul as early as 1964, making him the first of the British rockers to use it. Dave Hunter, *The Gibson Les Paul: The Illustrated Story of the Guitar That Changed Rock* (Minneapolis: Voyageur Press, 2014), 49.

222 *Furthering Clapton's interest in this Gibson model*: Clapton, *Clapton*, 72; Lawrence, *Early Years*, 248.

223 *from 1960*: Ibid.

224 *the whole story had been concealed from him*: Clapton, *Clapton*, 5.

224 *"It was like the Eric Clapton show"*: Dinu Logoz, *John Mayall: The Blues Crusader* (Zurich: Edition Olms, 2015), 41.

224 *Jim Marshall . . . far more of it than any Fender*: Austin Pittman, *The Tube Amp Book* (Milwaukee: Backbeat Books, 2003), 56–61.

224 *"Give God a solo! We want more God!"*: Ray Coleman, *Survivor: The Authorized Biography of Eric Clapton* (London: Futura Publications, 1986), 36.

225 *"In a way, I thought 'Yes, I am God, quite right' "*: Quoted in Michael Schumacher, *Crossroads: The Life and Music of Eric Clapton* (New York: Hyperion, 1995), 48.

225 *"I'm very conceited"*: Coleman, *Survivor*, 38.

225 *Studio 2 . . . March day in 1966*: Marc Roberty, *Eric Clapton Day by Day: The Early Years, 1963–1982* (Milwaukee: Backbeat Books, 2013), 48.

225 *tipsy bass player . . . what he was getting into*: Logoz, *John Mayall*, 43–44.

225 *a microphone immediately in front of the amp . . . carried it over*: Ibid., 44–45.

226 *volume knob to where he set it for a live show*: Clapton, *Clapton*, 73.

226 *asked him to turn it down . . . "Is this absolutely essential?" . . . "Give God what he wants!"*: Logoz, *John Mayall*, 44–45.

227 *"I was on top of my craft"*: Schumacher, *Crossroads*, 65.

CHAPTER 37

229 *"No British musicians have ever sounded like this"*: Quoted in Logoz, *John Mayall*, 50.

230 *hating to have his picture taken*: Clapton, *Clapton*, 73.

230 *recorded some earlier tracks . . . Jimmy Page*: Page claimed to have produced an unreleased version of "Double Crossing Time" in 1965 (Logoz, *John Mayall*, 31–32), and while Vernon did the later album cut, it has a Zeppelin-ish air.

230 *"Everybody started using the Les Paul Standard":* Gabriel J. Hernandez, "Kim Simmonds, Savoy Brown and the Incredible Journey from London, Circa 1965," Gibson .com, October 7, 2008, http://www.gibson.com/News-Lifestyle/Features/en-us/kim-simmonds-savoy-brown-and.aspx.

230 *luring his American followers to do the same:* Author interview with George Gruhn, May 29, 2018.

231 *"was better than any other possible rock 'n' roll guitar":* Quoted in Shaughnessy, *Les Paul,* 262.

231 *all but retired from public performance:* Ibid., 254.

231 *find some whippersnapper longhair:* Paul and Cochran, *Les Paul in His Own Words,* 297.

231 *One immediate effect:* Tolinski and DiPerna, *Play It Loud,* 204.

232 *"I'm going down 48th Street":* Paul and Cochran, *Les Paul in His Own Words,* 297.

232 *ceasing production of fully electric instruments:* Ibid., 296–97.

CHAPTER 38

233 *The first thing she noticed:* Cross, *Room Full of Mirrors,* 131.

233 *little Fender Duo-Sonic guitar:* Heatley, *Jimi Hendrix Gear,* 48–49.

234 *Sixty-Third Street . . .* Blonde on Blonde *for the first time:* Cross, *Room Full of Mirrors,* 132–34.

234 *"I don't have my own guitar":* Ibid., 135.

235 *pilfered a white Fender Stratocaster . . . a demo he had of a song called "Hey Joe":* Richards, *Life,* 186. Other girlfriends of Hendrix's around this time claim to have gotten him white Stratocasters, too, such as Carol Shiroky (Cross, *Room Full of Mirrors,* 135; Heatley, *Jimi Hendrix Gear,* 62).

235 *"This is rock 'n' roll history":* Richards, *Life,* 186.

235 *a fuzz pedal:* Cross, *Room Full of Mirrors,* 140.

235 *"H-bombs were going off":* Quoted in ibid., 142–43.

236 *Chandler showed up in a suit:* Ibid., 146–47.

237 *would certainly get an introduction:* Ibid., 152.

CHAPTER 39

238 *$208 per session:* Author interview with Carol Kaye, July 31, 2016.

238 *wore sunglasses inside:* Kaye, *Studio Musician,* 109.

239 *flipped the bird:* Kent Hartman, *The Wrecking Crew* (New York: Thomas Dunne Books, 2012), 146.

239 *Wilson pursued a mature sound:* White, *Nearest Faraway Place,* 251–52.

240 *Carol and the other session players had doubts:* Kaye, *Studio Musician,* 175.

240 *put him on a weekly retainer:* Alan Slutsky, *Standing in the Shadows of Motown: The Life and Music of Legendary Bassist James Jamerson* (Wynnewood, PA: Dr. Licks Publishing, 1989), 20–21.

241 *Thanks to a new eight-track mixing console:* Ibid.

241 *he invented the pulsing, unforgettable bass part:* Ibid., 29–30.

241 *a stunning 75 percent:* Jack Hamilton, *Just Around Midnight: Rock and Roll and the Racial Imagination* (Cambridge, MA: Harvard University Press, 2016), 123.

241 *"It was [Jamerson], me, and Brian Wilson":* Barry Miles, *Paul McCartney: Many Years from Now* (New York: Henry Holt, 1997), 271.

242 *Motown's success changed this:* Hamilton, *Just Around Midnight*, 138; Nelson George, *Where Did Our Love Go?: The Rise and Fall of the Motown Sound* (Chicago: University of Illinois Press, 2007), 103, 201.

242 *twelve altogether:* Kaye, *Studio Musician*, 169.

242 *as many as seventeen:* Barney Hoskyns, *Waiting for the Sun: A Rock 'n' Roll History of Los Angeles* (New York: Backbeat Books, 1996, 2003), 128.

243 *she thought it could be a masterpiece:* Author interview with Carol Kaye, July 31, 2016.

243 *cut off two words completing a lyrical rhyme:* Ken Sharp, "Mike Love of the Beach Boys: One-on-One (The Interview Part 1)," *Rock Cellar*, September 9, 2015, https://www.rockcellarmagazine.com/2015/09/09/mike-love-of-the-beach-boys-one-on-one-the-interview-part-1/2/.

244 *estimated by Brian Wilson at $16,000:* White, *Nearest Faraway Place*, 264.

CHAPTER 40

245 *Regent Street Polytechnic:* Roberty, *Eric Clapton*, 56.

245 *A familiar face walked in:* Schumacher, *Crossroads*, 80–81; Henderson, *'Scuse Me*, 109.

246 *God had a funny feeling about it:* Schumacher, *Crossroads*, 81.

246 *plug into the massive Marshall bass amp:* Cross, *Room Full of Mirrors*, 162.

246 *the slower version recorded by Albert King:* Ibid.

246 *thought it was particularly tough:* Clapton, *Clapton*, 80.

246 *Live recordings from this time:* A live version of Hendrix's "Killing Floor" was captured on October 18, 1966, at the Olympia theater in Paris and gives a good approximation of what had probably happened in London two weeks earlier.

247 *hands fell off the neck:* Chas Chandler, quoted in "The Birth of Rock," episode 1 of the BBC documentary *The Seven Ages of Rock*, BBC Worldwide, aired May 19, 2007.

247 *He'd been expecting this newcomer to hold back:* Clapton, *Clapton*, 80.

248 *"Eric was standing [there], trying to light a cigarette":* Chandler in *Seven Ages of Rock*.

248 *"They loved it, and I loved it, too":* Clapton, *Clapton*, 80.

248 *to meet Muddy Waters:* Murray, *Crosstown Traffic*, 38–39.

249 *found a deep commonality with Jimi:* Schumacher, *Crossroads*, 80–83.

CHAPTER 41

251 *"They were so unfashionable, Stratocasters":* Clapton, quoted in "Leo Fender Story."

251 *"As far as the new blues-rock hotshots were concerned":* Murray, *Crosstown Traffic*, 212.

251 *"I use a Fender Stratocaster":* Bill Kerby and David Thompson, "Spanish Galleons Off Jersey Coast or 'We Live Off Excess Volume,'" *Los Angeles Free Press*, August 25, 1967.

252 *small amplifiers suitable for rehearsals:* Mitch Mitchell and John Platt, *The Hendrix Experience* (London: Mitchell Beazley, 1990), 18.

252 *Chandler was then selling off his personal bass guitars:* Cross, *Room Full of Mirrors*, 163.

252 *"We tried everything to break them" . . . matching hundred-watt Marshall stacks:* Mitchell and Platt, *Hendrix Experience*, 18–21.

253 *employ it consistently:* This consistency was surprising given that in private, he played all sorts of different instruments and amplifiers, and would later make a habit of buying new gear en masse and at huge expense. Henry Goldrich and Holly Goldrich Schoenfeld, *The Wall of Fame: New York City's Legendary Manny's Music* (Milwaukee: Hal Leonard, 2007), 23–30.

253 *"the Black Bob Dylan":* Jan Waldrop, "Jimi Hendrix Shows His Teeth," *Humo*, March 11, 1967, reprinted in Steven Roby, ed., *Hendrix on Hendrix: Interviews and Encounters with Jimi Hendrix* (Chicago: Chicago Review Press, 2012), 17.

253 *"the Black Elvis":* Michael Lydon, "Jimi Hendrix: The Black Elvis?," *New York Times*, August 25, 1968.

253 *"the best guitar-picker in the world":* Michael Thomas, "The Persecution & Assassination of Rock and Roll, as Performed by the Jimi Hendrix Experience . . . Under the Direction of the Jumping Jimi Himself, the Cassius Clay of Pop," *EYE*, July 1968, reprinted in Roby, *Hendrix on Hendrix*, 98.

253 *"There was something about the way he played":* "Leo Fender Story."

253 *switched to the more commonly available SG:* Hunter, *Gibson Les Paul*, 51.

254 *"They're showing up at my house":* Paul and Cochran, *Les Paul in His Own Words*, 297.

CHAPTER 42

257 *highest-paid player in rock music:* Cross, *Room Full of Mirrors*, 255.

257 *"We got tired of 'the Experience'":* Jimi Hendrix, *Jimi Hendrix: Live at Woodstock*, MCA Records, 1999.

257 *"You can leave if you want to":* Hendrix, *Live at Woodstock*.

258 *"Everything just stopped":* Henry Diltz, quoted in Joel Makower, *Woodstock: The Oral History* (New York: Doubleday, 1989), 287.

260 *"A quintessential piece of art":* Ibid.

260 *"Before that . . . if someone would have played":* Cross, *Room Full of Mirrors*, 271.

260 *"It was probably the single greatest moment":* Ibid.

EPILOGUE

261 *Clapton knew he'd be seeing Jimi:* Clapton, *Clapton*, 130.

261 *behaving rather strangely:* Cross, *Room Full of Mirrors*, 329.

262 *scheduled to meet Sly Stone:* Mitchell and Platt, *Hendrix Experience*, 157–59.

262 *Hendrix had taken a heavy dose:* This account is from Cross, *Room Full of Mirrors,* 331–33, who offers the most credible account of Hendrix's final hours and death.

262 *"filled with a feeling of terrible loneliness":* Clapton, *Clapton,* 130.

263 *a lifetime of service:* Author interview with Geoff Fullerton, March 21, 2017.

263 *appeared on Forrest White's desk in 1966:* White, *Fender,* 172–74.

264 *flat and dull:* Smith, *Fender,* 253.

264 *abandoned the entire line:* Wheeler, *Soul of Tone,* 297.

264 *shuddered over the cheaper bridge:* Author interview with Charlie Davis, March 23, 2017.

265 *"And CBS come and said use it, use everything":* NAMM Oral History interview with Abigail Ybarra.

265 *took bets with his coworkers:* NAMM Oral History interview with Babe Simoni.

265 *out to Fullerton to work as punishment:* Author interview with Charlie Davis, March 23, 2017.

265 *earned more per year . . . "the 'fairyland' in which you were living":* Don Randall, letter to "all key salesmen," June 9, 1967, in Richard Smith Files.

267 *Two years after:* Gans, "Electric Guitar Pioneers," 37.

267 *skirted the edge of legitimate medicine:* Author interview with Geoff Fullerton, March 21, 2017.

268 *"a place to tinker and some friends around to have lunch with":* Smith, *Fender,* 268.

268 *a private phone line:* Author interview with Geoff Fullerton, March 21, 2017.

269 *He felt loneliness and profound guilt:* Author interviews with Phyllis Fender, August 4, 2015, and December 19, 2015.

269 *a shiny brown glass eye:* Ibid.

269 *Leo rejected the idea:* Smith, *Complete History of Rickenbacker,* 277–79.

270 *legal action over G&L's use of the name Leo Fender:* Michael Flagg, "Leo Fender's Legacy: G&L Sales on Rise," *Los Angeles Times,* August 11, 1993.

270 *Tavares . . . actually designed several:* Author interview with David McLaren, March 29, 2017.

270 *"Fred Tavares was employed in late 1953":* From copy of note given to author by Dave McLaren.

272 *Leo took a certain pride:* Author interview with Geoff Fullerton, March 21, 2017.

273 *Buffet tables stretched out in a long line:* Shaughnessy, *Les Paul,* 292–93.

274 *slapped Les on the right side of the head:* Ibid., 265.

274 *After five surgeries:* Paul and Cochran, *Les Paul in His Own Words,* 315.

275 *spend hours together on the phone:* Shaughnessy, *Les Paul,* 276.

275 *Mary would call him late at night:* Paul and Cochran, *Les Paul in His Own Words,* 312.

276 *shattered by her death:* Shaughnessy, *Les Paul,* 277; Paul and Cochran, *Les Paul in His Own Words,* 312–13.

277 *Peter Frampton approached him:* Shaughnessy, *Les Paul,* 275.

277 *jokes he'd collected and filed on index cards:* Les Paul Papers, box 3.

277 *extended, then extended again:* Shaughnessy, *Les Paul*, 286–87.

278 *Juszkiewicz had no choice:* Ibid., 292.

278 *"I had an LP at a very early age":* Page quoted in MTV News report on the party, posted at https://www.youtube.com/watch?v=U7KOOyzEfIA.

281 *until August 12, 2009:* Many sources list Thursday, August 13, as the day Les died; however, the date listed on his grave in Waukesha (and given by Gibson) is August 12.

INDEX